Summit
Books

DESTROY THIS HOUSE

A MEMOIR

AMANDA UHLE

SUMMIT BOOKS

*New York   Amsterdam/Antwerp   London
Toronto   Sydney/Melbourne   New Delhi*

Summit Books
An Imprint of Simon & Schuster, LLC
1230 Avenue of the Americas
New York, NY 10020

For more than 100 years, Simon & Schuster has championed authors and the stories they create. By respecting the copyright of an author's intellectual property, you enable Simon & Schuster and the author to continue publishing exceptional books for years to come. We thank you for supporting the author's copyright by purchasing an authorized edition of this book.

No amount of this book may be reproduced or stored in any format, nor may it be uploaded to any website, database, language-learning model, or other repository, retrieval, or artificial intelligence system without express permission. All rights reserved. Inquiries may be directed to Simon & Schuster, 1230 Avenue of the Americas, New York, NY 10020 or permissions@simonandschuster.com.

Copyright © 2025 by Amanda Uhle

All rights reserved, including the right to reproduce this book or portions thereof in any form whatsoever. For information, address Simon & Schuster Subsidiary Rights Department, 1230 Avenue of the Americas, New York, NY 10020.

This is a work of nonfiction. Some names have been changed.

First Summit Books hardcover edition August 2025

SUMMIT BOOKS and colophon are trademarks of Simon & Schuster, LLC

Simon & Schuster strongly believes in freedom of expression and stands against censorship in all its forms. For more information, visit BooksBelong.com.

For information about special discounts for bulk purchases, please contact Simon & Schuster Special Sales at 1-866-506-1949 or business@simonandschuster.com.

The Simon & Schuster Speakers Bureau can bring authors to your live event. For more information or to book an event, contact the Simon & Schuster Speakers Bureau at 1-866-248-3049 or visit our website at www.simonspeakers.com.

Interior design by Carly Loman

Manufactured in the United States of America

1 3 5 7 9 10 8 6 4 2

Library of Congress Cataloging-in-Publication Data has been applied for.

ISBN 978-1-6680-8344-4
ISBN 978-1-6680-8346-8 (ebook)

For Adam

AUTHOR'S NOTE: In the interest of privacy, certain names have been changed. Audio recordings, emails, interviews, journals, photos, letters, and especially newspaper archives helped ensure the veracity of the narrative wherever those materials were available. All other events and situations were recalled as faithfully and accurately as possible, given the shortcomings of human memory.

PROLOGUE

Suburban Detroit
2015

"My condolences," the florist said to me. Her shop was overstuffed with flowers and baskets. We sat squeezed together at a round two-person table decked in bridal tulle. A four-inch-tall, three-ring binder sat between us, page after glossy page of flowers on coffins, wreaths on tripod stands, towering bouquets on altars with BELOVED GRANDFATHER in scripty gold on a plaque.

I pointed to something sedate and white and pulled a checkbook out of my bag, hoping to leave both the shop and its claustrophobia as soon as possible.

"She liked white flowers?"

I nodded, realizing that I liked white flowers myself, but I had no idea what kind or color of flowers my mother liked. The florist thrust a cool, freckled hand across the table to grab mine. She did more weddings than funerals but found this caretaking part of her job very fulfilling, she told me. "I'm here for you."

I continued gripping the checkbook. I felt flushed but also cold, vaguely ill. I should have eaten lunch instead of the jelly beans I'd found in my car.

"How much?" I asked, and then I smiled a little, trying to reciprocate her warmth a few moments too late. I opened the folio and wrote the name of the flower shop on a check with a Mary Engelbreit motif. I didn't know my mother's taste in flowers, but in 2015 she still clung to a '90s Midwestern country-cute aesthetic for her personal effects. The check was trimmed in black-and-white checkerboard and in the corner, by my mother's address, was a pair of red cherries on a joined stem. As instructed, I printed "Four hundred twenty-five dollars." On the signature line I considered attempting her bubbly autograph but decided, like the color of the flowers, it didn't much matter. "Sandra Long" I scrawled, in my own narrow, tilted handwriting.

"When did she pass?" The florist took the check and stapled it to the order form, looking at me sympathetically. She'd interpreted my brusqueness as grief.

I admitted that she was still alive, but not for long. The idea was I wanted to get things all set up now, and I'd call the florist when I had a date for the funeral, probably next week.

The florist's entire body tensed. It's rare to see disgust materialize palpably, to envelop a body head to toe, a human body hardening.

Handing me the forms and the check, the florist suggested I return when there was actually a death in my family, not an illness. "Wouldn't a daughter want to be with her mother at a time like this?" she asked. Her revulsion was unsubtle. I wondered what she would think of me when she compared my name on the form to the check I'd just fraudulently written.

Thirty minutes ago when I'd opened the shop's door and its tinkling chime announced me, I had hoped only to be quick and to not appear coldhearted. I thought I could convey a businesslike grief long enough to order and pay for the flowers from my mother's bank account while she was alive. I expected that when she died, days from now, the IRS would seize the $1,900 in her account, or worse.

Already, it had been a long day. A September Wednesday, gray and humid. My job, in education, was busy at the start of the school year.

My daughter's sixth birthday was the next day. My mother was dying. She was sixty-four.

In the morning, I'd driven to her apartment in the dark, hoping to arrive before the crew. In eight separate loads, I took eight overfull black garbage bags to my car. Filled with my parents' financial paperwork, each one weighed about as much as my daughter—forty-five pounds or so of Medicaid forms, disability check stubs, insurance payouts and failed claims, class-action lawsuit filings, tax liens. My Toyota was full, but this was necessary. The trauma crew members coming to clean the apartment were all ex-cons. I'd been warned to remove financial documents from the premises for my own security; I'd been instructed to pay them in cash.

For years, my mother had dreamed of dying. I never knew her to be suicidal in the traditional sense, but anyone who knew her at all understood her reverence for death and illness, her fixation with it. As a hospice nurse, she became obsessed with the phase of life when all rules for ordered living could be abandoned. Diets be damned. Do only what pleases you. These are your final days. Administer the morphine. Increase it. Dying should be comfortable. She envisioned being surrounded and celebrated, our cherished matriarch, at last carefree, at last appreciated properly, and in a thick opioid haze if she desired.

Even my father joined the premature funeral procession for her. In his confused and paranoid years, he often misjudged her silence for an hour, napping, as sudden death. He could no longer climb the stairs to check on her, and they were not on speaking terms with any of their neighbors who might have indulged him by popping in to find her sleeping on a king-sized bed piled with folded and hangered clothing, the TV volume up, loud enough to muffle Dad's yells from below.

"Your mother is dead," his voice would announce evenly out of my cell phone. No hello. No reason, other than he hadn't heard from her since before the last TV show started. If I expressed doubt, he would insist, his voice now shaking with fear and sadness, angry that I didn't believe him. He placed a "your mother is dead" call to me at least monthly, but my reminding him of the last time provoked him. "Accept the facts," he would snarl into the phone. "She's dead."

Today it was actually imminent. For as long as the specter of her death had been hanging ahead of me, the looming dread of emptying her apartment was far worse, the cause of various fitful nights beginning when I was eleven. After she went to a live-in hospice from which I knew she would not return, I spent weeks dealing with her piles and her apartment's filth, sorting the important papers from the garbage and the things we could donate. Finally, I googled "hoarder clean up" and met Don, whose business served Detroit and its suburbs. Half the time he cleaned up hoarder situations like my mother's; half the time Don scrubbed domestic murder scenes of blood and hair and teeth.

That morning, I planned to let Don and his crew in and then leave them there, spending the rest of the day on funeral arrangements and other imminent-death errands before visiting Mom at the hospice a few towns over, then returning to meet Don to lock up and pay him before going home.

I had several meetings scheduled, beginning with the church where I left Mom's printed list of chosen funeral hymns. Later I'd go to an afternoon appointment scheduled with the undertaker. The florist was next. It would open in forty minutes, and I sat waiting in a McDonald's parking lot in the Toyota. It was jammed with the bags of papers, some of which had survived floods or bouts of black mold and carried their smell into the confined space of the car. The glovebox had two grand in cash—for Don—which made me feel jumpy, guilty for some reason. I tried instead to think about my mother's life, the love and frustration and despair she stoked in me, but I couldn't. My brain nudged me toward any distraction. The light of the cloudy day was diffuse, and I studied my pores in the rearview mirror. I imagined how many emails were accruing during this missed day of work. I scrounged for food and came up with some candy, which I ate while listening to upbeat music I liked in high school and asking myself, *Is this what a person does when their mother is dying?*

Don called me. "You have to come back. Now." I worried they were giving up an hour and a half into a daylong job. "No, we'll finish," he said, "but James can't be around drugs. Come back."

In a relatively short amount of time, they had boxed up all the canned goods from the living room. The hall closet was halfway empty, and there were at least twenty more black garbage bags stacked in the kitchen, tied neatly with yellow loops at the top. The crew of four included a Juliette Lewis doppelgänger, two men with extensive facial tattoos, and Don, who was the most clean-cut. He apologized for asking me to return.

"It's on me," another man said. James had two green-gray teardrop tattoos under his right eye, and he looked mortified that they'd bothered me with coming back.

Don handed me an untied black plastic garbage bag that was stuffed with two-inch-high cardboard boxes containing individual glass vials of morphine. "It's a parole thing."

"It's a *parole thang*," sang the Juliette Lewis–looking woman as she carried an armful of my mother's blouses out of the bedroom, bumping her hip on James.

Don reminded me it's $1,750 plus tips if I'm so inclined. I wasn't sure I was telling the truth, but I promised him there was nothing else weird in the apartment. I tied the bag of morphine, hefting it over my shoulder. "Cash," he said brightly one more time as I left them there.

Don, an impresario of the tragic arts, was practiced and practical in the quotidian end of end-of-life matters. He treated the family members of hoarders and murder victims with the same tenderness mixed with taking-care-of-business determination. Most everyone else in my life at that time tried to comfort me by insisting that things were not so bad. Don's clear-eyed acknowledgment of the situation—gut-wrenching mayhem—was perhaps the gentlest gesture ever extended to me. He believed that whatever happened between my mother and me was outside of his bailiwick. As far as Don was concerned, his chief duty was the writhing pit of filth that was my mother's apartment, and in that arena he was confident and capable. I felt honored he was willing to shoulder that responsibility alongside me.

He had asked me to text photos, and when he saw them, he replied, "Got them Amanda . . . any more? Are these the worst rooms?"

No, there were indeed more photos. I had been embarrassed to send him the worst rooms. I reminded myself that he had cleaned up gunshot-murder crime scenes and sent him images of the kitchen and one of the two bathrooms.

"Okay . . . it might go up just a bit, but we will figure it out . . . no worries," and followed that up with an email that included the contract and a cheery, "I look forward to meeting you on 9/9/15!"

Later, he wrote, "Hi Amanda, I am praying for you through this time. If there is anything I can do, PLEASE let me know. If you want to chat, I can listen. Here is the link to leave a review for us. Thank you for allowing us to help you. It means a lot to us. Don." Don was a man engaged in disgusting and dangerous work, with absolutely no interest in my motivation or meritoriousness. In the complex and superhuman feat that is his final five-line email to me, he extended genuine compassion while simultaneously requesting a favorable Yelp review.

Don and I understood each other. Without explicitly discussing it, I was certain he agreed: there is a time to mourn, and a time to work. This week, together, we would work.

Mourning my mother and father was an endeavor that had started so long ago I couldn't properly recall it. It began at some unknowable point in my childhood and continued for decades. Sometimes I was mourning their deaths. I more often mourned reality and sanity, the facts as they appeared to everyone on Earth except my parents. At other times, I mourned the imagined normal relationship with them I longed to have, something like the one I thought we'd had before I got old enough to know better. In a thousand revelations over thirty-some years I stuttered toward understanding them amid their endless contradictions and mysteries and deceptions. The more I knew, the less I understood. I grieved incessantly. I lost them little by little.

One of our financial crisis years was 1989. Money and the lack of it were so prominent on all of our minds that Mom and Dad, in their counterintuitive way, decided I would receive an allowance for the first time: $5 per month. I spent the first installment on one issue each of *BOP* and *Big Bopper*. After hearing my parents argue and cry about money and bills in the following weeks, I felt terribly guilty that I'd used our household money to read about Corey Haim. The next month, as soon as Mom gave me the $5 bill, I folded it in half twice and stuck it inside the Patty Duke memoir on her nightstand. This book, *Call Me Anna*, was the only book I ever saw my mother read, and she'd had it on her nightstand with a bookmark in it for at least two years. The five, apparently discovered by Mom, was unfolded and put onto my dresser while I was at school, in sixth grade. I folded it and returned it to Patty Duke that evening. I never received another allowance, and we never spoke about it. We both knew Mom needed the money more than I did, and not talking about it felt like proof to me of something palpably dark but otherwise mysterious.

In 2007, secretly and once again, my parents were on the precipice of financial ruin. Their new house, purchased with a daftly optimistic adjustable-rate mortgage, was untenable. Their other bills were impossible given their semi-employment and spotty health. They'd done this before. And I'd tried but failed to help them avoid it this time.

One Sunday morning that May, my father sat in a reclining lawn chair and announced, "I am going to die today." He fetched the wooden pirate's chest jewelry box on his dresser and a metal case he called "the strongbox" and set them on their living room floor. "These are my papers," he said.

We were supposed to play along with his premonition, but even in 2007 we were already tired of his hyperbole. My husband and I left my parents' house to mow our lawn, Dad's papers in their latched boxes on the area rug in their living room. Before our front yard was fully trimmed, I received a call from my mother, who spoke softly into the phone, even in the clamor of the hospital emergency room.

"Come back," she told us. Dad had been very close to correct. A catastrophic stroke an hour after we left had stolen my father's ability to speak or walk.

To stanch the flow of cash shooting outward in all directions, I colluded with my mother. Under fluorescent lights on plastic waiting room chairs we wrote an emergency budget. We would not touch his bank account. We would not drive his leased car. The physician would help us legally declare Dad disabled, and we hoped against hope that we could isolate Dad's massive debts and find a way for Mom to financially survive with her salary and maybe some disability payments to cover Dad's lost income. It would be easy for Mom to simply drive her own car and use her own debit card so we could sequester Dad's liabilities. They had not blended their banking in many years.

Through the next hellish ten days, I slept in their messy guest room and helped Mom navigate Dad's hospitalization and their ruinous financial situation. Mom kept primly to our plan. Any costs were paid directly by me or out of Mom's own account. Dad's massive black, leased SUV sat like an $800-a-month elephant in the driveway. The vehicle was a shrine to him—his goofy comedy CDs in the console, crumpled Coke cans and Bible study worksheets on the backseat floormats. It would remain untouched until I could make a case to the dealership to let us off the hook for the payments. We were trying to cordon off Dad's debts, a grasping effort to help keep Mom afloat.

On the eleventh day, I finally drove home, eager to smell my own shampoo in my hair and sleep next to my husband. To catch up at my job. To at least briefly exit the emergency mode we'd been in: vending machine food, the crater of debt, wondering if Dad would die. I called Mom that evening, which was the first she'd return to an empty house, perhaps the first time in many decades that she'd be sleeping alone. She wasn't home.

"Are you still in his room?" I wanted her to be home, to rest. Dad had not yet spoken since the stroke. Days at his bedside were draining—endless digital beeps from medical machines and exclusively one-sided conversations. The longer you stayed, the deeper the demoralizing effect. It had fully depleted me in the last week and a half.

"Nope, pumping gas," she reported. It was an upbeat declaration—and an odd one. I'd paid to fill her gas tank just before I left less than twenty-four hours ago.

She was driving Dad's big, black Honda SUV and using his debit card to pay. Our financial scheme may have been nonsensical, but there was comfort in it, while it lasted. She ditched our plan roughly five minutes after I left. I felt betrayed, not least because filling the very large gas tank was ridiculous; we hoped to turn in the car in two more days, on the weekend. I was too angry to speak. Mom filled the silence.

"I wanted a cheeseburger," she said petulantly. There was no reason provided why she couldn't get a cheeseburger with her own car and her own bank account. Or when I was still there. She declared this with unspoken certainty that I'd been denying her cheeseburgers, oppressing her. She was miserable. It was my fault. She was defiant.

Then I remembered: Mom was getting something for herself out of this interaction—rebellion, I guess. Independence.

Years before, a member of our church held an annual Super Bowl Sunday party centered on his wife Linda's regionally famous chili. Guests were to bring beer, or chips, or anything but chili. This was Linda's moment in the sun. For three consecutive years, Mom brought her own chili to Linda's in a Crock-Pot, the electrical cord wrapped around its belly. The fourth year, she was not invited.

Back in 2007, after Dad's stroke, I was worried about how to stretch the dollars in her account, how to find a rehab facility for Dad, how to emotionally navigate whatever tornado was subsuming the Longs. Mom was doing those things, too, but more powerful, and more peculiar, compulsions gripped her. For some years now, she had been experimenting with shifting parental responsibilities away from herself and on to me. I thought Dad's near-death might bring our relationship into a more elemental, rational phase. It did not. Nothing would. This exact hollowness is the feeling of losing your mother. In 2007, I did not know when she would die. She was gone already.

In many ways, I had already lost my father in 2011, when I visited him the day after he was discharged from the hospital after a tenuous open-heart surgery. He spun his wheelchair around a tight corner toward the kitchen of my parents' new-construction, all-beige house in Pontiac, Michigan, leaving a greasy black streak on the laminate floor. "I'll get your snack, Dad." I'd made the hour-plus drive to see him for the explicit purpose of helping him navigate the house post-surgery.

"No," he snapped at me, insisting I stand back and watch his labored trip to the edge of the counter, his hand shaking and reaching for the wheelchair brake lever, which he eventually engaged. Slowly, he began picking up items from the counter and stacking them in an arbitrary pile, making space for his snack project. Mom had covered every surface in catalogs, food packages, clean dishes that wouldn't fit in the cabinets. Dad took several silent minutes to get organized; the task required his full concentration. He shushed me every time I tried to help, so I stood, silent myself, and waited. Onto a red ceramic plate, he placed a large wedge of Danish pastry from a Panera Bread package. The cordless phone in his lap rang. He raised it to his ear without pressing a button to answer it and grew annoyed when no one spoke. A glass Pyrex measuring cup half full of chicken broth was on the counter, and Dad placed the ringing handset there, quieting it. With a serrated steak knife, he spread an inch-and-a-half-thick lump of soft salted butter onto the pastry. He added a fork to the plate, disengaged the brake, and began wheeling toward his hospital bed in the living room.

"Dad, I really could have gotten that for you." He had been fully disabled for four years at this point, which didn't lessen the pain I felt in seeing him in such a diminished physical and mental state. Until 2007, he had been vital and robust. My adored father. Even though his politics skewed far to the right of mine, even though his bragging, exaggerated stories were insufferable, we loved him. With this confused and obstinate man as my counterpart, I was a different version of a daughter now—impatient and sad in the kitchen of the new house where they were now dangerously behind on mortgage payments. I was also annoyed that I'd made the trip to spend the day helping him, and he refused.

The red plate teetered on his bare knees. Dad now always wore collared polo shirts, white underwear, and thick-soled orthopedic shoes but no pants. Today he still wore the plastic hospital bracelet printed with his name in caps, STEPHEN F. LONG. He brought his wheelchair to a stop in front of the TV, haltingly reached for the brake and set it, turned down the volume on Fox News, then spoke to me over his shoulder. "You wouldn't have added butter."

In December of 2012, having lost the house, they lived in a low-income, assisted-living apartment building, which my mother said Dad would never leave without my hands-on assistance. He was shaky, making uneasy transitions from wheelchair to car. The staff at the home or the visiting nurses or physical therapists could have helped, but Dad refused help from anyone but me. This was either a compliment or a whole lot to ask of someone who lived an hour away.

His heart, his brain, his mobility, and his mind were all compromised when, finally, his face deteriorated, too. The pink scar on his right cheek since his college football days had grown a plump sore. It oozed. It pressed his loose jowls taut in one spot. It was melanoma, maybe a vestige of his sunny Miami childhood. But after he'd had a stroke, and heart surgery, and a nervous breakdown, and so much more, how could he succumb to a bump on his face?

Mom scheduled an outpatient oral surgery to remove it. "Be here at eight thirty a.m. on Tuesday," she told me. The problem was I had to drop my daughter at school at eight, and then I had a work meeting at eleven and then—it didn't matter. There was no way whatsoever to move the surgery appointment, and Dad flatly refused anyone's help leaving the apartment except mine.

Keys in hand, I pushed through the stacks of fabric and clothes by the door and mustered a cheerful "Let's do this!" I expected to see Dad in a coat with his wheelchair rolled up to the door, ready.

"Not going." He was in his white underwear. The television hummed. President Obama was asking Congress for relief for Hurricane Sandy victims. "We were in a New York City hurricane once," he said.

"Okay, Dad, let's get some pants. Let's put you in the car. Let's get you into surgery."

Dad's focus was on Fox News. His cheek bled gently and he dabbed it. He thought Obama was being more generous than necessary. "None of this socialism," he grumbled. "Reagan wasn't giving any handouts in '85."

"Dad, we have an appointment. I took the day off work."

Mom emerged from the bathroom. "He's not going. He doesn't feel right about it today." Having already canceled my work and family plans for the day, I sat on their couch and talked or did chores in the apartment for a couple of hours, until I had to go to the bathroom. Long before today both the bathrooms in the apartment had become untenable, graphically gross. I left. On days I was visiting my parents, I used a restroom in the McDonald's two miles up the road.

Six weeks later, the bump was larger, and I took another day off work. Dad was in his coat when I arrived. Mom could have come with us, but she said she needed a break. "On your way home," she said, "could you stop at Tim Hortons and bring me a coffee, four creams?"

The oral surgeon was officious but kind. "After you," he said. The room was quite small. I hesitated.

"After you," he said a second time.

I suggested I'd find a spot in the waiting room, but Dad said, "You came all this way," and I went in.

Dad's wheelchair was pushed forward by the nurse. His chair was wider than the usual model, and when it didn't quite fit, she rocked and pushed until it did. The trim of the doorjamb snapped once, then hung loose on the inside. Little nails stuck out.

The surgeon followed. I took a step backward and felt a stool bump the backs of my knees. I sat, spinning unexpectedly. Four adults. One wheelchair. One immovable, plasticky, blue, reclining dental chair. The room was small.

I started physically negotiating my way out of the tiny space but found I was stuck, everyone and everything obstructing my way to the door. If there was another feeling in those years, besides the hollowness, it was the everything-is-closing-in feeling of being unwillingly confined. I'd looked for various ways to escape my parents and their problems, and I'd failed to find any routes out. All their lives, my parents built their own world—an island—with their own rules and their own truth. The harder I tried to get away the more permanently stuck I became. This February morning, Alcatraz was a suburban Detroit dental surgery office.

"I'll leave," I said.

The oral surgeon entered with a syringe held high. "This will be quick," he said. He numbed my father. Most people have melanoma growths removed when they are the size of a dime, or a pea. A golf-ball-sized cancer protruded from Dad's face.

Dad looked sideways over at me. He was probably terrified or possibly angry. I couldn't tell. His eyes watered. I closed mine. I didn't have the nerve to watch the golf ball emerge. The sound—muddy suction—and the smell—deathly—were enough.

★ ★ ★

After my father died, my mother was alone in their apartment, and I managed trips to see her as often as I could or whenever she summoned me.

"The freezer won't close," she told me on the phone. "It hangs open, and the food will spoil," she began to cry. I reminded her that in her assisted-living building there was a maintenance staff and they would help her and it wouldn't even cost anything. She cried and gasped and rebuffed my suggestions.

"Just come up and you can fix it," she told me. I had never fixed a refrigerator. I almost always felt like I was doing as much as I possibly could to help her, and I knew she was never satisfied. She wasn't shy about assessing how I was parenting my daughter as a full-time working mother, and yet most days she seemed to need me more physically and emotionally than my kindergartner did.

"I'll come up Saturday, but I'm going to call maintenance now and we'll see if they can help," I said.

"Don't you dare. Don't ever." Mom explained that she had received several warnings about her stacks and piles, which the management characterized as a fire hazard. She was on her last warning and they seemed to have forgotten about returning to make sure that she'd cleared a path for safety. "You'll have to fix it yourself. Or I'll get evicted and will have to live with you."

Days later, when I arrived, the once-frozen food in the freezer was soft and smelly. I hugged Mom quickly, but the odor indicated an emergency-level situation, so I went directly to it. She was right: the freezer door would not close. However, the only thing preventing it from closing was the abundance of things inside it. I removed one box of Eggo waffles and heard the assuring sound of the rubber gasket meeting its frame and sealing.

I should have hidden my annoyance but could not. Her freezer was "fixed" and now we were left with a fetid pile of melted ice cream and old, seeping, raw chicken. The smell spun my head. My stomach heaved. I agreed to clean it but sat down first to drink my takeout coffee and look within to try to find a more charitable version of myself.

"So, Mom, if the management is considering eviction, we have to talk about that." I moved a pile of hangered clothes from the sofa and sat down. A box of Stove Top dehydrated stuffing was tucked in the cushion behind my back. Years before, I had covertly called the Pontiac Fire Department to try to intervene with the hoarding situation in their house, and I was unsuccessful. Hearing that some other authorities—her apartment management—might be able to help me somehow was a beacon. It was leverage.

"They are nasty people, sending me nasty letters," she said. "It's not about the mess. They don't like me." Mom directed me to the table by the front door, where she'd kept the letters of warning. It was stacked heavily with sewing projects, notebooks, magazines, nail polish, canned food. She'd uncharacteristically cleared out a space in the center of the table's surface where three printer-generated letters sat atop a thick paperback book. "See for yourself," she urged me. "The letters are horrible."

I held my breath and walked to the table. I grabbed the letters, and because it was so clearly part of this display she'd staged for me, I glanced down at the book beneath them. It was titled *When Our Grown Kids Disappoint Us: Letting Go of Their Problems, Loving Them Anyway, and Getting On with Our Lives*.

The smell in the apartment was apocalyptic, and I began filling garbage bags and bleach-wiping surfaces. I returned the letters to her dining table. I did not know what to say, so I said nothing at all. She left for Kroger.

My throat burned from the ammonia odor of the old meat. My eyes leaked. My now-cold paper cup of coffee sat next to the book about adult children who are disappointing.

Mom returned with several bags of frozen food, more than would ever fit into her freezer. I went to McDonald's. I got a mediocre coffee for the drive home, but every time my hand neared my face for a sip, a little whiff of Mom's freezer came with it.

The years I spent with my parents are preserved by vivid extrasensory memories, but the actual facts of what happened feel impossible to pin down. My parents made things up. We hid our true selves from other families. Our stories changed. We pretended. We imagined. We lied, each in our own ways. The Longs were masters of reinvention. Our lies were aspirational, or desperate, or occasionally genuinely deceitful. We built our own island where whatever fictions we'd crafted were Gospel. We were the Longs, and we lived on Longs Island. We shaped the truth to evade consequences, and we definitely also lied for fun. My dad told and retold stories in loops, weaving in new information—real and imagined—anytime it suited him. The story of the years they were married, 1975 to my mother's death in 2015, is at once unforgettably hyperreal and the fakest, strangest, most ever-changing, tallest tale there is.

I lost them little by little, and since they've been gone, I've discovered more and more about them, little by little.

My period of mourning my parents was prolonged and peculiar. By the time they were gone, I had finished. I saw a therapist for the diabolical year and a half after my father died, before my mother died. At the session scheduled after her funeral—my last—I couldn't think of what to say. "I feel good," I managed eventually. It was difficult to admit.

And though I didn't have any more grief, or regret, I did have a monumental mystery ahead of me. I lived alongside my parents, closer than anyone, for thirty-seven years. Still, our time together was over before I had any idea at all who they were.

Dad's stories, even after his devastating stroke and aphasia, persisted until the day he died, complaining about President Obama in an Affordable Care Act–funded nursing home bed. In the year and nine months she outlived him, Mom's storytelling flourished, filling in unknown details about their life together. When their stories diverged, or departed drastically from my own memory or from widely accepted rationality, I checked with other sources. Newspapers and other media were the backbone of my research but, like most of us, many periods in my parents' lives were undocumented in the media. I used photos and letters and emails. I found audio recordings from the '90s. Check registries. Criminal court records. Traffic violation notices. Voicemails. The mold-scented garbage bags I loaded in my Toyota the day I ordered my mom's funeral flowers yielded precious clues.

An hour after I picked up the bag from Don, as the florist leveled her judgment at me across the little table covered in white netting, I thought about my car—sitting at a parking meter—and its contents. Eight garbage bags of financial papers, one garbage bag of morphine, and two thousand dollars in tens and twenties. My desire to leave the cramped shop took on a panicked, by-any-means-necessary urgency. The florist told me to take care of my mother instead of worrying about flowers. She said I should come back and go through the binder with her again and make some decisions, without rushing, whenever that sad day arrived.

"Any day now," I said, scooting my chair backward. I put the form and my mother's check on the little table and flew to the front door before she could protest, the perky chime following me onto the sidewalk.

PART ONE

Martinsville, Indiana
Huntington, West Virginia
Outer Philadelphia
Long Island, New York

1975 to 1986

ONE

Wedding announcement etiquette in small-town Indiana dictated that the bride's name should come first, but someone at the *Martinsville Reporter* decided that flipping the order of my parents' names would improve the headline. The May 5, 1975, edition proclaims "LONG-COX VOWS" in all caps beneath their nervously smiling faces.

Toward the end of the three decades I knew them, I often wondered which of the things they'd told me were true. I'd settled on roughly half, which factored in scant evidence like this *Reporter* clipping and accounted for me being trusting in my childhood and skeptical in my thirties. But fifty-fifty is really another way of saying you have no idea.

My father—split from both his birth family and his first marriage and kids—was a solo operator before they married. A businessman. A ladies' man. For part of 1972 he was simultaneously the manager of the Indianapolis Press Club and homeless. The following year, my parents met at a party where she was evading someone else's attention and asked him to pretend to be her boyfriend. They were pretending from their very beginning. My father agreed and followed her home that night, carrying an overstuffed Thom McAn shoebox.

Everything Dad owned in 1973 fit inside the shoebox. Without an apartment of his own, he most often slept on his friend Mike's couch, entering and exiting by squeezing his six-foot-four, former college football player body through the kitchen window during Mike's frequent business trips. He had not been entrusted with a key. He may not have actually had Mike's permission. Except for the shoebox, my father was entirely unencumbered.

He quit sleeping at Mike's the night he met my mother. The night before the party where they met was the last night either of them was ever truly alone again.

Rent for my parents' second-floor apartment was $16 per week and was collected Saturday mornings by their landlord, a Jehovah's Witness whose wife enforced a no-television rule. For over a year, there were very few Saturdays that my parents had $16 available when he arrived. At the first sound of the landlord at the front door, my father would conspiratorially whisper "Hey, Boo" to my mother. He'd turn the TV volume up while she took the week's empty glass Pepsi bottles out the back door. The noise of a cartoon laugh track covered the clanging sound of the bottles bumping together in the paper grocery bag she carried.

The landlord would lean heavily against the doorjamb, refusing to sit on the furniture. Dad would engage him in conversation, crouching strategically to keep sight lines open.

"Good show," Dad would say, gesturing at the screen.

"I don't watch TV," he'd answer, craning his neck for a better view. Once this routine was established, the landlord came later and later in the day, to avoid the kids' stuff in the morning and, hopefully, catch a football game. Dad retold this story in the '80s and the '90s, always ending it by wishing that Saturday morning TV would have shown something more salacious—some cleavage, maybe. He could have stalled the landlord for hours.

Mom had to return with the bottle deposit money before the landlord became impatient. She walked in the back door and added her coins to any bills in the apartment and usually made it to $16. One more week. If they were short, the landlord might stand longer at the threshold, taking his tax in black-and-white entertainment. He often forgave their arrears.

The week before the wedding, they paid their $16 and packed what they could of the apartment into their car. Mostly clothes, some papers, and kitchen things. Their dining table was aluminum and faux-wood grain with brown plastic handles on each side. When folded on its hinge, it fit into the backseat. They would be married on Saturday evening, then leave immediately for a new state and their new jobs the following Monday morning.

In a little brick Lutheran church in the town where my mother grew up, my father wore a ruffled, powder-blue tuxedo shirt under a black bow tie. Mom, whose long red hair had been pressed straight on an ironing board, smiled defiantly into the pews at her own mother and stepfather who'd said that at twenty-five she'd never meet anyone, that it was too late for her to avoid being an old maid. Her two best high school friends were already married. She dropped Cox. They became the Longs.

No meal was provided, only cake, champagne, and an oversweet red punch in a wide tureen. The post-ceremony celebration was in the community room of the Home Building Association, and the *Martinsville Reporter* also notes that "nuts and mints were served from silver bowls." Pelted with rice, laughing, holding each other, they walked into the church parking lot, where her brothers had tied the wedding gifts onto the car's roof with a thin rope.

Waving royally, they crept out of the lot, out of town and south and east toward West Virginia. The laden car shot through the dark night. The rope loosened around Louisville, and they watched their unopened wedding gifts spin onto the berm beside the highway. One by one, glass fruit plates and parcels of towels flipped off the roof and into rural Kentucky. They didn't stop the car.

When I was growing up, there was no evidence that any wedding gifts had ever existed. We had no matched set of fine china. But as long as I knew them, my parents' favorite pastime was inventing a version of reality that suited them better than actual reality. This story may or may not be true. It's absurd. Why wouldn't they stop the car? But also: Wouldn't they have at least one wedding gift? A single salad bowl? A candlestick?

All I know for sure is that I often heard this story, and every time I imagined my mother's straightened, burnt-orange hair blowing in and out of the car window at night, and unknown Kentuckians picking their way through the middle-class loot the next morning. Maybe their copious wedding haul filtered through the pawnshop ecosystem during lean months or was left behind in one of their middle-of-the-night moves. Or maybe a generation later in the Bluegrass State, bourbon is served in delicate matching glasses with another origin story that begins on the side of the road in 1975.

In the '80s, my mother told me that people with matching sets of plates—or silverware, or towels—looked down on us. I didn't feel that people looked down on us for being poor, which we were on and off throughout my childhood. It's possible they looked down on us for any number of other reasons, like our four-foot-high backyard grass or my parents' duplicity. She was right that people knew we were different. I knew, too.

As a girl in the suburbs of New York City, I ate dinner with a favorite fork, a heavy-handled number with a fleur-de-lis in relief below the tines, the only one like it in the drawer. Plucking it from the bouquet of other mismatched forks was a nightly ritual I enjoyed. No two towels in the hall closet matched; I was drawn to the one with the Toys "R" Us giraffe rendered in mint and peach on terrycloth. Our best glassware came in sets from Arby's at the holidays. There were the Garfield mugs from McDonald's and narrow, clear tumblers that held Kraft Old English sharp cheddar spread before they held our orange juice.

Eating dinner at a friend's house in first grade, I asked about her favorite fork and learned that every last one their family owned was identical. And they were poorer than us! I sat at the table with Karen and her mom and siblings under a fluorescent light, and we all waited for her dad to come in and tell each child how many chicken nuggets we were allowed to eat. It varied, seemingly based on both the child's size and their recent behavior and demeanor. I was allowed four—a guest's portion—and Karen got three. My meals at home had never been regulated this way. Her brother begged for a fourth nugget and was denied. I snuck him one of mine, sweaty palm to sweaty palm under the table. He and I never spoke.

Mom picked me up later that evening. Unable to hide my shock and disappointment at the fork situation, that was the aspect of the evening I mentioned, not the food rationing. "Karen's family's forks are *all exactly the same.*"

"I'm glad you enjoyed your fancy night out." Mom was always subtly checking to see how we measured up with other families, and if she felt someone had a leg up, she'd set the record straight. Dad would back her up. The two of them had concocted a bizarre world together—the myth of our family, the Longs—and were its loving, fiercest defenders.

Our across-the-street neighbor was sometimes lauded for her exotic beauty (one blue eye, one brown) and her inimitable Italian gravy, slow-cooked on Sundays and infusing our neighborhood with fragrant tomato and onion scents all afternoon. These accolades were never mentioned without at least one rejoinder.

"But her husband yells at her," Mom would say anytime the aromatic gravy was mentioned, which made her jealous. He did yell. Nightly, we'd hear Jimmy shout her name across six angry syllables, "An-gel-ah-ah-ah-ah!"

"And he works construction," Dad might add, derisively.

"There's more to life than gravy." Case closed.

On the car ride home from Karen's, Mom repeated the "wedding gifts on the side of the road" story. "We *had* a full set of dishes and silverware," adamant, "but we never got to use them."

TWO

The summer before their wedding, my mother was the subject of a full-page story in the *Indianapolis Star*. "Woman Finds Career Fixing Typewriters More Interesting." The story purports that typewriters are normally "women's entry to the white-collar office world," and my mother, in plaid pants, is pictured winding the inner mechanism of a typewriter, which has been pulled apart and is upside down. She was IBM's first female engineer in 1973, and she visited offices throughout the city, carrying wrenches and a primitive beeper. Men in offices gaped at her over their wide, wire-rimmed glasses and pinched her bottom. The article says she likes this work better than doing secretarial work herself, which she'd done in New York at a new building called the World Trade Center in 1971 and '72, the first years it was open. In the photo, her glossy, naturally curly hair is ironed straight as a broomstick.

IBM transferred her to their Huntington, West Virginia, office, and my father's job, selling paperbacks on commission door to door to retailers for Simon & Schuster, had allowed him to continue with his work from their new home. He later told me that in Indianapolis, all the gas stations had spinning wire racks of books. He'd drive around with his suitcase of new releases and an order pad and talk up the proprietors, setting them up with stock. He excelled at talking to people, persuading and flattering and small-talking like no one else. In Huntington, there were fewer readers, or at least, fewer gas stations with spinning racks for books. Dad had to drive farther and farther into the hills each day to make a sale, and the deeper into Appalachia he went, the less likely he was to find anyone interested in what he was selling.

Mom worked for IBM in the daytime and at night plunged herself into the red-and-white-checkered *Better Homes & Gardens New Cook Book*. In the shadow of Mary Tyler Moore, Mom was part career-driven Mary Richards and part homemaker Laura Petrie. She made ham with brown sugar and raisin sauce. Ketchup-slicked meatloaf and scalloped cheddar potatoes from a box. Chicken à la king with canned creamy mushroom soup and frozen peas beneath a crust of tubed biscuits. Dad's favorite was porcupine meatballs, the sauce tangy and the beef stretched with rice.

They invested in a glamorous, full-sized brass bed whose knobs spun and slid on its hollow pipes. Either to distinguish herself from what they called the hillbillies around them or to keep herself occupied after hours, my mother took up antique collecting and refinishing, filling their apartment with broken-legged chairs and toxic fumes. Their West Virginia landlords—altogether different than the Jehovah's Witness landlord in Martinsville—lived on the lower floor of their duplex and didn't mind the smell.

The landlord couple downstairs were about their age, and they were loud. She wore denim shorts cut off as high on her thigh as possible while still technically being shorts. His beard was part mountain man, part hippie. They had a lot of visitors. They fought and shouted at each other. My clean-cut parents fought, too, but mostly with glares and silent treatment.

"Hey, Boooooo!" the wife called out their front door. My mother looked at my father, wondering if he'd betrayed their secret Boo name to Miss Short Shorts downstairs.

"Don't holler at me, Boo! Go round back," her husband shouted in reply. She went to the rear window, giving him hell while my parents listened upstairs. After hearing them argue, my mother decided she liked them and especially enjoyed that they also called each other Boo. My father liked that rent was only due once a month, not once a week.

The two couples played cards some Friday nights, drinking beer, sometimes whiskey. Downstairs had more furniture, so gatherings were usually in the landlords' apartment. Mom complained about being ogled at work. Just like in Indiana, here in West Virginia she was the only female IBM engineer in the state. Dad complained about the lack of books in gas stations.

"Peanuts," the landlord said, laying his cards on the table. The house was warm, and smoke from four cigarettes lingered around them. You could smell that my mother had fried pork chops upstairs earlier. "Peanuts. There's money there," he said.

In the back bedroom downstairs, there were several cases of peanuts and mixed nuts. The landlord explained that his income came from sourcing these vending machine nuts and then refilling them in venues around Huntington. "You think I live on just your rent?" He laughed.

"It's so easy," he told Dad. "And you're already driving all the hell everywhere to gas stations. You could join up, help me get some new accounts."

Dad wondered if more people in West Virginia might be interested in peanuts by the handful than they were in paperbacks. Mom considered the money. The landlords' apartment was nicer, their lifestyle plusher, with fully intact furniture and whiskey to serve guests. A life of luxury, built on peanuts.

Dad quit Simon & Schuster, stars in his eyes.

A massive amount of nuts was shipped to the duplex.

"Damn," the landlord said, helping Dad haul the cardboard cases up the exterior back stairs. My parents had found enough money to lay in a large order to get started. Dad was not a halfway sort of guy. The landlord stacked box atop box. One of them had greasy dark splotches where oil and salt leached through.

Mornings, Dad dropped Mom at IBM's parking lot and then returned home to load up. Plenty of places housed these peanut machines—glass globes on metal columns with a coin slot and turn knob. The problem was efficiency. A handful of nuts cost only a dime, and the time and gas money to drive to a remote location and restock a couple dollars' worth of nuts didn't leave much yield. At less-trafficked gas stations the nuts would go stale or even rancid before they all sold. Some places didn't have a machine, but they'd be willing to take one. Dad would call a 1-800 number to order it and then he'd be responsible for the cost of the machine until it turned a profit, maybe a year later. It was, in short, a peanut racket, sending my parents into peanut debt.

"Pass," Mom said.

"Pass," the wife said, ashing her cigarette into the tray in the middle of the table.

"Pass," Dad said.

"Screw the dealer, I guess," the landlord said. "Hearts." They played euchre most Fridays now, always downstairs. The closer Dad got to the nut business, the more he realized that he was the only guy in Huntington who was actually in the nut business. The landlord, a prescient ancestor to West Virginia's twenty-first-century opioid crisis, was full-time in the drug business. Because he had a bank loan, he also needed a legit, on-paper income stream: that was peanuts. Strange pickup trucks arrived most nights for quick exchanges at the front door. The downstairs phone rang at the oddest hours. There was cash stacked in squared-off piles behind the dishes in their kitchen cabinet. These are not the lifestyle characteristics of a vending machine peanut salesman.

A loud bang popped outside. Neither of my parents could be sure whether it was gunfire. Mom considered crawling under the dining table. Dad's eyes widened when the landlord scooted his chair back and reached into the dining room hutch behind him, pulling out a massive black shotgun without even standing up. He stalked the noise into the dark, humid night, gun on his shoulder, until he found a raccoon, who was likely responsible for the ruckus. By this time, Mom noticed that the wife had gone to the kitchen to put the stacked cash inside her underwear beneath her short shorts, and she was holding a smaller gun of her own, aiming it out the back door.

The card game resumed, one of its players with a couple thousand dollars down her pants. The Longs won. They were playing for points, not money.

It was nice that rent was only due once a month, but less nice that the amount they owed was so much more than the weekly $16 they'd paid in Indiana. Some months were worse than others for nut commissions. My mother's paycheck vanished into groceries and clothes, which had always been a primary creative outlet for her. After high school, she'd left Martinsville to study fashion design at Pratt Institute in New York, where she lasted only a year as a student but carried forever what she learned in Brooklyn in 1970: that clothes make the man—or woman.

In 1977, a year and a half into living in what they now called "West by god Virginia," they knew it was time to leave, in part because they didn't have the coming month's rent. They used a portion of the rent money they did have for a U-Haul truck, which Dad parked two blocks away on a Friday afternoon.

After dinner, euchre and drinks downstairs proceeded as usual, except that my parents took on the role of topping off their hosts' whiskey tumblers whenever possible, hoping to induce sleep, or at least incoherence. The game went long past midnight, the hosts finally succumbing to exhaustion. My parents went upstairs and started pulling apart the brass bed, putting forks and mugs in boxes and bags. Ever so quietly, they unloaded all they could out the back stairs and onto the rear lawn, whispering and tiptoeing as they hauled bedrails and spaghetti pots. Dad pulled the truck around, then cut the engine and let the driveway's slope pull it down near the yard. They loaded it all slowly and quietly, without a single crash or a thud. The only things left in the upstairs apartment were some antique furniture in disrepair and cases and cases of unsold nuts. Dad turned over the engine, and the U-Haul rumbled to life around dawn. They drove to Pennsylvania.

THREE

I was born in a Philadelphia hospital in the summer of 1978. A few months before, the Blizzard of '78 tore through the East Coast and created in my mother a desperate craving for peach ice cream. Dad couldn't dig out the car and walked through 16-inch snowdrifts to 7-Eleven, where he found a pint and trudged back to their apartment complex.

The Thunder Hollow Apartments were hundreds of townhome-style units with private entrances arranged on a loop called Thunder Circle. They all looked the same: ecru siding, sliding glass doors in the back, little shuttered windows up top. They only lived there one year. Dad told the ice cream story and another one over and over throughout my childhood.

"You couldn't tell these places apart," he'd say. Every door in the complex was the same color. Every window had long, off-white vertical slats as blinds. "We had a terrible problem there with drunks." Arriving home late from a bar or boozy dinner, some men couldn't tell one apartment from the next. They'd stumble between concrete stoops, peering into dark windows to try to recognize a sofa or a wife—anything to provide a clue of which apartment was theirs. "Sometimes these lowlifes were even putting their keys into our lock, trying to get in the wrong place." Dad was incredulous, telling this story years later. The gall of these wanton men.

At least twice, a drunk had tried and failed to get home and was found sprawled on the steps outside in the morning. Hearing this story as a kid, I envisioned this: a large, dark-haired, mustachioed white man holding a briefcase and wearing a khaki trench coat with the belt undone, asleep outside in the early light. The man I pictured was basically Dad, but, unlike Dad, this guy was despicable, smelly. A societal blight.

"But people could put different things in their windows," I'd suggest. I heard the story enough times to begin poking holes in it with grade-school-level logic. Was it really that hard to find your way in the Thunder Hollow Apartments complex? Couldn't you tape something to the door handle or put out a flowerpot or something? It plagued me as a kid, trying to understand this.

"Nothing worked," Dad declared. "You simply couldn't tell them apart. I was lucky in the Blizzard of '78. I guessed right. Your mother would have killed me if she didn't get her peach ice cream."

I was in pursuit of the truth. "I thought only drunks couldn't tell."

"Yes, drunks, but can you imagine finding your way with a foot and a half of snow on the ground? You couldn't."

I have limited information about our year in Philadelphia. There's one photo of me, five weeks old in August 1978, held by a blissed-out, long-haired Lutheran pastor at my baptism. My twenty-eight-year-old mother wears a black sailor-style dress, piped in white, a subtle curl in her dark-red hair, hazel eyes. She looks exactly the way I did when I was twenty-eight. In addition to this photo, the peach-ice-cream-in-a-blizzard story, and the drunks-on-the-stoop story, there is just one more artifact, a tale from my birth.

The doctor was a woman and Indian American. It was a novelty that Dad was in the delivery room, a signal that women's lib had burst into all aspects of life, even its beginning.

Like my father, I'm big. I'm five eleven, broadly built, strong. He was six four, played varsity high school and college football, and for a month or two the Dallas Cowboys flirted with recruiting him. He shopped exclusively at Big & Tall stores. I have the woman's version of his big and tall body, and when I was born, headfirst, my shoulders got stuck.

"'Oooh, big baby!'" Dad retold the story with a cloying Indian accent. "You like to have a football player with big shoulders?" the doctor asked him.

The doctor reached for forceps and extracted me, mushing my face square. It stayed that way for a week, enough time for the nickname Buickface to take hold and carry on into my childhood.

"Well," she said to him when I was finally released into the world nude and newborn and not a boy, "girls can play football, too."

FOUR

Two and a half months later, in the fall of 1978, my father got a job in New Jersey as a janitorial product sales rep for SC Johnson Wax. They began house hunting near the office but found what they could afford was smaller than their vision of their first home purchased together. In an ever-expanding outward circle, they scoured exurban New Jersey and even stretched into Connecticut but still didn't find what they wanted. Finally, they landed at the least sensible of all their options—a three-bedroom, one-and-a-half-bath colonial in the middle of Long Island's South Shore in the town of Medford. Dad's commute would be at least two hours each way; he'd be driving through Manhattan at rush hour both times.

Separately and together, my parents had a knack for self-made obstacles, a proclivity for building situations of extreme hardship for themselves. It made them happy. I came to understand it as something sacred about their true selves. Buying a house whose location promised four hours of commuting each day brought them a distinctive sense of satisfaction, their travails validated and the chaotic world momentarily clicking into precise alignment as they signed the real estate paperwork.

With an advance from his new job, they took a mortgage for the house and a lease for a new silver Chrysler New Yorker Fifth Avenue with wire-spoke hubcaps. He would be on the road a lot.

Mom would be home a lot, with me.

As an adult, I've spent some time trying to sort out if one or the other of them was propelling their shared values on childrearing, which were retro in a gendered sort of way but also the distinct opposite of old-fashioned. We didn't live near or talk to any family members. My mother, who had stopped working when they left West Virginia, had a few pen pals in Indiana but no friends in New York. Even though only a decade before she'd lived in Bed-Stuy when she was going to Pratt and later working in Manhattan, Mom had no social life outside our little house.

In the early '80s, a new archetype of a woman was emerging. Laura Petrie and her homemaking were out. An '80s woman would, as the Enjoli perfume commercial showed us, "bring home the bacon *and* fry it up in a pan." TV was telling my mother that she could have it all, but she had no interest then in balancing both a career and a family. Dad agreed.

"I'm so glad you're not one of these selfish women that put their kids in daycare," he would say to her, with genuine love and admiration.

"Those poor children," Mom would agree.

It was insidious, their way of translating the world into who could do what. It gave them comfort. Even though my mother said over and over that being a mother was the most important thing and it was why she was put on this earth, and it was the only thing that truly made her happy, and that I as her daughter was the very best friend she could ever or would ever have, I think she was probably lonely. I was.

Before my brother was born, and even after, most of my time was split between Mom and my imaginary friend Himbee, a miniature guy who looked a bit like the comic strip character Ziggy and drove a pink sports car the size of a football.

Mom—perpetually annoyed that I wasn't the kind of kid who would nap—bribed me with strawberry-banana milkshakes in exchange for thirty minutes of daytime sleep, which I faked when I couldn't avoid it. In sharp contrast to Mom, Himbee was omnipresent and undemanding.

After too many listens of the "Jesus Loves Me" song at Sunday school, I'd developed a conviction that the line "Little ones to him belong" was a reference to the name of a family member I'd not yet met. I was Amanda Long. My parents were Stephen and Sandie Long. "Him belong" was

Himbee Long, a stalwart companion during the languid early '80s of my preschool days home alone with Mom while Dad was driving to New Jersey and back. We were not park people or outdoor people, thanks mostly to Mom's debilitating phobia of snakes. We were inside types. My mother sewed. I watched *Sesame Street* in the mornings. In the afternoons, she'd spread a blanket on the living room floor and pull the blender onto the kitchen counter—an enticement for me to sleep, to give her a break.

"Let's take a nap together," she'd say, checking the freezer for ShopRite strawberries.

"Can't do it," I'd say. "Himbee needs me in the other room." Himbee and I hung out in the downstairs half bath, where my father had about twenty *Penthouse* magazines under the sink. Himbee spoke what I called "Spanish," just a jumble of nonsense, really, but it was unintelligible to adults.

"What are you saying in there?" Mom called through the locked bathroom door.

"Himbee and I are talking," I said. Himbee often asked me why the women in the magazines didn't wear clothes, and I had no idea what to tell him. This was discussed, in Spanish, often. We emerged from the bathroom to find Mom asleep on the living room floor. The carpet was textured and rust colored, and one full wall of the room was an entertainment center made of particleboard with wood-looking veneer over it, golden handles on its many drawers and doors. A boxy TV sat right in the middle.

Mom lay under a blanket with her eyes closed and mouth open. Richard Dawson's *Family Feud* was on, and I always liked to see who he would kiss. It seemed like a glamorous honor to be recognized that way. He always wore a boutonniere, sometimes a tuxedo.

Afternoons were long while my father was at work. Mom and I shopped after her nap. Modell's, Swezey's, Caldor, the drugstore. Sometimes we just drove around until the radio played Hall and Oates, which was Mom's favorite music. If the shopping had been particularly exhausting, we would go to Carvel afterward for a flying saucer ice cream sandwich. Or we'd go home and she'd mix powdered strawberry Quik into milk for me and add ice and cream to the leftovers in the morning coffeepot for her. We'd drink it on the back deck if our neighbor wasn't outside.

Next door, on the other side of a tall, impenetrable fence, our neighbor had two black rottweilers and a primitive sound system. Mom and I found both deeply annoying. The dogs would growl and bark, disturbing our peace. But worse was the neighbor, who was a Pentecostal preacher with no family we ever saw. His rear upstairs bedroom had a balcony where the sound system's speaker was permanently installed on a pole. Weekday afternoons he stood on the balcony, trying out new material for the weekend worship service, beginning with quiet sincerity and winding up to breathless, fevered intensity. *You will be SAVED*, the last word shouted. He'd try again, with different emphasis: *You WILL be saved*.

Praise GOD. He will DELIVER you from your enemies. The dogs snarled menacingly below. *YOU will be saved*.

One afternoon when the neighbor was particularly impassioned, we got in the car. Mom wanted to shop and have an extended browse at makeup in the drugstore, and I didn't.

"It's hot. Just come in," she said.

I refused.

"You'll be bored."

"Himbee's here."

"I might be awhile."

"I know."

The backseat of our emerald-green '76 Mercury Cougar was black Plasticine leather, sticky hot on days like this one. Each side of the back had an oval opera window, which I pretended was a portal into Narnia or a fast-food drive-up window where I was taking orders. On a previous afternoon outing, I'd gotten McDonald's Happy Meal stickers that turned out to be the exact size of the button to depress on the Cougar's seat belts. A white, yellow, and red image of Ronald McDonald was affixed to each end of each seat belt. In the heat, the adhesive was slipping off a little. Even with Himbee there, I grew bored. Hot. She'd cranked the windows down before going in, but I cranked them back up, then down again, spinning the translucent spool at the end of the handle.

Sometimes we went to the bank, whose drive-up teller in heavy mascara always wore a silk blouse with a tie, as sophisticated to me as the women on *Family Feud*. She spoke to my mother through a microphone on a long, metal stem, like game show microphones and so similar, I now realized, to the Cougar's gearshift. I moved to the front seat.

"How many dollars?" I asked Himbee into the gearshift microphone. He replied in Spanish, and we continued a volley of banking conversation together. I found it frustrating that the microphone didn't move. The gear—in park—was immobile. I spun the heating knobs, pressed the radio buttons in and out, ran my hand over the burled, faux-wood steering wheel.

My mother's keys swung from the ignition where she'd left them. I'd seen her do this move so many times that I knew I could replicate it. I turned the key forward, and the Cougar's engine came alive with a four-year-old at the wheel. And now the microphone seemed willing to move, to glide up and down. Himbee agreed it was worth trying, and I slipped the microphone downward, putting the car into drive. My legs kicked loose, feet nowhere near the pedals. We crept forward toward the pharmacy, Himbee, the Cougar, and me, until a woman began yelling. She ran toward the car and put her arm inside, jamming the gearshift up into park again. Her nails were long and frosty pink. She was shrieking, "*What are you doing?*"

My mother came out of the pharmacy. The pink-nailed woman shrieked at her, too, but my mother said, "She's only four. She didn't know."

A small crowd gathered to shame my mother, and she made a quick pivot to stop defending me. She needed to deflect.

"You could have rolled backward into the street and been killed!" she shouted at me. "You could have wrecked the car! Or run into the building!"

I cried. The pink-nailed woman seemed happy that blame had been meted out to me, if not my mother. Mom got in, put the car in reverse, and stopped yelling.

She looked at me in the rearview mirror and said, dispassionately, "Well, we can't go back there again, thanks to you."

Neither of us told Dad. Mom sighed heavily whenever we drove by that drugstore or whenever she schlepped to the next town over, to their drugstore where she hadn't been shamed. The store took a weird hold in my head, reminding me I *could* have gone inside with her that day. Or I could have just not played bank or shifted the gear. Or I could have not been stopped by the pink-nailed woman and maybe the Cougar would have coasted into the bricks and glass of the building, the kind of thing you see on the local evening news: car smashes into building.

FIVE

Himbee and I looked forward to our long afternoon breaks in the downstairs bathroom, which was wallpapered in blue and white and had a framed pencil drawing of a walrus in a bathtub. When we tired of examining the walrus, we looked at the magazines under the sink. The nudity I took in stride. But the Technicolor makeup, the extreme height and fluff of the models' early-'80s hair was fascinating. These women were putting themselves in such hilarious situations—roller-skating with no pants!!!—that I couldn't look away.

The afternoon that I saw a woman lounging by a rainforest waterfall with her legs wide open, in high heels, I just had to invite someone else to marvel at this absurdity with me and Himbee.

Mom was pregnant and napping on the floor of the living room. Her original offer to give me a milkshake if I slept alongside her had long since been replaced by the offer of a milkshake if I allowed her to sleep undisturbed. I considered that as I walked out of the half bath, my finger holding the page of this foolish, you'd-have-to-see-it-to-believe-it picture. Sacrificing the milkshake, I shook her awake.

I expected Mom to commiserate with me. I imagined her incredulity would match mine. "*Heels, in the jungle?!*" she might laugh. But instead, she screamed about Dad, who I learned was the real owner of the magazines I'd been looking at every afternoon with Himbee. Mom didn't know that I knew they were there, in plain sight in the under-sink cabinet. She called Dad's office, but his secretary, Geraldine, said he'd already left for home.

All the *Penthouse* magazines were stacked on the front porch next to our firewood when the Chrysler Fifth Avenue pulled into the driveway that evening, and I never saw them again.

Dad decided that Mom's pregnancy was making her ill-tempered, and he doubled down on his own parenting efforts.

He made breakfast most days of the week, clicking on the Mr. Coffee and composing one of his two mainstays: eggs-mixed-with-toast or coffeebread.

Combine a runny fried egg with buttered white toast cut into a crosshatch of sixteen cubes: eggs mixed with toast, a workaday breakfast that was also served religiously the day after a stomach flu to all members of my family.

More often, he and I ate coffeebread while Mom slept in. Dad claimed that his Miami upbringing had taught him this special Cuban recipe. "No one else in New York eats this," he told me. He'd eaten it himself in diners in Miami on mornings after his late nights as a nightclub booking manager there in the '60s. He'd eaten it with his own dad, who swirled Carnation evaporated milk into the coffee instead of half-and-half, which we favored. Everything about coffeebread seemed cosmopolitan to me, especially that it was a breakfast eaten in a restaurant.

Our kitchen wallpaper was rusty orange and brown with a psychedelic '70s farmer motif. EGGS and MILK were rendered in stretched bubble letters beneath stylized illustrated cows, farmers in wide-brimmed hats, and aproned milkmaids. Our appliances were avocado. I studied the wallpaper, learning to read *eggs* and *milk* as my earliest words, and Dad made coffeebread.

Take soft white bread and spread thickly with room-temperature butter. Put it into a low bowl and cover its surface with white sugar. Add hot coffee, and top with enough half-and-half so that the liquid is no longer hot and no longer very brown. The hot coffee melts the butter and turns most of the sugar liquid. If you use enough sugar, a few crystals will still crunch. I pushed my spoon into the now-spongy bread to cut a bite, floating in cream. I felt so lucky, so genteel.

"This is our morning routine, right, kiddo?" Dad spooned sugar onto buttered bread. "Shit, shower, shave, breakfast, then we go!"

I barely noticed the swear, but he corrected himself. "Oh, let's use your Grandma Long's version, a *PTA*." He declined to tell me what those letters meant.

Dad watched me eating and made a beckoning motion with his right hand, curling his fingers toward himself.

"What?" I asked him, my mouth full of spongy, sweet bread.

"You have to tell me you appreciate it. Tell me it's delicious."

"Oh, I like it!" I answered. And he hung his head in a faux-bashful puppy slump. "I love it, actually!" I said, and he was happy. Dad lived for my praise, my laughter.

In 1982, he took me, at four years old, to see *Annie* on Broadway.

More memorable than the show, for me, was the drive through Lower Manhattan before the performance. At a stoplight I saw two men on ten-speed bikes, one with acid-green hair puffing out in gelled tufts and the other who had shaved but all but a narrow strip of black hair down the middle of his head. His mohawk defied gravity, standing upright in triangular points a foot off his scalp. I was afraid and intrigued, and I pressed my face against the glass window separating us.

"Don't stare," Dad told me. I insisted on knowing how their hair achieved those heights, but Dad was derisive, disinterested. "Egg whites," he finally muttered. I watched the men weave their bikes dangerously through lanes of Union Square traffic, impressed that their little bikes had agility and speed, unlike our car. "Don't worry about it. They're freaks."

Dad bought a battery-operated electronic keyboard that he rested on the front passenger seat for his long drives to his office. West off of Long Island on the Long Island Expressway, into the city and directly across it to New Jersey, he drove with his left hand, and with his right noodled out doo-wop melodies every morning. On certain Fridays I was invited to ride with him for an office day. "The Buickface will ride in the Chrysler!" he'd announce.

The two-hour drive between our house and Northvale, New Jersey, went by very quickly. We listened to *Imus in the Morning*. I asked to stop in Manhattan and see the punk hairdos, and I was almost always refused. Dad told me stories about a girl named Penelope who apparently lived in the tall pine tree behind our house and who I imagined as a prim, independent girl in a white dress. He ranted about his secretary Geraldine. "What kind of name is Geraldine, anyway?" he asked me over his shoulder. "It sounds like a prescription medication. *Take your geraldine*," he whined to get me to laugh in the backseat. "I think she must be Jewish," he said.

After *Imus*, Dad sang and played one-handed piano versions of late-'50s Black artists' hits. "Get a job," he'd sing, "sha na na na, sha na na na na," somehow pulling off the melody while he merged into the Lincoln Tunnel.

He always tried to close with his favorite, "Silhouettes." "Took a walk and passed your house *late last night*," he cried out, adding volume to the last three words like a nightclub singer. "All the shades were pulled and drawn *way down tight*."

He'd learned piano riffs, and how to belt out a song on key, twenty years earlier when he was in a college frat-rock band called the Hustlers, and after that in his Miami nightclub days when he was booking music and selling hotel rooms. Every day in the late '60s, even weekends, he wore a suit and a thin tie, along with a bracing cologne, and his hair was trimmed into a tidy cut he called a "duck's ass." He was a regular at several hotel bars, buying mai tais for Playboy Bunnies and dancing to Afro-Cuban music until he was eventually hired to book the bands himself at the McAllister Hotel.

It was in his blood. When Dad was a kid in the '40s, my grandfather worked evenings at a shoe store in downtown Miami, and my grandmother played drums in a lady jazz band. She sometimes did hair but would not call herself a beautician, a term she reserved for graduates of cosmetology school, which she was not. Dad's parents were heavy drinkers.

Dad's little brother Billy died as a toddler, just before the advent of penicillin. His parents drank more after that.

Summers and weekends, Dad slept at his grandparents' apartment in the pink stucco building they owned and operated, Littles' Apartments, while his own parents stayed out late in Miami Beach bars. Early mornings, with Grandma and Grandpa Little still asleep, Dad would slip out and visit the other five apartments, asking for breakfast, telling a sad story. He might pick up scrambled eggs in apartment four and then oatmeal in apartment six before sitting down to pancakes with his grandparents midmorning. He was good at talking to people, convincing. Even during years when WWII food rationing was still in place for things like sugar, he swindled his way into many-breakfast mornings during his parents' hangovers.

"You lied?" I asked him, years later. "You said you didn't have any food at your house?"

"Of course I didn't lie," he insisted. "I told them I was hungry. I was."

SIX

After my brother Adam was born at the end of 1982, Mom and I stayed home even more. She announced that with this pregnancy behind her, she would be fulfilling a yearslong dream of frosting her hair, which she now wore with its natural curl. She began by adding an ashy blond only to the tips of her dark, red-brown hair. Over time, the blond gradually dominated.

We watched TV. I colored. She took care of Adam and sat at her sewing machine anytime she could. After a fresh snow, she'd send me outside with a Tupperware bowl, a spoon, and Hershey's syrup to make snow sundaes while she fed Adam a bottle. Before I started school, neither she nor I ever had any friends over, though occasionally she sat at the kitchen table and pulled the coiled phone cord across the room for a conversation with her mother in Indiana or her friend Gwen.

I knew to never interrupt during long-distance calls.

There were fewer afternoon shopping trips. I rarely visited Manhattan after that, and my father's work was changing from his day job at SC Johnson to new endeavors that involved multiday trips away from home.

First, he was promoted, and there were trips to the SC Johnson headquarters in Racine, Wisconsin. His boss's boss worked in the outrageously grand Frank Lloyd Wright–designed office building, all salmon-colored carpet and soaring columns, a Busby Berkeley film set come to life in a small Wisconsin city. In Racine, Dad learned about kringle pastry, which he carried home for us smooshed flat into his suitcase. But he was straining at the edges of his work life, looking for something more.

Around 1983, without consulting my mother, he bought an oil derrick somewhere in Texas, a fact we learned when he wore a cowboy hat home from the office one evening. It went well with his mustache. Dad had bought the hat at a Western shop in the city, where he was making more and more frequent detours on his drive home. He'd bought the oil well from a man he met in a Greenwich Village bar on the way home.

The hat, of stiff tan felt with a patterned-ribbon trim, was not authentic, but that didn't dissuade me from wearing it whenever I could get my hands on it. I paired it with a quilted mauve coat that hit my leg mid-calf and felt to me—like coffeebread and like the Andes mints we occasionally unwrapped after dinner—glamorous. I wore the hat and coat when lip-synching to Mom's Barry Manilow records, my new afternoon activity now that there was a baby in the house. I never wore it when Dad was home.

He went on a trip to Texas to check his oil well's progress and returned to Long Island no longer its owner. Dad expected that being in the oil business would be lucrative, but after most of a year, he owed money instead. He was officially out of the oil business. Dejected, Dad gave me the hat. I wore it often.

I also wore dentures. In preschool, kindergarten, and first grade, the same years I was obsessed with the cowboy hat and the elegant mauve coat, I was without my four front teeth. When I was two or three months old, Mom learned that I loved apple juice. I liked it more than milk or water, and she filled Playtex-nippled bottles with Mott's apple juice for me several times a day. I stopped crying whenever I got apple juice. She put me to sleep nightly for years with a full bottle I'd drain while I drifted off. "It was like magic for you," she later told me.

By the time I was four, the enamel on the backs of my teeth had been eaten away by the acidic juice that pooled in the roof of my mouth, eroding my teeth. From the front, the problem was invisible, but after I complained about what I called a "headache in my teeth," a dentist looked at the backs of my front teeth and found them black and mottled.

He pulled all four of them and fitted me with a translucent plastic plate with fake teeth attached.

Mom felt guilty. She wrote to a friend of hers back in Indiana, confessing, and in anguish.

"You couldn't have known," her friend Penny replied in 1982. "Little Mandie will be just fine."

I was fine. I must have been sedated for the actual tooth-pulling because I only remember the aftermath, and the pulpy holes in my top gums, into which I'd poke my tongue and taste a bit of blood. I took it all neutrally, though once the rotten teeth were out, I felt different. I'd had a "headache in my teeth" for years. Without a permanent toothache, I was a new person.

I fed the dentures to our cat. Once my painful teeth were removed, the problem was solved as far as I was concerned. Toothlessness was irrelevant, and the dentures were annoying. The plastic plate hit the roof of my mouth deep in the back, triggering my gag reflex.

Given the enormous cost of kid dentures, as soon as they brought the dentures home, my parents began joking that it would be just their luck that one of our cats, Lucy or Ethel, would find and destroy them. I'd only ever seen them eat Meow Mix, so I wondered what a cat would want with dentures anyway. During one of Mom's naps, I held them in front of Ethel gently: pinkish plastic, a wire, four little white knobs nestled into fake gums. I was right. Ethel was mostly disinterested, but I'd done the necessary damage by having her chew them a bit. I left the dentures in her food bowl for Mom to find later.

When the cat-gnarled denture plate was replaced with another expensive set of false teeth, I hoped to permanently lose it. I tried squeezing it between the boards of our back deck. I thought my parents wouldn't so quickly replace something that might still be found. Mom caught me crouched on the deck, unsuccessfully trying to jam the little teeth into the gap. She pulled the dentures out of my hand and wiped them on her pants.

She told me I'd be eating a lot of Cream of Wheat between then and whenever my adult teeth grew in. Which I did, along with eggs mixed with toast and coffeebread and other foods that don't require incisors.

By the time she retold this story to me in the '90s, she'd apparently worked through the guilt she cited in her letters from 1982. "Apple juice made you so happy," she told me. "I wouldn't have given you so much, but you just demanded it."

SEVEN

Dad worked for the Johnson Wax part of SC Johnson, and floor wax was their bread and butter. Stripping and waxing commercial floors were all part of the demonstration he did to sell a whole package of cleaning products to a school or a corporation. Every sale began with floors and grew to include hand soap and glass cleaner and furniture polish. On the side, Dad began to tinker with ideas that SC Johnson hadn't yet: a new kind of soap dispenser for public restrooms, an innovative mophead.

Evenings after work, he'd stop in Manhattan regularly for business meetings with prospective investors and partners. He wanted out of his regular job. Dad had a Ziggy coffee mug that said "I hate paperwork!" and seemed to embody his approach to working life. Talking to people and making sales calls was always fine by him, but he hated the slog of day-to-day tasks. He didn't care to have Geraldine looking over his shoulder, reminding him of appointments and deadlines. He wanted to patent something of his own. He wanted to be rich. He certainly also liked his evenings in New York City bars—Jack Daniel's, hair-sprayed women, meeting new business contacts, raucous conversations that lasted into early-morning hours.

Brian was older than Dad and still single, a successful New York businessman of the early '80s. He lived in a high-rise in Midtown but also owned a place on Fire Island.

"Brian will invest," Dad told Mom. "He's the bucks, and I'm the brains. Give us some time to develop this thing. I'll be just like him."

"Not *just* like him," Mom joked.

"Well, no." Dad and Mom both called Brian a *fairy*, an image that I never removed from my head. He was mostly bald, about fifty years old, and wore reading glasses at the end of his nose. He was like no fairy I'd ever imagined. Over drinks in New York, Brian and Dad had developed a winning, get-rich, can't-lose idea to meld their business savvy, Dad's janitorial connections, and Brian's significant cash investment: an AIDS-resistant toilet seat.

Brian came to our house for dinner one evening. Mom had spent days putting the meal together, a designed-to-impress spread whose centerpiece was roast lamb served with mint jelly. When Brian complimented her cooking, for some reason she said, "Oh, this is nothing special, just a typical Tuesday night," indicating that this was our workaday fare.

Our dinners were normally Crock-Pot-made or casseroles from the *Better Homes & Gardens New Cook Book*. Mom liked and often made molded Jell-O with suspended layers of fruit and cottage cheese. A fancy night was something called Turkey Manhattan, an open-faced whitebread sandwich drenched in Heinz turkey gravy.

I had never before—or since, actually—eaten either lamb or mint jelly, which I mentioned to the three adults. Mom's face turned angry. It was probably also turning red, but I couldn't tell in the candlelight, which was also a first at our dinners.

"Don't be silly," she said with her eyes directly on me. The lamb part reminded me of Vacation Bible School and the idea of jelly being mint flavored just seemed wrong. I insisted that I thought I would have remembered if anyone had ever given me mint jelly before.

Mom let everyone know that I'd had lamb many times, but this was the first time I'd been told it was lamb and also the first time I'd been allowed to have the mint jelly with it.

Brian smiled at me across the dim table.

Their work progressed over several months. Sample toilet seats arrived at our Long Island house, and scrolls of drawings were laid out in

Dad's den, where he sometimes took evening calls on our ivory-and-gold French rotary phone. "Something that kills the germs will be embedded in the plastic," he explained to me. "Baked in." He hadn't been this excited in years.

"Can you get it from toilet seats?" I asked him. "AIDS?" I thought of all the times I used the bathroom at Friendly's or visited the backroom at Modell's department store when I couldn't hold it.

"Probably not, but it doesn't matter. People are afraid they can. That's what will sell."

On a summer weekend in 1984, our whole family went to Brian's Fire Island house, a red clapboard beach house with a cutout of a pelican by the door. No cars were allowed, so we had to take a ferry across.

Brian and Dad worked while Mom and Adam and I swam. There were men everywhere on Fire Island, and their swimsuits were smaller and tighter than the ones Dad wore. Men laughed together in a way I hadn't seen before. A lot of them had mustaches. Some of them held hands.

Brian's house had tall stacks of magazines I'd never seen—*The New Yorker* and *National Geographic*. I was only about ten miles from home but felt very far from what I knew. Yes, I was vacationing in a legendary gay enclave in its heyday. But also, the water was saltier, the waves harsher, and the sun hotter than other beaches I'd visited. "It's a different undertow," Brian told me, taking a spot next to me on his leather couch. I'd never seen or sat on a leather couch either. I'd flopped there with a *National Geographic*, drinking in the pictures.

"What's undertow?" I asked him. Talking to Brian made me realize that most adults I knew were cloying and weird. Maybe teachers and other people's parents had to be a certain way. Brian was different. He explained undertow to me in a very rational, adult way.

A few weeks later I began receiving *National Geographic* every month, a subscription in my own name, with a note indicating it was given by "Uncle Brian."

"He thinks girls can be interested in more than hair and makeup,"

Dad told me. He said this in a way that indicated slight admiration, much mystery, and a twinkle of judgment. It was the same way he might have said, "They worship cows in India."

"And he won't be having kids of his own," Mom said.

Later that summer I woke up, very late at night, to Mom and Dad arguing. I peeked between the wrought-iron slats surrounding the stairs and I saw Dad with crutches in his armpits and one of his feet wrapped in a bandage. The next day I heard that after too many drinks with Brian, Dad had fallen down the stairs at a bar in the city, breaking his ankle. Mom blamed Brian, calling him a "fruit." World domination via their AIDS-resistant toilet seat was now doomed.

Dad had moved on to another endeavor anyway. The idea of HIV being transmitted via toilet seats was on its way to being debunked by then, and Dad had hand soap on his mind. After years of selling products for commercial restrooms, Dad knew the current standard dispenser could be improved. In most bathrooms, a plastic globe filled with bubblegum-pink liquid soap was accessed by bumping your palm up against a metal stem. Some places even kept a slimy sliver of bar soap by their sinks. He could do better.

Working with a Johnson Wax colleague, they developed a valve that would squirt a just-right amount of soap when depressed. Imagine pushing a button and having a perfect teaspoon of soap spill into your open hand. It would be sanitary! And innovative! Dad's den filled with different iterations of samples of the little plastic valves. They gave a satisfying pop each time I pushed them.

His new partner began filing patent paperwork. In the meantime, Johnson Wax started using a version of the valve in its new soap dispenser, but Dad was undaunted. He quit his job and took his version of the valve to a Swedish competitor of Johnson and sold it to them for their soap products. He found yet another partner who was working on an ice cream machine. They agreed to add Dad's valve to his machine—tentatively called the "flurry." It would regulate squirts of flavored syrups to be added to treats sold in ice cream shops. He told us we'd be opening an ice cream shop of our own on Long Island one day soon.

Dad went to Sweden to sell soap valves to the Swedes. He went to Hong Kong to sell soap valves there. Dad returned from every single trip with a rubbery blue Smurf figurine for me. New ones were tossed into the pillowcase where I stored them. The pillowcase was half full with fifty Smurfs.

When he wasn't traveling, Dad spent days in the den amid his sample valves and stacks of papers. He continued to wear a suit daily, even in the den, having nearly nothing in the way of casual clothes from the Big & Tall shop. Evenings he kept his dress shirt on, but the pants would go, his white underwear a fixture at our dinner table. He owned a threadbare blue robe, for weekend mornings. The rest was suits.

Pinned to the wall of the den was a pencil sketch of the word FLURRY rendered in blocky caps with melting ice dripping off the letters, as though the word itself had been snowed upon. It wasn't quite the patent he'd hoped for, but having his valve as part of the flurry trademark would be a huge step. Dad made business cards printed with thick, glossy brown and black ink. Beneath his name it said "International Marketing Consultant." He made slick ballcaps, too: black with gold oak leaves on the bill and his logo on the front.

Dad had grown used to a commute and without those daily hours in the car, he was restless. Our evening family activity was to take a ride. After dinner he would cry, "*Llaves!*"—the Spanish word for keys, an echo from his Miami days—and either Adam or I would run to find them, usually in his suit pants. He'd move the electronic keyboard off the passenger seat so Mom could sit next to him. We might have gotten ice cream or seen Christmas lights, depending on the season, but those were an afterthought, never the reason to leave the house. The car itself was our destination.

Adam sometimes slept; he was barely more than a baby and would nestle in, pacifier in his toddler mouth, and chill out. I listened. My parents talked in the front seat, sometimes for hours, and always about the most pressing and most personal things they were feeling. They spoke at home, of course, but the TV was usually on, and their conversations were lighter and more transactional. Dad saved his soliloquies for these drives. Mom rarely snuck in a word but affirmed and agreed as we tooled through town. One night we might be treated to a lecture on Dad's theory about how his valve would revolutionize the janitorial supply business, and the next he'd hold forth on Colonel Gaddafi.

"I can see your ears flapping back there," Dad said, catching my eyes in the rearview. We were driving by a piece of real estate that Dad said would be the Long family ice cream shop. Seat belted into my parents' car as a first grader, I was pretty much the definition of a captive audience, but they both always accused me of interloping in their conversations.

"She's smart," Mom reminded him. Their theory was that as a chronic listener to adult conversations I was gaining vocabulary and knowledge, becoming world-wise beyond my years. Also, according to them, it was impossible for me to mind my own business. Mom claimed that *Sesame Street* had first stoked this hunger for words and learning, and they found it amusingly quaint and mildly annoying.

For Dad's part, he seemed to need these rides. His driving lectures may have been colloquial, but they were also professorial, semireligious. He was unapologetically opinionated and in order to hone his perspective, he needed to talk it out, with an audience. With his immediate family confined to a Chrysler, he had the rare chance to focus and develop his ideas without interruption, to be himself.

When Dad was traveling, Mom, Adam, and I continued to do our thing at home.

I paged through my *National Geographics*, which continued to arrive for several years even though Dad said he and Brian were no longer speaking. Adam watched an impressive number of different cartoons—considering we didn't have cable—and collected G.I. Joes. He wore T-shirt-knit army camouflage pajamas every night and any day he could get away with it.

Mom sewed. She made clothes for me and for herself almost compulsively: ruffly dresses for me and bold, geometric tops she wore on our grocery and shopping trips. She said boys' clothes were boring and never made anything for Adam or Dad.

There were three bedrooms upstairs. I slept in their old brass bed, which was now outfitted with a yellow Holly Hobbie bedspread and a pillowcase stuffed with Smurfs under it. My parents' bedroom had a crib where Adam slept, and the third bedroom was dedicated to Mom's fabric, which was stacked in boxes and plastic bags waist-high all over the room. One corner was reserved for her sewing machine, which hummed hotly when she pressed her foot on its pedal. The *zzzzzzz* of it runs in my brain as the background noise of my childhood.

EIGHT

My after-school routine for first grade was solid. After riding the bus home, I came in the house, where Mom handed me a prewrapped Entenmann's brownie and a cup of milk. I positioned a kid-sized rocking chair a foot away from the TV and watched *Inspector Gadget*.

When the show ended, I played with my yarn-haired Cabbage Patch doll, hard-won by Mom who'd braved the Long Island Rail Road for a December 1983 trip to the Caldor in Queens, elbowing her way through a throng of other mothers a little less desperate or determined than she was to please their little daughters.

Sunday evenings, we watched *The Muppet Show*. If it wasn't a school night, I was sometimes granted permission to stay up for *The Carol Burnett Show*. We had broadcast TV, and one of those handful of channels was on most all of the time: *Sesame Street* and *Mr. Rogers' Neighborhood* in the morning, game shows or cartoons all afternoon, and sitcoms or variety shows at night. If we were awake, so was the TV.

When I'd started first grade at the building attached to our Lutheran church, it was the first time I'd been away from my mother and the nest of our home she'd built for us. The world swirled darkly beyond our walls, I learned. The feeling of mystery reminded me of my glimpse of New York City punks or my look at Brian's magazines—something different than anything I'd seen or experienced on the Longs Island of our little home or even on its omnipresent TV. I met a kid named Theresa who owned two parrots, a concept so deeply foreign to me as to be mystical. Someone at school spoke Spanish at home—*actual* Spanish. A policewoman came to our classroom and told us that angel dust may sound like something for kids but warned us never, ever to take it. An older kid on the bus made fun of the Jacques Cousteau diorama I was carrying. "You can't make cotton balls look like a glacier," he sneered. As startled and hurt as I was, I remember being drawn to the bully, Jonathan, and wondering whether he lived the way I lived at home. I thought my household was altogether different than anyone else's, and hearing that Jonathan's mom also had cotton balls made me wonder.

In the summer of 1985, between my first- and second-grade years, Dad was going strong with the Swedes. The ice cream shop had not come to pass, but soon no one in Sweden would be washing their hands without a squirt from Dad's soon-to-be-patented soap dispenser. It was going so well that he'd begun to bring a children's version to the US market, too. He named it Kleen Kids and announced that Adam and I would be part of this brand and heirs to the vast fortune it would create.

He arranged a photo shoot at the Lutheran school. The idea, he told me, was to remind people that kids are diabolical germ-spreaders, putting toys in their mouths, eating boogers, and distributing contagious colds and worse. He'd market the product to schools and parents to keep kid hands clean and germ-free. The preschool classroom was staged, and Adam was dressed in red shorts and a red-and-white-striped polo shirt. A photographer set up a tripod and two lights, and I asked Dad if I should change into something more model worthy.

"You're not in the picture," he told me. I was gobsmacked. The photographer continued setting up, and Adam and some other three-year-olds started playing with blocks. I couldn't speak for a full minute. Wasn't *I* supposed to be a model for Kleen Kids, too? Until that moment I'd thought I was one of two people who were Kleen Kids royalty. It was horrifying to realize that all along, the photos were to be of Adam and other kids a few years younger than me.

"You're seven," Dad said. "We need cute *little* kids here." He also mentioned that blond-haired, blue-eyed Adam was going to sell more soap than brown-haired, hazel-eyed, almost-second-grade me. "You're going to draw the logo anyway," a flourish he invented during this conversation.

Genuinely wounded and feeling not-cute for the first time in my life, I took to the logo-drawing task with determination and resolve. It was a logo, yes, but it would also be proof that I was something *better* than cute and blond. I imagined I'd be lauded for my artistic insight on this soon-to-be-famous brand. I used markers to draw grass and flowers under a sunny sky, leaving room in the middle of the composition for the brand name. I carefully printed "Clean Kids" and handed it over, letting Dad know I'd also done him the favor of correcting the spelling. He had me redo it.

Large, glossy photos of Adam playing blocks and soap dispenser labels with my flowers-and-grass logo started accumulating in Dad's den. In a shaggy '80s italic, *KLEEN KIDS* was pasted over the photos. He was working hard, and even though the patent paperwork was lagging, money had begun to roll in, showing up in subtle and obvious ways around the house.

Mom's fabric room became denser. She mail ordered rare fabrics from a catalog and also made big hauls from our local Jo-Ann Fabrics. The stacks of fabric bags and boxes were now deep enough that Adam and I could rearrange things and play inside a fort of fabric. More often, he wanted us to arrange things so the boxes of fabric made a car, like the one on *The Dukes of Hazzard*, which we'd jump into as though jumping through the windows of welded-shut doors. I refused to be Daisy, whom I deemed stupid, and agreed to be the non-blond brother instead.

Dad was bringing home electronics. First, we got a Commodore 64, a taupe-and-brown behemoth with a rainbow logo on all its components. We didn't have any personal computing to do in 1984, and Mom and I didn't know how to use it. Neither did Dad, actually, but the computer and the particleboard desk it sat on took up a chunk of our living room. It was also the fulcrum of the following conversation, which repeated, verbatim, intermittently.

Amanda: "I'm bored."

Dad: "I bought you a *computer*."

He bought us two VCRs: a Betamax and a VHS player. He wasn't sure which one to get and, faced with such choices, my parents usually went with the more is more option: both. We were the only family I knew that had these gadgets, and I don't remember ever having or seeing a commercially made VHS tape we could play. Dad explained that they would pay for themselves in convenience: we could tape things on TV to watch them later. Mom taped a broadcast—commercials and all—of the 1981 Tony Danza movie *Going Ape!*, which also stars Danny DeVito and three orangutans. I watched it obsessively, in part because it was the only tape we had for a while and also because using the tape player helped Dad feel like his significant investment was worthwhile. If we neglected it, he would feel like he'd wasted money and that would be not only tragic but also our fault for not appreciating that he'd gotten it for us. If we didn't praise him for buying it at least once a week, he'd ask us to. In this case, I found *Going Ape!* a hilarious and heartwarming cinematic masterpiece, so it was no bother at all to keep watching it and continually thank Dad for providing the experience.

"You'll be able to watch some tapes," Dad told Mom. "I can't imagine this will be anything worse than a rainstorm. You'll stay home and watch a movie. That's it." Near the very beginning of my second-grade year, Dad had a scheduled trip to Sweden. There was also a forecast brewing about an unprecedented hurricane that might actually hit Long Island.

"By myself, during a hurricane, with two kids?" Mom was distinctly not okay with this plan and urged him to cancel. Dad couldn't imagine canceling on the Swedes. They'd been the source of the funds for the VCRs, the Commodore 64, and would be funding the aboveground backyard pool we'd been discussing. The Swedes were his future. He was going.

As a compromise, and out of what felt to him like extreme precaution, Dad bought another gadget: a kerosene heater. "Look, hurricanes never make it this far up the coast," he told her, speaking as a native Miamian. "It will rain, that's all." He said that if a hurricane hit, really the worst that could happen was a power outage for a night. The kerosene heater would live in our garage and be our fail-safe should something happen. Dad highly doubted we'd need it at all.

We received news that the hurricane, now named Gloria, would be arriving a few days ahead of schedule. Dad would be here when Hurricane Gloria hit, that is, if it was even still a hurricane by the time the storm made it this far north.

Local schools were set up as Red Cross shelters, but we stayed home. The four of us sat in our house's very center, its slate-tiled middle hall, between Dad's den and the staircase. All along it ran a white heat register near the baseboard, which meant we couldn't sit leaning against the wall but had to hunch forward, looking out the front door's citrus-slice window or the larger windows over the kitchen sink at the back. For a long while, nothing happened.

It was quiet, barely a car on the street. We only heard the wind. Adam kept darting up to go to the living room; he didn't understand why we were all sitting so still on the hall floor.

We ate bologna on white bread with yellow mustard. Dad fiddled with a radio, and we tried to discern where it would make landfall and where the eye would hit. We heard it was Islip, about ten miles west of us. Outside, the trees began to sway and dip in the ever-louder wind. The weeping willow sagged in the rain that was now heavily pouring down and across our windows. Branches slapped the side of the house. The wind roared like a train.

Our power went out, and the house became dark, even though it was still midday. First we heard creaking, then we turned to see that the massive pine in our backyard—the one where Dad's imagined stories of Penelope took place—was in danger. Its trunk was so massive I couldn't put my arms around it. And its height, so perfect for Dad's stories, was immense enough that none of us could really distinguish the topmost branches. They were so high above our heads that it was easy to imagine little Penelope up there, just out of sight.

Penelope's massive tree moaned and stretched in 85-mile-per-hour winds. There were woods behind our house. If the unimaginable happened and Gloria's fury tore down the pine, it could fall southward into those woods with very little consequence. Alternatively, it could snap and drop its weight northward, in which case it would surely hit the roof of our house and crush it. "Do not go upstairs," Dad admonished Adam, who continued his restless toddler wiggle.

With a sharp smack, the pine split under pressure from the wind, and we watched the trunk of Penelope's tree race to earth southward, toward the woods, sparing us.

In the evening, we ate more bologna sandwiches because the fridge food wouldn't last forever. Our phone line was dead. Dad heard on the battery-powered radio that LaGuardia and JFK were both open, so he decided he'd keep his plans to fly to Stockholm the next day. How long could the lights be out? A couple days at most, he was sure.

Before he left, he pulled the kerosene heater out of the garage and set it up in the kitchen. He added the strong-smelling fuel with a turkey baster–style bulb and tube and showed Mom how to light it. He took his suitcase and drove to the airport.

NINE

The power was out on Long Island for eight days. This was the closest my mother had ever come to camping, and she was miserable. No lights. No stove. No TV. And a seven-year-old and two-and-a-half-year-old.

We were warned off going outside because of the many downed power lines. Our battery-operated radio was to be conserved because the batteries in it were the only ones we had, and Mom said there was no way we could find any batteries at stores anyway. The phone remained dead, but who was there to call?

The three of us spent most of that week sitting on our kitchen floor around the kerosene heater. White and squat, a wire cage surrounded its enamel body. "Don't touch it," Mom said to Adam over and over. She explained that the metal would be hot and the stove inside it even hotter. A warm, orange flame pulsed in it. Mom squirted in kerosene to refill it, as Dad had done with the turkey baster, and the sharp, oily smell of it was inside my nose the whole week.

I wanted to watch *Going Ape!* I wanted to go to my dance class and to school. Instead, we looked out the back window at the underside of Penelope's tree, its dark roots twisting upward now, the trunk having smashed my swing set on its way down.

The house and everywhere around us was supernaturally quiet. Days passed without the sound of the preacher neighbor's amplified voice seeping into our yard. No one knocked on the door.

We hadn't prepared by laying in food or batteries, but Mom had us covered. Later in her life, as a bona fide hoarder, she proved florid in her illness, in her unstoppable impulse to have and collect food in particular. In the '80s, these urges must have begun, gently, borne of her insecurity or their iffy financial situation or whatever else makes a hoarder a hoarder. The fridge was unusable after a day or two. No more bologna sandwiches. But Mom had dry goods to last us.

I was allowed to open the pull-top on a can of Vienna sausages, whose delicious contents splashed in meaty water. There was also vanilla pudding in cans. Mom warmed water on the kerosene stove and added powdered Lipton chicken soup, which we drank from mugs with a seashell pattern. Dehydrated noodles stuck to the gray mugs' interiors when we were done. Our sink's tap water ran icy cold that week. In order to wash the dishes, or wash us, she had to warm big pots of water on the kerosene heater, which took much longer than one might guess. Everything did.

A few days in, when our only baths had been cursory armpit washes and our hair was greasy, we watched workers remove the jumping, blue-sparking power lines in our yard. They left, and Mom said it was safe, so we explored the wreck of the play structure out back. My deepest fascination was with the felled tree. Our neighbor Jorge, whose daughter babysat me sometimes, lived on the other side of us from the preacher, and he came over to investigate. Jorge told us the roof had blown off the ShopRite; we'd better continue eating our powdered soups. The great pine's upturned roots were taller than Jorge, maybe over six feet. I walked the tree's trunk like a balance beam, easing toward its top and Penelope, who I never found in the mess of branches in the woods.

Time stood still. The phone was reconnected, but of course we didn't hear from Dad, who was doing "god knows what" in Sweden, according to Mom's mutterings. On Day Eight, with the three of us sitting in the dim, psychedelically wallpapered kitchen on the linoleum, the overhead light suddenly blinked awake, and the fridge began to hum.

Mom was never happier. She turned the TV back on and cooked something on the stove. We all bathed in luxuriously warm water. When Dad came home the next morning, the fridge was full again, the lights on, and the kerosene heater had been wrestled back to the garage.

TEN

"Warm up my coffee, *woman*," Dad said to Mom from the couch, exaggerating *woman* and winking at me. Christmas 1985. He was both exactly like this all the time and not like this at all. He adored my mother. He needed her. He also had an ongoing joke that involved having a dog with the same name as my mom: Sandie. "Yeah, Sandie peed on the carpet and I rubbed her nose in it!" Dad would say in his joke voice. "The dog has the same name. Get it?"

After he told this joke, his eyebrows raised up, his brown eyes expectantly waiting for me to get it. Even as a kid, my response was lukewarm, confused. "I'm not the kind of guy who makes those jokes, anyway," he backtracked, even though he just had.

"Whatever you do, don't get into this women's lib thing," he warned me.

"Hubba hubba is a compliment, always has been," he reminded me.

That morning, Dad held out his mug to Mom. I stared hard at him, the effect of my indignation surely muted by what I was wearing: fuzzy, forest-green footed pj's embroidered with Winnie the Pooh on the chest. Dad stared back at me, his ratty blue robe vibrating with suppressed laughter. He didn't dare speak, and I couldn't read the look in his eye. We were all quiet. He held the coffee cup outward—one of the seashell mugs we'd used for our powdered soups during his trip to Sweden. Mom picked it up on her way around the corner. I pulled Adam, dressed identically to me in a Pooh onesie, away from the pile of presents spilling out from our Christmas tree onto the lumpy, orange living room carpet.

Mom screamed. The sound from the kitchen was beyond language at first and then morphed into "Oh my god" delivered with such heft and volume between high-pitched scream-laughs and scream-sobs that I had no way to distinguish it. She was elated. Or horrified. "You didn't!" she shouted to Dad.

I took a quick swig and then set down my orange juice, which was in a footed goblet with holly berry trim, from Arby's. Adam, who was three, set his pacifier beside it on the coffee table. He'd had a rough go trying to be without it, and we now expected he was a long-hauler with the Nuk.

Adam and I tore into the kitchen, the soles of our vinyl-covered feet tacky on the smooth linoleum. Mom was standing in front of a massive, wood-paneled and smoky-glassed box. It was so deep that its edge spilled at least an inch over the front of the counter. Mom turned one of the knobs left and right and pressed a lever to open its door. "A microwave," she said and looked at Dad, glowing.

"A microwave," he answered, "from Montgomery Ward." It was what she had most desperately wanted.

The demand for a coffee warm-up had been a ruse, a loving lead-up to the wow Christmas present of Mom's life—a microwave. Dad gloated, gently.

She warmed his coffee mug, and the bell dinged.

The grudge that Hurricane Gloria had left between them began to evaporate.

"Nothing bad will ever happen to us," Mom insisted anytime I mentioned things that scared me, like Colonel Gaddafi or famine, which I learned about from the *We Are the World* cassette she bought me. I knew about AIDS, too, but it was not going to happen to people like us, she promised.

When a classmate's parents divorced, she pledged, "Your father and I will never get divorced, no matter what." She sputtered on with a convoluted and completely invented explanation that they were legally unable to divorce.

"But Dad is divorced from someone," I reminded her. Many times when I was out for a ride with Dad, he'd mentioned his first marriage. I knew he had children other than Adam and me. I knew his first wife was Jewish. Dad never called her by her name or "my first wife." When it was only him and me in the car, driving and talking and listening, he would begin, "When I was married before . . ."

"Yes, that's part of why we can't ever divorce. We won't. We can't," she said.

I thought maybe they could, if they wanted to or if they needed to.

"We are different," Mom often said of the four of us. It was a solemn promise.

PART TWO

Martinsville, Indiana

1986 to 1989

ELEVEN

In 1986, a microwave was a status symbol. For Mom and Dad, it was the first external indicator that we were rich people. They'd believed this about themselves for years, and the microwave proved it in a way the VCRs, the Chrysler, the overseas trips, and the rest somehow couldn't. Mid-'80s cash was flowing through their joint checking account, and Dad was no longer tied to a forty-hour workweek. He was a self-proclaimed "international marketing consultant." Even though we'd just installed a moss green aboveground pool in the yard where my swing set once sat, they announced we'd be moving later in the summer of 1986, right before my eighth birthday.

"To be closer to family," Dad said, and he meant Mom's. I was an infant when his mother met me, once, in 1979, and she died before meeting Adam. Dad's father had died in 1963 when Dad was twenty. His living brother, David, still lived in Florida. They were estranged.

Mom's family was in Martinsville, Indiana, and we Long Islanders were moving there. We'd be near my mother's mother and stepdad. One of her two brothers and their kids lived in town, and so did some of Mom's friends from high school and from the church where they were married in 1975. Martinsville was a town of about eleven thousand, halfway between the college town of Bloomington and the state capital of Indianapolis. It all sounded very folksy and small-town homey. Mom told me about the county fair in the summer, the livestock, the oversized vegetables and complex quilts on display, the long line to get yourself dizzy on the Scrambler, and a vaunted fried pork tenderloin sandwich whose meat dwarfed its bun. Thanksgivings on Long Island she'd been making the most delicious, tangy, sweet persimmon pudding—a Hoosier classic—for dessert. We'd previously made a few visits to my grandparents, who lived high on a hill in a dark wood above the town. The orange-and-brown pictorial upholstery of their couch was covered in slick plastic, and Grandma hung a nail clipper from the lamp switch on the side table. In the middle of their dining table was a bowl of polyurethane fruit. I didn't think to ask what Indiana would be like. I felt I already knew.

Furniture catalogs arrived, and Mom studied them, folding top corners of certain pages and eventually calling North Carolina long distance to order several rooms' worth of high-end beds, tables, dressers, and armoires. Dad extended one of his Hong Kong valve-selling trips by several days in order to shop for Chinese furniture and arrange its passage to rural Indiana. I don't know what happened to the suite of particleboard furniture in our Long Island living room, or most of the rest of the items in that house. I imagine they would have packed everything, but Long Island is the last time I saw the burgundy, paisley bedspread my parents slept under and the tall tumblers Mom used for afternoon iced coffees: smoky glass with a white, puffy dandelion design. These things show up in the photos I have of our time on Long Island but disappear in 1986. With a few exceptions, our Long Island household evaporated when we moved to Indiana. We took the microwave. We took the brass bed, our butcher-block kitchen table, Mom's sewing machine. It took many days to pack all of her fabric, but we took that, too. We took the VHS player but scrapped the Betamax. We didn't take the Commodore 64; no one knew how to use it.

My mother had minimally prepared me for what the house itself would look like. Her descriptive phrase, "great big," indicated its size without specifying it was more than 6,800 square feet, about 5,800 more square feet than we'd had on Long Island. And "great big" was one of several Hoosierisms she had not shaken in the years she'd spent away. Words like *yonder* and *britches* were imprinted in her vocabulary irrevocably, microwave or not. And now Mom's twang and dialect were mixed with a little NYC vernacular. Our bagels were topped with a *schmear* and served with light and sweet *cawfee* for the adults.

Undeniably, she was correct. Our new house was great big. How else to describe this palace—front yard across from the golf course, backyard opening onto a lake with our own dock—in a gated subdivision? There were two kitchens. Formerly owned by a diamond broker, one of the rooms in the basement was a walk-in safe larger than our Long Island dining room had been. In total there were eighteen rooms plus six and a half bathrooms. That was before counting the cedar closet, the walk-in safe, or the decks, one of which had a hot tub that would spontaneously burble now and then. The house was an entity unto itself.

My mother stood under the foyer's double-height, vaulted ceiling with her freckled arm slung tight around my shoulder and whispered a vow: to fill it.

TWELVE

The driveway in front of our mansion was a near-perfect C shape. I biked its perimeter over and over, taking brief breaks to flip a cassette tape in the pastel boombox I'd strategically placed in the grassy half-moon that the driveway carved out. The boombox and the bike—a purple Huffy with a unicorn banana seat—were purchased new that summer. Almost everything we had was new.

For once, Dad's business deals were going his way, and hefty checks from the Swedes were arriving often. It wasn't only that my parents suddenly had a lot of money. More importantly, they were pressing reset on everything in our lives. There are real or imagined points of no return in adulthood—driving a new car instead of used ones; having a dishwasher instead of scrubbing by hand. For Mom and Dad, in some arcane way, getting that Panasonic microwave and then moving back to Martinsville was a way of traversing a threshold, wiping away their entire past and beginning anew. Everything changed.

On Long Island, I took my meals with milk most of the time, or my beloved apple juice. Once we got to Indiana, a new norm took hold: everyone got a can of soda with every lunch and dinner, even Adam.

We got new cars. My mom had a fairly straightforward station wagon, but Dad's car was an eye-popping 1986 Lincoln Town Car in deepest navy, hearse-like and pure opulence at once. There were soft leather seats and a built-in hush in the car's interior. Dozens of silver switches were sunk into glossy, burled panels on the dash and doors. Dad had a briefcase-sized car phone, which he sat next to his upgraded, battery-operated piano keyboard in the front seat. With slight horror and deep fascination, I learned that the illuminated buttons by the driver's door held a simple four-digit code for entry. I pressed 0-5-0-6 again and again, my own obsessive ritual that ended each time with the satisfying *pop* of the door locks shooting upward. I slowed down when Dad suggested I'd eventually wear out the keypad. Like him, I knew that having to stick a metal key in that door would be primitive, a little shameful. I didn't want to go back.

Dad began wearing dress shirts with "SFL" embroidered in tight blue stitches at his wrists. Hung side by side in the closet on dry cleaner hangers, his initials lined up in a row at their cuffs. It didn't seem improbable to me that his business exploits were ascending even as we were moving away from New York. Instead, I saw that he was dressing the part of CEO, even if his new office would be one of the downstairs rooms in our house and if the Town Car would be mostly used for family outings rather than to shuttle clients. Wearing these shirts, under a long shiny tie, was Dad's uniform for our new life.

Mom wore a new trio of rings Dad gave her from Hong Kong. Her left hand was still for her modest diamond solitaire engagement ring and gold wedding band. On her right were three rings of gems in continuous circles: one ring each of rubies, sapphires, and emeralds.

While we had attended church sometimes in New York, we began going every week in Indiana. Even though I went to a Lutheran school in New York, we didn't really socialize or connect with the church members in any meaningful way. In Martinsville, there was a church supper or a Bible group weekly and worship service every Sunday morning. It was part of our new way of living.

When I was almost eight years old, they decided that I would now be a teen girl and that Adam would remain the family baby, indefinitely. He was three and a half, and his bedroom was the nursery attached to their master bedroom, though in a six-bedroom house there were other options. The nursery was tricked out with sailboat wallpaper, and there was no door between my parents' suite and his room. They installed a twin bed shaped like a race car and a lifetime supply of the pacifiers he still used and would until he was five. Adam spent hours "driving" the car-bed and persuaded me to be his passenger, removing the silicone-and-plastic plug from his mouth to bellow "Need a ride, lady?" at me. Instead of looking at the Nuk situation as a parenting challenge to conquer, which might have been in Adam's best interests, they viewed it the same way they viewed my years as an apple-juice-in-a-baby-bottle fiend: kids want what they want.

At the opposite end of the massive house was the formal dining room, pristine and built for guests who never came. The room had navy, textured wallpaper and was outfitted in a luxe set of black, lacquered furniture from Hong Kong, replete with a soapstone folding screen, shimmering mother-of-pearl inlaid into its black surface. The white carpet in the dining room felt knee-deep.

I was set up right off this dining room, where we never ate, in an enormous bedroom with its own bathroom. Mom had chosen a suite of North Carolinian furniture for my room that was dark cherrywood with a cluster of dusky roses on the headboard and on the top drawer of every bureau. There was a desk, a tall chest, a low chest, a nightstand, a mirrored cabinet, a glamorous, freestanding, full-length mirror on a pivoting hinge, and a twin bed with a pink poplin canopy. The soft carpet was pistachio green, and the bathroom's towels were trimmed in roses like the furniture. One day Dad came home with a small pink Emerson TV, which he set up on the tall dresser.

"Let me guess, you're going to be sitting in here watching MTV all day, ignoring us," Dad said, standing in the doorway of my new room. He shook his head, giving me the dad-of-a-surly-teenager treatment before I ever considered being surly. The luxury subdivision where we lived was outside the area served by Cablevision, so we actually didn't even have MTV. It felt a little like they were trying to avoid me or, at the very least, trying to rush me into grown-up and teenage things, for which I didn't yet have much interest. When I turned the pink TV on, it was to watch the daily afternoon broadcast of *Scooby-Doo*.

Right after we moved, Mom decided to provide me with a candid and thorough sex education conversation ranging from armpit hair to menstruation to masturbation, which she indicated I might want to begin soon, so as not to succumb to curiosity with boys later. Hickeys and hand jobs were also presented as things I should consider in a multipronged approach to preserving my virginity.

This first conversation was pretty eye-opening and not unhelpful. I was eight years old and this was all very new information. The lengthy and frequent follow-up conversations became horrifying. "Any questions about intercourse?" Mom would ask lightly at least weekly. Once, without my asking, she explained, "That's why some people call it *screwing*," as she went over the concept of friction and cited the phrase "in and out" as though I'd be taking a standardized test on the subject one day soon.

"I can't wait for you to become a woman." Mom looked at me, holding my shoulders in her hands. Her skin was always slightly dewy, and mascara had flaked into a subtle dark smear in the corners of her eyes. She smelled citrusy, having dotted her pulse points with Giorgio Beverly Hills earlier that day. We'd lived in Indiana only half a summer and already I felt like we were different people in a totally different world. Her voice shook, but her grip was firm.

I looked back at her, hoping I could do what she was asking. The way she said it made me wonder if I'd be able to pull off menstruating, procreating, and the other projects she'd laid out for me. I nodded back at her, determined not to fail.

THIRTEEN

"Sixty-eight hundred square feet, and you're out here," Mom said, her arms crossed over her chest as she watched me loop through the C of the driveway, singing along to a cassette of the Bangles.

One of the double front doors was open, and Freon-chilled air poured out of the foyer and into the southern Indiana humidity. Mom didn't like the outside; she was terrified of snakes, and the very idea of encountering one kept her indoors with few exceptions. I didn't like the empty feeling of our house, even as it was quickly filling with furniture deliveries and mail-order fabric. I could rely on the front yard to be mine alone because Mom and Dad almost always parked in the second driveway, around the corner.

I was young enough to not yet be embarrassed by my parents, so it didn't occur to me that I could possibly be embarrassing to them. I wore a neon leotard and leg warmers to do my driveway laps, which served double duty as time I'd spend memorizing Duran Duran and Madonna lyrics by singing them off-key. I'd recently acquired a curling iron, which I used to style my bangs into a lofty, hair-sprayed puff.

Dad had an idea. "You can join the swim team," he told me. I was surprised. I'd been enrolled in a dance class on Long Island, but sports were not really in the range of options I knew to be possible for girls. Dad said swimming was not really "dykey" like other sports and that I'd probably do well. I was tall. He also seemed to think it would be good for all of us if I wasn't looping around the driveway in a leotard in full view of the golf crowd.

Mornings, I wrapped a packet of powdered Jell-O mix and a bologna, mustard, potato chip sandwich inside a beach towel and rode my Huffy half a mile to the country club. I wouldn't start third grade for another few months, so I stayed all day.

My eight-and-under swim practice lasted most of the morning and was followed by lunch with my teammates, who'd shown me the delicious move of dipping pool-wet fingers into an envelope of dry Jell-O and licking them clean. Fueled by my sugar-chlorine cocktail, I swam all afternoon, bending my legs and then shooting them hard against the aqua concrete wall for lap after lap of backstroke. I remained afraid to dive and was poor at the breathing maneuvers required for the other strokes, but I was a backstroke star. I liked gathering speed right away, folding my palms flat enough to alternately gather water and push it behind me, then slice through it on the return. With backstroke, there's a quick glance at the lane and then blind faith. You charge backward at top velocity, no way to heed whomever or whatever is behind your head and in your path. There are no tentative backstrokers.

I memorized the tree canopy over the pool and the fence edges I could see in my peripheral vision. On breaks, sunscreen-less, I'd wrap my towel around my shoulders to keep them from burning, and I'd sit directly on the pebbly concrete, pilling the butt of my one-piece. Mom said that because my body took after Dad's, I was not then and likely would not ever be a two-piece kind of person.

I rode my bike home whenever I wanted to go home, which was usually dinnertime, and tossed it on the lawn. The sun set late, and I always hoped I could do a driveway ride after dinner. I had on my white one-piece with the towel draped on my head. "Did you taste the good life?" Mom asked. "The lap of luxury all day long," she mused, browning hamburger meat in our big kitchen. It meant something to my parents to give Adam and me a certain lifestyle, an abundance of comforts.

Dad, in his monogrammed shirtsleeves, wandered up from his office, immediately followed by my cousin Heather. Across from the exercise and sauna room downstairs was a large room with stringy, white shag carpet and two desks, each with a two-line phone. This was the headquarters for Dad's new company, called REN Americas, Inc. A sliding glass door in the office led out to our backyard's sloping grass and eventually to the dock on the lake. Dad had to stand from his desk in order to see the pontoon boat bobbing there below, which he did, several times a day. He could; the phone didn't ring often.

In a bullish bid to encourage the onslaught of calls Dad knew his business deserved, he had hired my cousin Heather, who was nineteen, to be his receptionist. Heather's only other paid work was intermittent modeling for the Victoria's Secret catalog.

Dad trained her to press the hold button and then announce, "Line one for you, Uncle Stephen." He spoke on his business calls with his forefinger extended over his upper lip, a futile measure of privacy against his booming voice. He only spoke this way for business conversations, not personal ones. Given the infrequency of incoming calls, I mostly saw Heather filing her nails at the second desk or flipping through Victoria's Secret and the other lingerie catalogs to which she aspired. She once showed me her picture in one of them. She was wearing white underwear and lying down on satiny peach sheets and had a blank look in her eye.

Heather told us goodbye and then Adam, Mom, Dad, and I ate our dinner around the oval oak table in the kitchen.

"How was your day at *The Club*?" Dad asked me, flipping his wrist extravagantly. There was an understanding in my house that I was snobby about going to the country club to swim every day, even though they'd pretty much made me do it. It hadn't been my idea.

"Good," I said, mid-bite, and meant it. I loved having a place to be and people to see most days of the week. I could also see it gave Mom and Dad something to be proud of, that I was part of something a little grand. I liked making them happy.

Adam and I both were obsessed with the fridge on the other side of the wide kitchen. On Long Island, the fridge was a plain aluminum box of avocado green. Here, it was sheathed in a reflective black plastic and had a port in the door that dispensed ice and water. It had a lightbulb and several buttons that illuminated to a lime green when pressed. Adam scooted over and punched several buttons to fill a plastic cup with ice for his Coke.

Dad said he had an announcement.

"We're joining The Club," he said, laying his fork beside his plate, waiting for our response.

The Tudor palace next to where I swam every day also served as an elite membership club where dinner was served Friday nights in the gloomy, chandeliered and draperied rooms of its main floor. It had been owned by the millionaire founder of Barbasol who had also died there, and my swim teammates believed he'd hung himself from a beam above the steep spiral staircase. Some said he fell. Or he killed himself, but his family made up a story that he fell, which was a gentler gruesome death than the other rumored gruesome death. In 1972, the *Indianapolis Star* reported, "Mr. Shields died in 1946 after a fall down three flights of a dramatic spiral stairway in the mansion." Even if I'd had access to this clipping in the '80s, it wouldn't have dissuaded any of us girls that the manor house, specifically its staircase, was haunted.

Dad paid the fee. Now we had Friday night plans, in perpetuity.

FOURTEEN

"This is not the damn *Beverly Hillbillies*," Dad announced as he entered the double front door. "Amanda, your bike . . ." his voice trailed off, but I knew what to do.

Passing him in the foyer, I raced out to pick up the Huffy, which, as usual, I'd tossed onto the lawn out front. Dad had recently received a gruffly worded notice from the homeowners' association that bicycles lying on their sides in yards were unacceptable. With swim season over, I was back to laps in the circular driveway most afternoons. I couldn't seem to remember to put the bike in the garage, or even leave it upright.

It was weird how Dad never complained about Mom's endless and teetering piles of stuff everywhere, while my bike on the lawn was a nagging, burning annoyance. I'd learned that Dad seemed to not see Mom's messes, or any of her flaws. She returned the favor and for each other, they were blameless.

"Are they calling you Mandy?" Mom asked.

Jumping in on my parents' urge to reinvent ourselves, I rechristened myself Mandy at the very start of school. I immediately regretted it, and ten days later tried to undo it.

"Yes," I reported glumly. It was too late to go back. My teacher had already laminated a sign for my desk labeling me "Mandy Long," and so I was. As Mom well knew, change came slowly to Martinsville, whose residents usually liked things familiar, the way they were.

People there knew Mom as she was in high school before she left, restless and glamorous and heading off to study fashion design at Pratt Institute in Brooklyn. In 1972, the *Reporter* even made note of her arrival for a return visit: "Miss Sandie Cox of New York City will arrive early Sunday morning by jet to spend a few days with her parents . . . She will return to New York on Wednesday evening." It appeared in the "Social Scene" column for which a typical entry was that two Martinsville women would be in Indianapolis for a weekend attending a conference on African violets. Or that a serviceman was home and would be traveling 100 miles north to visit his grandmother during his leave. Mom's trips to and from New York, and her sophomore-year study-abroad trip to France, were memorable aberrations in the column. People saw them and took note. Even in the mid-'80s, if we bumped into someone in town who knew her in high school, they might say, "What was it like in fashion design school, Sandie?" eyeing her floral culottes and white Reeboks.

She liked being known as posh and fashionable, a persona she'd cultivated in her late-'60s Martinsville high school days to counterbalance the dominant narrative about the unhappy household where she grew up. My step-grandpa Earl's cross disposition was legendary. Kids at my school knew of him as fearsome and bad-tempered, a looming presence high on his hill, and even my classmates knew he wasn't Mom's real dad.

She was born in 1950, enough years after her brothers to be called "a mistake" by my grandma, Dolores. Mom's biological father fixed radios for a living and had a drinking problem. Mom said he would throw her brothers down the cinderblock stairs outside their little house in Indianapolis, though she was too small to remember him. Grandma understood she couldn't end the marriage amicably, so she developed a plan to escape with her two school-aged boys and little Sandie. Dolores devised ways to shave down their family's food costs from her allotted grocery money each week, and the extra went toward cream cheese and graham crackers and sugar. Dolores quietly began a clandestine side business selling one or two cheesecakes a week to neighbors and stuffing the cash proceeds into a shoe in the hall closet. All three children had small bags packed, which lay waiting under their beds for the right moment, when the cheesecake money was sufficient enough for them to leave.

Late one evening they did, the three kids and Dolores carrying their bags quietly out the door while the children's father slept off some liquor. Mom was two.

Earl was proprietor of a laundromat in a seedy part of Indianapolis's west side, near the family's new apartment. He was divorced, just as Dolores was. They met when she took her family's laundry there every week. By the time I knew them, it wasn't clear precisely what Earl and Dolores saw in each other, but by then it hardly mattered. Mom's childhood from five onward had unfolded in the stale air of their quiet house in the woods. The curvy road to get there and the deep plunge into the woods below the house were reminiscent of Appalachia. Though they died and were replaced, their house always had a black Doberman with a German girl's name—Heidi, Schultzie, Ilse. A lava lamp on their end table squirted its claret goo into puffs and blobs day and night. The glass was boiling hot; the lamp might have been running continuously for twenty years. Transfixed, I couldn't stop myself from tracing the shapes on the glass, burning my fingers.

Other than living in an honest-to-god mansion, my girlhood was shaping up in the image of Mom's. My face was, too. We shared a hazel-green eye color and identical noses and chins. As I inched toward my teens, I looked more and more like Mom's high school senior picture. We were a loop. Me growing into a version of her was thrilling to Mom, the most primal joy of all parents, to replicate and to live again, or at least to live on.

But some parts of this stasis and repetition were uncomfortable for her. Mom's personal reasons for returning to Martinsville involved proving Earl and her mom, and her big brothers Steve and Tom, wrong. They generally thought she was foolish for flying off to New York after high school. Coming back eleven years later had a purpose: recasting her story for all the people who knew her early years, who would only ever think of her as a weirdo high schooler obsessed with Marimekko fashion who lived in the woods with a big, black dog and humorless parents.

Now she was someone else. A country club member in a finely appointed, great big house. Wife to a high-flying businessman with monogrammed cuffs. Adored mother, twice over.

"Should I call you Mandy?" She gave me a salty look, then a loving squeeze. She knew I hated the name, and she thought it was funny that I'd be stuck with it.

Mom stood up from where we sat together at the kitchen table. "Change it in college, maybe." Neither Mom nor Dad had finished college, but it was assumed that I'd go, and finish. She dug through a paper grocery bag on the floor and pulled out a box of au gratin potatoes, whose dehydrated slices rattled as she headed to the stove.

"I think you should play with Kimberly," Mom said as she started dinner. Adam rarely socialized outside of his preschool, but Mom was very focused on lining up some friendships for me.

"Go, go, go, go, go!" Dad yelled at the football game on the TV downstairs. His voice carried up the stairs when he was excited about a game. His frustrations were more likely to be mumbled.

Kimberly, who I saw at the pool once in a while, was not someone I cared to see more often than that. She wasn't a swim team member and wasn't much on my wavelength in other ways either. She was freckled and blond and tiny. I'd never been in it, but I could see her house, and her parents' matched set of forest-green Jaguars, at the top of the hill across the golf course.

"Pass the damn ball!" Dad bellowed, his voice hoarse already in the second quarter. The Florida Gators were his old team, and he still had his heart in the game. "PASS IT."

Mom smiled toward the stairs. She was happy when Dad was happy. And she wanted me to be happy with some classier friends.

"I guess so," I finally told her. It was the most enthusiasm I could find for the idea.

Eventually I was cajoled into going to Kimberly's house on Saturdays and sometimes after school. Mom thought it would be much better to pal up with a girl like that than with the kids "from town" who lived more like my uncle Steve did, with cars on bricks in their yards. Kimberly's family's backyard was Hole Seven.

Home alone at Kimberly's, we tried on the black lacy underwear her sister had left behind when she went to college. We snuck into her father's personal library with leather chairs and framed pictures of golfers on the wood-paneled walls. On a side table was a tray with an empty liquor bottle and two extremely heavy, cut-glass tumblers. The first time I saw it, I imagined Kimberly's father had just recently set out this tableau for himself and a guest and would be back momentarily to catch us.

"Dick?" She called her father by his first name. "He's out of town on business." I learned that Dick was perpetually ready to receive guests with scotch. The tray was always there, fully set. I didn't know people lived this way.

We had an unspoken rule at my house, a truth that had established itself back on Long Island and was one of the few things we opted not to change when we moved to Indiana. No visitors. Exceptions were justified along a two-axis system: potential visitors' value to Dad's business dealings or their capacity to be dazzled, with a special carve-out for family members. Cousin Heather, who only lasted two months in the basement with Dad, scored well on both fronts.

Whether we were in a thousand square feet or sixty-eight hundred, what happened in our house was our business and was for the Longs only. As a rule, friends didn't come over.

At Kimberly's, things were tidier than they were at my house. The house was whiter and brighter, with a shiny piano in the front room and an austere set of couches the color of fresh snow. The main part of the house could've been a set for *Moonlighting*, Cybill Shepherd wearily dropping her attaché case on the clear Lucite coffee table after a long day.

Mom had done our house in furnishings from two schools of design: Chinese traditional and American '80s country. A dark cherrywood end table whose legs were carved with dragons held a gray-blue carafe adorned with geese wearing ribboned bonnets. Our decor may have struck an unlikely balance, but it held to a straightforward dogma: it was what Mom liked.

Afternoons, Kimberly and I would arrive at her house, and she'd immediately hand me a red plastic tumbler with the logo of the Indiana University basketball team. In third grade, she introduced me to ice water.

"Why don't we drink ice water?" I asked Mom one evening, after downing a few bracing cups of the stuff at Kimberly's. I'd never seen either of my parents drink water. When taking pills, Mom would pour a scant inch of water in a glass then barely part her lips, letting in the least possible amount before snapping her head backward to swallow the pill. Most of the inch of water remained in the bottom of the glass.

"We could if we wanted to," she told me, gesturing at the shiny fridge. We only used the ice portal, not the water.

"But at Kimberly's they drink it all the time. For fun."

This was years before hydrating oneself was seen as either a sacred act or de rigueur, but she was still a little defensive.

"I guess at Kimberly's house they're very virtuous with their water drinking. Let me guess, there's not a speck of dust and the place is always so freshly vacuumed that you can see the sweeper stripes in the carpet?"

I declined to answer. It was eerie how she'd correctly assumed there were vacuum lines, and Mom was right that the foot-wide stripes in their carpet did fascinate me, like the green-on-green, waffle-print lawn mowing outside The Club.

"We don't *have* to drink water." Mom spoke slowly, revealing her wisdom. She explained that we could afford to drink Coke, or juice or Tang or whatever else we wanted, and that was better. When you had the kind of options we did, drinking water was like sleeping at Motel 6 when you had Four Seasons money in your pocket. She added a bit of science as backup. "When you drink Kool-Aid, or root beer, or anything, if it's *made* with water, it's the same as water to your body."

Kimberly and I drank ice water out of her dad's crystal whiskey tumblers whenever we could be unobserved, which was often. It felt as subversive as wearing her sister's underwear.

FIFTEEN

While gathering the accoutrements of the rich, my family and I were also putting on the airs of our new town, populated mostly by people who disdained the very idea of a country club. If you didn't live in the golf course subdivision we did, your community meeting place was Poe's Cafeteria, and our family ate there, too, for our own reasons. We were filthy rich country folk.

Dad and Earl went in together on a red-and-white Ford pickup truck. Magnanimously, Dad offered to pay the note on it but keep it in Earl's name, which, in Dad's explanation, was a way for Earl to keep his pride about the whole thing. Earl drove it more than we did, up and down the winding driveway from his hilltop house outside of town. We borrowed it a few times a month so Dad could drive us to get ice cream with Adam and me ricocheting around the truck bed.

Most evenings, we took a destination-less outing in the Town Car.

"Martin Luther is spinning in his grave," Dad said. "I swear to you." He directed this at Mom, sitting next to him up front. Adam and I were in the back of the Town Car, pretending it was a Jell-O factory where we worked.

She wasn't in a position to argue his point. Mom had not grown up in the church at all, but Dad had Lutheran roots back to Miami and the generations before, and he didn't like the hippy-dippy way this Martinsville church was running things. The Town Car crept out of our subdivision and onto the rural roads between it and the proper boundary of town. Dad pressed on.

"Didn't we have a little something called the Reformation that dealt with all this?" His complaint was that the small church we attended, where they'd been married, was either too liberal or too Catholic-seeming. Or it may have been something else. The theology was over my head, though I listened with one ear and played the game with Adam with the other. The car drove on and Dad kept sermonizing.

He loved this time in the car with us. Dad was increasingly thinking about his faith, and our family drives were where he developed his ideas, out loud, with us as the captive audience turned congregation.

It takes about fifteen minutes to circumnavigate all of Martinsville, and we drove up and through it a dozen times while Dad talked. Dad wanted to orate. The state of the contemporary Lutheran church bled easily into Reagan-era politics, which bled easily into business and money and life and college versus pro football. He talked. We listened.

"The liberals will do anything to make you feel bad!" he cried, citing the term "acid rain," which he was convinced was made up. Dad clicked on the turn signal and steered the enormous boxy nose of the Lincoln into a gravel lot.

"Here's where we'll do it." He roused Adam and me from our gelatin-manufacturing operation and directed our attention outside the car. We were in an empty lot just across from the town's main ice cream purveyor. Dad said we'd be building our own shop right across the street, and we'd specialize in Flurries.

"We should pick another place, not so close to this ice cream place," I said. The other shop was lined in purple neon tubes that threw a violet glow onto the rocks where the four of us stood. I questioned the sanity of the across-the-street decision. That place had been serving cones since Mom was a kid, and people liked it. I brought this up because the idea of my family operating an ice cream store was extremely compelling. Imagine if instead of *playing* Jell-O factory with Adam, he and I were pulling the levers of an actual soft-serve machine ourselves. It was hard to envision a more fulfilling future.

Dad explained that Burger King will always pick a spot near a McDonald's when they open a new store. We'd use the same principle, and because Longs' Ice Cream would have a superior product, we'd just be driving more people to buy ice cream, not taking away their customers.

"Sometimes the line at our place will be so long that people will end up over there," he promised, pointing across the street. "They'll thank us." I was in awe of all that Dad knew, not just about religion and business, but everything. He was as confident navigating the business world of New York City as our new town and all its proclivities and history. He never wavered.

That first Indiana summer, I began accumulating a stockpile of blue ribbons in backstroke. It was as though I couldn't lose the event, whether I swam one lap or four and no matter which decorated swim club was our opponent. It was truly astounding that I'd taken to swimming, having been nudged into it as I was. Swim-meet Saturday nights, my accomplishments were celebrated with a visit to Poe's Cafeteria.

Any time of year, visitors walking into Poe's were greeted with a gust of warmth, followed by a buttery, yeasty aroma. A steaming table with containers of old-fashioned, homestyle food lay just beyond a stanchioned line. Evenings, families would wait twenty minutes or more to get a tray and start filling a plate.

After the winding line, diners took a plastic tray, placed it on the rails and spoke to the women on the other side of steamy, angled glass. Desserts were the first choice you'd encounter. The women presided over meatloaf, Swiss steak, country fried chicken, beef and noodles, soft carrots floating in yellowed water, golden corn kernels, planks of pink ham. The cooks there made their own rolls and pies, including gooseberry. Mashed potatoes were served with an ice cream scooper in a perfect whitish dome. At the end of the line, patrons chose one of the gravies—the salty brown one for beef or the creamy one studded with black pepper. It went with everything.

We took our trays to the dining room and found a spot with people we either knew or soon would. Tables were communal.

Gently sunburned from my day at the swim meet, I sat with my family in front of a platter of bread and meat and gravy with other families I knew from school or town. One of the Poe brothers approached, wearing a smock-like shirt with two front pockets on his hips. He bore a strong resemblance in my mind to my step-grandpa Earl, though I don't think they actually looked alike. They were probably the only two men in their seventies I knew. Grandpa Earl had 1960s black glasses and a gray-white goatee, a rail-thin and unsmiling version of Colonel Sanders in a sweater vest. Mr. Poe smiled always.

"Swimming today?" Poe asked us, looking at me jovially.

I nodded and he said, "You must be wore out." He pulled from his left pocket a little jewel for me, a plastic monkey or mermaid or giraffe, setting it on the edge of my glass of Coke.

Adam and I had an obscene number of toys, but these trinkets were treasured differently. Adam lined up his rainbow menagerie on the nightstand by his race car bed, and mine were in a paper cup secreted away beneath the sink in my rose-themed en suite bathroom. The little toys, and not the menu, were why I chose Poe's every week, for all three summers I swam backstroke.

I may have been blind to them, but my parents must have perceived—maybe even orchestrated—the alternating rags and riches aspects of our life. Our dinners out at Poe's and the nights we bounced through town in the red-and-white pickup were interspersed liberally with country club evenings and international vacations. Dad bought a full complement of tackle and took me fishing for little silver bluegill we tossed back. He also booked our family three times at the Acapulco Princess luxury resort, where I backstroked over to their swim-up bars for Shirley Temples. We were far from where we'd started, but the new experiences, from picking out worms in the local live bait shop to poolside virgin piña coladas in Mexico, didn't feel new for long. They felt normal.

SIXTEEN

"Her parents are getting divorced," Katie, an eight-year-old who was a friend of Kimberly's, said to me while raising a footed glass of 7-Up to her mouth. Her little finger pointed across the room to another girl eating Friday night dinner at The Club. That girl's mother was scowling, and her father was red-faced, scooting his chair back for another trip to the bar.

"Tragic," Kimberly answered. "Divorce is a very bad money decision." The three of us, all third graders, sat together at our own table Friday nights. Our parents had their conversations, and we had ours.

I looked down at my plate of steamed fish and wild rice. There was no homestyle black pepper and cream gravy at The Club. I didn't know enough people yet to meaningfully contribute to gossip, and I could only think of one thing I knew about divorce, one person I'd heard about who'd done it.

"My dad is divorced," I told them. I knew this was true, even though we never talked about it together at home. Dad had talked to me about it, and Mom had told me her own version.

"So she's not your real mom." Katie and Kimberly both looked across the room at Mom, whose frosted hair curled wildly out from her head. She was wearing a black-and-white silk houndstooth top with hot-pink slacks. Her big gold earrings bounced in the candlelight.

"I didn't think so," Katie said, adding that she'd always suspected something.

My head spun. "No, she is." How could my mom not be my mom just because my dad had been divorced? This had never occurred to me.

Katie was authoritative on the explanation. "That's what divorce means. You have another mom somewhere, and this is your dad's number two."

I sat in my upholstered seat in the dim room, my face quickly growing hot. I looked over at Mom, who laughed encouragingly at something Dad said to someone across their table. I looked just beyond them to the steep, twisty staircase, site of the untimely death of the Barbasol magnate.

I went in for a full non sequitur. "How did that guy really die?" I wanted to ask Mom about this whole thing before having to discuss it with anyone else, least of all these two.

"Killed himself. But anyway, I don't think there's any way in the world that's actually your mom," Kimberly said.

Did she not notice how much Mom and I looked alike?

I laid it all out for them as Mom had done for me years before. Dad was a high school football and basketball star. He went to the University of Florida on a football scholarship and his high school sweetheart followed him to Gainesville. She was beautiful and popular and her father was the kingpin of something called the Miami Jewish Mafia. Dad excelled at football, so much so that he was invited to a tryouts week for the Dallas Cowboys. He joined a frat rock band in the offseason, let his girlfriend wear his letter jacket, and generally fulfilled all the Big Man on Campus stereotypes available to him from 1961 to 1963. His college and football careers were cut short when he and his girlfriend dropped out before junior year. She was pregnant. They married in a hurry and moved back to Miami, into a house purchased for them by his new wife's father. They were raising three kids when Dad said he caught her in bed with the Miami chief of police. Dad was summarily and forcibly removed from the state of Florida by men he indicated were members of the Jewish Mafia. At the time, Dad was the vice mayor of Miami suburb Biscayne Park and the manager of the Miami Press Club. These ties were swiftly cut by his father-in-law's associates, along with any ties and obligations to his young family. Mom understood that the children were told their father was dead.

Two men deposited Dad—very much alive—in Indianapolis in the freezing cold March of 1972 without a winter coat but with his small suitcase. They had arranged for him to take the currently open position of Indianapolis Press Club manager. Dad's father-in-law wanted to keep an eye on him in addition to keeping about a thousand miles between Stephen and his daughter.

In the face of scant other options, Dad took the job. He slept on the floor behind the bar at the Press Club at first, later transitioning to his friend Mike's couch, and eventually to my mother's bedroom in mid-1973, beginning that first night they met, at that party. Telling the whole story out loud reassuringly locked the facts into place in my mind: she *had* to be my real mom.

If Katie and Kimberly were titillated at the first whisper of a divorce in my family, they were now agog. I felt amazing. I'd not only delivered them far juicier fodder than they'd ever expected but had also established my own maternity, which had been in question for a terrifying ten minutes or so.

An hour later, in my pink and green bedroom at home, Mom tucked my rosebud quilt around me and asked if I had any questions about sex, reminding me that sometimes, if a boy was really bothering you, you could just tug on his penis a few times and, if you did it the right way, he'd be satisfied and leave you alone. I didn't have any questions.

Mom's own sex education had been wan, as she'd told me before. She wanted to be sure she did things right with me. Taciturn and gruff, Earl would not have raised the subject under any circumstances. Cowed by him, naturally meek, and already divorced from another domineering husband, Dolores would not have been forthcoming either. Mom aimed at a utopian middle ground between the free-love late '60s of her destructively experimental high school and college years and puritanical silence.

These opposing ideologies flared and merged into Mom's recompense, which she packaged as a gift for me.

"I can't believe the boys aren't after you already," she said. "Just wait."

She asked if I'd had a nice time with the girls at dinner. Unguarded and with the full emotional range of any eight-year-old, I told all. The same way I'd done at dinner, I went on and on, to her increasing horror. The Jewish Mafia thing. The chief of police in bed with the wife thing. Mom's face was a little gray when I finished with, "I'm just so glad you're my real mom."

She sat on the edge of my bed and explained that some things were only for us to know, never for anyone else.

"Secrets?" I asked.

"Private information is all," she said. "I've told you about Santa Claus. You're never to tell your brother that information; he could not comprehend it. I've also told you about sex and puberty. Would you tell Adam those things?"

I had felt so good at The Club, but now I felt ashamed.

Mom had a plan. She told me that next Friday night I would sit with Katie and Kimberly and tell them I'd been joking, just trying to get their attention. I would say I'd been wrong to lie. And I was never, ever to tell Adam about Dad's divorce. He didn't know now, but Mom promised they'd tell him when he was mature enough.

"He's a baby," she reminded me. Adam was four, and I already knew about Dad's other family when I was four. On top of Dad's dresser was a small brown box, a miniature pirate's chest with grommets and a latch, a pewter skull and crossbones on top. He called it his jewelry box, but he never opened it or wore jewelry other than his wedding ring. Inside were photos of the children in Miami—two girls and one baby boy. I had seen the photos once but was afraid to look in it again.

I pledged silence. I could see that it was very important.

"Act like it's not true. It won't be true anymore, for us."

SEVENTEEN

Dad went to Sweden so often that the *Reporter* asked him to comment on the 1986 assassination of Olof Palme, which Dad did, from a thoroughly uninformed perspective.

He returned from Sweden with "hundred-dollar," vibrantly colored wool sweaters for Mom and me that were too warm to wear even in the depths of winter and too itchy against our skin to be appealing. Adding to their discomfort was the constant warning, "Don't spill anything on that hundred-dollar sweater." He also brought a matched set of bright-blue down parkas with the Swedish janitorial company's logo embroidered at the breast. Made for Swedish winters, they were generally too hot to wear comfortably, but Adam and I did, boiling and sweating inside them because of how cool they made us look.

Our whole family went to Sweden twice, both business-pleasure hybrid trips for Dad. The first trip was in August, just before I started fourth grade, and when Swedish sunsets occur near ten in the evening. My father was feted with what seemed to be a town-wide celebration of the business and riches he'd brought to the janitorial supply company there. Dad's Swedish business partner lived in a village with a castle about three hours outside of Stockholm. His family and dozens of villagers welcomed us Longs like royalty. Our first night there, under late-evening sunshine, several tables with disposable white paper on top were arranged outdoors. We were taught to pinch the tails and suck the heads of boiled crayfish, which were spilled out onto the paper tablecloths. Thousands were boiled that night, and we ate dozens of them from our perch at the head table. Gradually, the sky darkened and the party grew louder as the adults refilled tiny, frosty vials of aquavit. Later, we collapsed into austere-looking beds made of blond wood.

In the morning, hungover adults spread Nutella on bread for us, and it was quiet enough for me to have a conversation with the kids of the house. Flushed, blond Hans was my age and wore long socks with his shorts, which I found embarrassing on his behalf. His sister was a teenager, much more sophisticated and better at English than he was. Minna took it on herself to be my guide.

I watched carefully as she was sweet and deferential to her father, a janitorial businessman like my own father, while he poured us milk at the breakfast table. She held the chocolate bread up and said, "It's good, *ja*?" The night before I'd seen her make the same raised-hand gesture when she held up a paper cup to her friend, pouring from an absconded bottle of the semi-frozen, golden liquor, unkindly imitating their parents' singsongy toasts.

"*Ja*," her dad said. Hans and I *ja*-ed, too. I silently marveled at Minna's duplicity, mild as it was.

As my parents had noted during Dad's car ride soliloquies, I was introverted. A listener. An agreer. An observer from two steps back. I knew in my heart, and I'd been told again and again, that my family was different. We were, according to Mom, much smarter and had much better taste than anyone we knew. Dad's reckless optimism veered into the conviction that nothing bad ever could or would happen to any of us, a maxim he repeated with varying levels of divine intervention from "God won't allow anything to happen to us" to "We're the Longs. We cannot be unhappy."

This exceptional quality seemed fragile and sacred. I worried sometimes that I would ruin it if I took advantage of our immense good fortune and also, conversely, if I failed to utilize it. I was worried that I'd already let an important secret, Dad's divorce, out into the atmosphere, and it would be impossible to rein in again. At times I was terrified that my friends would learn that we were like this—invincible, chosen—and at other times I thought it was futile to hide it. It must have been obvious in our gigantic house, my straight-A report cards, our membership at The Club.

"One of the biggest struggles we have as a family is that everyone envies us," Dad said at the airport in Stockholm, heading home. "God is holding us in the palm of His hand. That's not true for most people."

On the plane ride, Mom asked me if Hans had kissed me. She was disappointed when I said no.

Home in Martinsville, I didn't understand why Mom kept referring to our trip as "Europe" when we'd only gone to one country: Sweden. She must have enjoyed the way it sounded. Uncle Steve rolled his eyes every time she said it.

Steve had never left Martinsville. In a bizarre coincidence, Mom had married a person with her brother's name, and her brother Steve had married someone with hers. Mom's other brother, Heather's dad, Tom, married seven times—twice to the same woman, none named Sandra. When our family wasn't jetting back from Sweden or the Acapulco Princess, sometimes my parents, Steve and Sandie, would have dinner with my uncle Steve and aunt Sandy.

They lived outside town on a triangle-shaped piece of land with two rutted country roads making a V shape around their property. Steve was a tool-and-die maker who fixed cars on weekends. Cars that were not yet fixed, or perhaps doomed to never be fixed, decorated the front and back yards. If the needed repair was tire related, the cars were propped on cement blocks. If they were window related, tarps stood in for glass. A growling dog stood guard.

Inside their narrow, one-story house, Sandy served us burgers, the buns topped with a three-quarter-inch-thick layer of Shedd's Spread Country Crock margarine scooped from a very large taupe tub. Dad asked for mustard and pickles, which my uncle reluctantly delivered from the fridge with another roll of his eyes. I ate mine as served, and it was velvety rich. Chips were the side dish.

On the way home Mom and Dad complained that Steve and Sandy would never come to our house. There were things about our house that were private. My mother's ever-increasing shopping habit had resulted in heavy clutter in most rooms. She despised cleaning. But certain guests were desired even if they rarely if ever made an appearance: Steve and Sandy, Earl and Grandma Dolores. If they'd ever agreed to come, Mom would have cleaned up the front four or five rooms, ordered a takeout beef Wellington from someplace in Indianapolis, popped it onto one of her own newly purchased platters, told everyone she'd made it, and lit a Yankee candle.

Uncle Steve had been invited again and again but consistently refused.

"He's not too busy," Mom protested. Dad noted that if he was actually that busy, they might see fewer cars on the lawn awaiting repairs.

"I mean, are you fixing cars or collecting broken ones to sit around like lawn statues?" he asked us. Mom and Dad were both prone to these sort of withering, condescending remarks about family and friends, which I received neutrally.

Dad raised the power windows of the Lincoln Town Car. We were driving past the fisheries north of town, which stank. As we turned off the main road and passed the stone gates guarding the dark golf course, Mom reminded Dad, "Some people like to live that way."

EIGHTEEN

By the spring of 1987, life in our mansion was just normal life. Dad traveled a little less than before, but his work with the Swedes was going strong, and we'd agreed to host Minna as a summer exchange student of sorts. She'd sleep in our lower-level guest suite and live an all-American teenager's life for eight weeks in June and July.

I loved the basement. Downstairs was cozier than the formal upstairs with its Chinese furniture and tall ceilings. We'd stuffed the creepy walk-in safe with board games and puzzles, and I spent winter afternoons in the safe or just outside it, playing Clue or working a jigsaw with Adam. I was grateful Adam was emerging from his army fatigues era but couldn't say I really identified with his new interests of playing sports and whizzing Matchbox cars on the slick floor of the downstairs kitchen. He was younger and more content as a homebody. I was usually antsy, striving like Dad for something beyond our weird walls. As the only witnesses to my parents' constant chicanery, he and I stuck together anyway, finding our middle ground in front of the video-game console or rerun episodes.

On one of our Mexico trips, Dad had caught a nine-foot sailfish, which was taxidermied and mounted on the family room's rear wall, shimmering blue and silver, its nose pointed toward the lake out back, its single glass eye watching us watch TV.

Adam and I had figured out the VCR, and we timed it to tape the late-night broadcast of *Cheers* so we could watch it after school. He was enamored with Rhea Pearlman for some reason, and I wanted to be glamorous Diane, whose actor's real last name was Long. I paused the tape and announced I'd get us some snacks from upstairs. The downstairs kitchen only had soda in the fridge and Mom's surplus fabric in the cupboards.

In the kitchen upstairs, snacks were abundant. Whether or not we were eating out at The Club or at Poe's, and in the absence of any dinner guests, Mom grocery shopped as though we were stocking up for war or famine. Around this time, she developed a habit—doubles. If she wanted a box of Bisquick, she'd buy two. She may have needed only a cup and a half out of one of the boxes, but she'd get an extra. If she needed marinara sauce for dinner, she put two jars in her cart. Buying a single item became foreign to her, unnecessarily spartan.

When she arrived home, the groceries were schlepped indoors, but it was hard to find room for new things and harder to make room for twice as much. I'd once suggested to her that we put the surplus groceries in our kitchen downstairs, but she reminded me we needed that one for fabric.

The overstuffed pantry was in the hall between the kitchen and her sewing room. I could hear Mom's sewing machine going *zzzzz* as I trudged up the stairs.

I pushed open one of the louvered saloon half doors at the sewing room entrance and gave her a goofy hello on my way toward the pantry. The bags and boxes and cans had just begun to bother me in a low-level way I didn't understand. I loved my mother so much, and I tried to be extra sweet and loyal to her to compensate for my increasingly dark feeling about all the mess, all the stuff. There was just so much. At Kimberly's house, their groceries fit in their cabinets. And I wondered sometimes about the older stuff—would the eighth-newest Bisquick ever get used? I looked for an older box of granola bars. I always did this—sought out the oldest item, the thing to use up, to make space. Waste not, want not. Someone in the house had to think that way. There were about twenty boxes in the pantry, enough that you could trace the graphic design evolution of the Quaker Oats Company.

I grabbed two bars from the most vintage-looking of the boxes and opened mine so I could eat it on my way back downstairs to *Cheers*. I took a bite off the top and then looked down at the foil-wrapped bottom half of the bar, which was crawling with white mini-worms. It looked like wiggling rice. Mom told me they were maggots.

"Just spit it out," she said. "You're fine." She continued sitting at her sewing machine.

I yelled and spit and rinsed my mouth until Adam came upstairs. Mom looked at me the way Uncle Steve had looked at us when Dad wanted mustard and pickles on his burger. She explained that sometimes food got buggy. It wasn't worth making such a big deal about.

"There are plenty of other snacks," she suggested.

NINETEEN

Clothes shopping was Mom's second-favorite hobby, next to clothes making. Her new sewing room spilled over with fabric, piled in plastic bags and boxes in that room and several others. Martinsville had only chain fabric stores, and Mom liked to order unusual fabrics to supplement local shopping trips. Catalogs would come with page after black-and-white page of information about different materials and a stack of zigzag-cut, 1-inch squares of samples. Mom spent hours matching the squares to their page and Scotch-taping them in place. Then she circled the ones she'd phone in and order. In her fabric room, most of the packages that arrived remained sealed, a folded-over polyethylene bag stuffed with fabric she'd never see or use. Her primary joy was in choosing them.

She did finish sewing projects, but she began exponentially more than she completed. "The fun," she explained, "is in the choosing." Her creative process was primarily around selecting a pattern and a fabric to complement it, ciphering the math to get the right amount of material, choosing buttons and other notions, envisioning it. Once the project was actually done, she might feel dissatisfied with the result. Disappointed. Mom preferred to limn the vast region around a potential failure without getting close enough to actually risk it.

"How long would it take?" I asked. I stood in her sewing room, her hands and a vinyl tape measure circling my waist. She wanted to make me a skirt. It would take her about a week to make it, using just one of the hundreds of folded pieces of fabric. I wanted to know how long it would take her to use it all up, one dress or pillowcase or T-shirt at a time. To be finished.

"Oh, years, I guess."

She slipped the vinyl measuring tape around my elementary-school hips and reminded me how lucky we were that she could make clothes for me that would be flattering for a big body like mine. I was the tallest in my class. (Dad's take was upbeat, "Listen, Christie Brinkley and all these people are tall. You'll grow into your football-player body. You'll probably be a model.")

We took frequent shopping trips. I enjoyed looking around, picking up a shirt or dress, and rubbing the fabric between my fingers.

"You like it?" Mom asked. She flipped a fuzzy, lilac sweater and its hanger into our cart. I'd been looking at it closely, touching the sleeve, thinking it was an eye-catchingly awful sweater.

"Oh, I just wanted to feel it," I answered. Mom plowed on through Kohl's, adding to our pile.

"Try it on."

I learned that anything I touched would go in our cart, and anything in our cart was going home with us, even if I didn't actually like it. I'd argue, "But I already have a neon-green sweatshirt," or "I changed my mind. I don't like it. I won't wear it."

None of this mattered.

"You're afraid to say what you like, Amanda."

I was growing more and more afraid of something else. The longer we lived in our huge house with our huge number of things, the more generally uncomfortable I felt. It was a nonspecific malaise that I couldn't name. I understood that the same thing that made me anxious was the exact thing that gave Mom joy. To me, it felt like the things we owned outnumbered us, were taking over.

When I was nine or ten, I began to have a recurring dream in which I was given a solemn mission by some unknown authority figure: I was to destroy our house and everything in it. I dreamed this at least once a week for eight or ten years. Some weeks I dreamt it nightly. Each time I would hesitate on my mission at first. "My parents will be so angry their stuff is gone," I'd protest. "I could never do this." I'd beg to be let off the hook even though my dream self and my waking self both wanted to annihilate it all. It felt like the only thing that could satisfy the persistent uneasiness.

After being assured that a full duplicate house and its possessions awaited us elsewhere, I set to work night after night in this dream. Our spice cabinet had seven jars of cinnamon. I removed six of them, dumping the auburn powder on the floor. I filled garbage bags with Mom's folded fabric, plaids and corduroys stacked together for the dump. I squirted dozens of shampoo bottles onto the Oriental rug. I opened windows and tossed out canned goods and sheets and towels and all the things we simply had too many of. Purging it all made me feel content and balanced, and I had to sleep to feel those things.

"Don't buy it. I don't like it," I told her in Kohl's.

"But you do." She reminded me that not every mother would take their daughter shopping for anything she wanted.

"I don't even wear the white pants I already have. I don't want more white pants."

"You will." She said it with love and anticipation. "And you should wear white pants as much as possible now, before you get your period." I would thank her one day, she said, blowing me a kiss across the cart.

TWENTY

Minna arrived in June 1987 with the expected amount of fanfare from the *Martinsville Reporter*, which ran a photo of her under the headline SWEDISH VISITOR. Her blond hair was permed in a style similar to the way Mom had permed my brownish hair. She wore a preppy, cable-knit sweater in the photo, and Mom told the newspaper that her children were looking forward to having a "Swedish big sister" for the summer. Adam and I were four and nine; Minna was seventeen.

At the far end of our house's lower level was a guest suite. (Upstairs, the old West Virginia–purchased brass bed sat in a fairly utilitarian guest bedroom.) The white shag carpet in Dad's office repeated around the corner into a large room that had somehow maintained decades-old wallpaper that would have matched my grandparents' lava lamp. Two of the suite's walls were covered in an aqua-and-chartreuse, oversized floral pattern. Sliding doors led directly outside to the sloping yard and its lake. A cozy en suite bathroom had two deep sinks, and Mom had stocked it with soft new towels. The furnishings were from Hong Kong: a queen-sized, black lacquer bed with gold trim on its arched headboard, a squat, shiny, black nightstand, and a dresser to match. Minna would be the first person to ever sleep here.

"She needs her privacy," Mom told us. Neither of my parents had ever supervised a teenage girl, much less a teenage girl who had the gumption to travel across the world and live with virtual strangers. When my parents used the word *au pair* and indicated she might be like a sister to me, they were imagining a different kind of summer than the one Minna had imagined for herself.

She tumbled into the guest suite, Dad carrying half of her many suitcases. I followed them in. In just the same way she was sweet and polite to her own dad, Minna paid my dad the favor of a bubbling laugh and warm "thank you, *tack!*" for helping with the bags. Dad told her we would have dinner the next night at The Club, where he'd introduce her to some families with high schoolers. "For now, just rest and settle in," he told her, leaving her luggage near the door as he left.

She smiled at him, then looked over at me lying flat on my back on the queen bed. For a year now, I'd had the run of the place, from the butler's quarters to the hot tub to the mod-and-Oriental guest suite, where I tried on dress-up clothes and used the bed as a stage for elaborate pop song lip synchs. I watched my own reflection in the varnished black panels of the dresser. I studied the floral wallpaper and recalled my dream from the night before—peeling it off the walls in long, jagged strips, tearing it to confetti I stomped into the white shag carpet under my feet. I didn't anticipate my habits would need to change now that Minna was here.

She cleared her throat and said something in Swedish that may have betrayed her impatience with me. I understood that she was asking me to leave her alone. I asked if I could just watch her unpack. I wanted to see what Swedish teenage clothes she'd brought along. She wasn't unkind, but she still refused. "You're my brother's age. There are things you can't see." Minna closed the door of the guest suite and waved goodbye as she said this.

I speculated with Mom about what things she might have in her bags that I shouldn't see, and Mom made an extemporaneous list of embarrassing things, including a gentle suggestion about a vibrator. I was sorry to have asked.

Minna may not have been sisterly that summer, but I believe she found her way and likely achieved some of the 1980s American high school goals that had inspired her to want to stay with us. I knew, though

I don't think my parents did, that she entered and exited via the downstairs glass sliding doors after hours, and that she drank beer with some members of the Martinsville High School football team, which she told me herself later in the summer.

I was only a little disappointed not to have Minna at my side all summer, which helped me find new things to do. My parents' bathroom had a mustard-yellow Jacuzzi tub; I played with Mom's impressive array of makeup bottles and tubes and stole a look at the pirate chest on Dad's dresser during the half an hour it took to fill the tub. I continued to bike our driveway and neighborhood indefatigably and had another winning season of backstroke. Mom kept up with her sewing and her shopping. Dad kept up with televised football, while Adam and I cultivated our sitcom and cartoon acumen with hour after hour of *He-Man*, *Full House*, *My Two Dads*, *Perfect Strangers*, and whatever else was on our four channels. At the pool, friends tried to stump me by asking sitcom esoterica. (Name all the family members on *Just the Ten of Us*. What was the dad's job on *Family Ties*?) Like my backstroke competitions, I never lost.

Meanwhile, Minna just floated in the background and popped up for dinners at Poe's or afternoons at the pool, where I sat with my friends eating powdered Jell-O and doing TV trivia, and she behaved as if she were filming a John Hughes movie where a blond, Swedish teenager allows the small-town American boys to pinch her bottom under her bikini.

"Your parents know this goes on?" Kimberly licked pink sugar crystals off her pinkie.

"Pretty much." I had already learned the power of being discreet.

While the rest of us enjoyed our preferred summer activities, Dad spent more and more time in his downstairs office. I'd creep down the hall to spy on Minna, whose door was closed and locked at all times, and find Dad's office door the same way. His voice sounded muffled through the wood door, but I could hear he was upset, probably on a long-distance call. Years ago an opponent's football cleat created a pink, feather-shaped scar on Dad's right cheek. It was barely noticeable most of the time, but when he was angry, the arched line burned as red as it must have when it was a fresh gash in the early '60s. I stood outside his office, strings of the white shag peeking out beneath the door. By the tone of his voice, I knew his cheek was flushed crimson.

The valve patent was languishing, and while the Swedes were still providing business for him, Dad needed to develop more projects, get clients beyond Minna's dad. The valve would be our long-term financial security, but the short term needed attention, too. Dad's answer: air fresheners. He'd begun to work with some of his old janitorial business clients on a motorized air freshener. Plug it into a wall outlet, and a small fan would generate a breeze and blow it over a cartridge of scented gel, infusing a room with the smell of mint or lavender. Not only was it high tech but it also addressed the environmental concern of the moment—chlorofluorocarbons in aerosols. Spray air freshener—like we constantly saw spritzed by coiffed mothers wielding cans of Glade potpourri scent on commercials—would be a thing of the past. Dad soundly rejected the environmental issues, but nonetheless, to him, this air freshener was the future. Or at least, our future.

TWENTY-ONE

Mom was a solid cook on nights we weren't at Poe's or The Club, but meal preparation and cleanup was the extent of her housework. She didn't vacuum. She didn't dust. Neither did Dad. A bathroom sink would be wiped of its blobs of toothpaste and food detritus at the point it was deemed too nasty to use, not a moment before.

Some rooms became harder to clean as clutter accumulated. Because we had more food than our pantry would hold, paper bags full of cake mixes and canned beans, in doubles, sat in the hall. Doing laundry was necessary, but we had so many clothes that the chore could be delayed almost indefinitely; a dirty clothes pile the size of a Volkswagen Bug was always on the floor near the washing machine. A plastic honey bear split down its seam inside a kitchen cabinet, and flies feasted on the sticky puddle for months. Stacks of slick catalogs were piled on the living room coffee table until they tumbled off where they'd stay splayed on the hand-knotted Oriental rug. None of us picked them up.

In part to keep up appearances for Minna, Mom hired an older lady named Della to clean for us. For good reason, hardworking Della looked at slothful Adam and me with annoyance and pity. She looked at Mom with scorn, and no pity whatsoever, and it was mutual. Mom huffed about having to clean *before* the cleaning lady's visits—by picking up various piles about the house—as well as *after*. Notoriously absentminded Della would leave the vacuum somewhere in the cavernous house and forget where it was or move some objets d'art to dust a shelf and then leave them tucked elsewhere because it slipped her mind to repopulate the shelf afterward.

For his part, Dad hired a crew of lawn men to care for our outdoor spaces. The enormous backyard and its steep incline would have been a daylong project to cut without a riding mower, and the front yard had to be kept pristine for the golfers who walked by every day and for the ever-watchful homeowners' association.

That summer, as my discomfort in the house grew, I gravitated outdoors. I asked Dad to take me fishing early on Saturday mornings. My second summer at the pool, I was an established blue-ribbon backstroker, so I'd earned the respect of the teenage lifeguards and became a fixture with the other kids who spent long afternoons there. Rainy days or days when the grass was being cut, I'd be forced to stay inside, searching for a way to build a world of my own inside the world my parents made for us. That impulse was usually satisfied by burrowing within the massive dirty-clothes pile to create a damp fort, its walls made of soiled jeans and mildewy towels, whose sharp smell was everywhere. I longed to be out of the house with its piles of stuff and TVs on in every room. I could only truly escape in the yard outside our house. Except for the lawn men and me, no one else set foot in it. Dad was in his office; Mom was snake-phobic, and young Adam was deemed a drowning risk because of the lake out back.

Our dock was made of soft wood that had been sponging up green lake water for twenty-some years, but it served me well as a place to watch dragonflies touch down on the water's surface or daydream while I smelled the gently sulfurous shore. When I got tired of sitting there, I'd go up front and lie down, arms above my head at the top of our grassy hill, and roll myself down it or play store with rocks as money along the split-rail fence by the lower driveway. I even liked the summer humidity. Upon reentry to our ultra-chilled house, the sweat instantly iced over behind my knees and in my armpits.

"Have fun?" Mom assessed the lawn cuttings in my hair and grass stains on my butt when I came back inside, brushing debris off me. "See any snakes?"

I had not. It was probably unavoidable that she'd passed this deep and irrational fear to me. When I was very young, she saw a picture of a snake in *People* magazine and was so startled that she abruptly threw the entire magazine in the trash can without reading the rest. She screamed if a snake ever appeared on TV. On a kindergarten field trip, I was invited to touch a snake and declined based on what I'd gleaned about snakes from Mom up to that point. When the teacher made me touch it anyway, it sparked in me a fear as deep as my mother's. If I see a snake, my body floods with ice-cold terror, not of being bitten or constricted, but a hybrid of fear and hatred of the snake itself. I abhor the way they move, the way a snake's body touches itself as it repositions. I despise that they approach with threatening silence, their leglessness. Whether via nature or nurture, my mother transferred her phobia to me as efficiently and undeniably as she passed me her chin and hazel eyes.

Even though Mom always asked about snakes, I never saw one in our yard and really never thought of them, certainly not when I was most vulnerable, skittering down the hill barefoot and bare-torsoed, or astride the old dock with my feet in the swampy stuff between grass and lake.

"Now she knows what a real summer's like," boasted the July 8 edition of the *Martinsville Reporter*, under a photo of Mom, Dad, Minna, and me. The short article states that she ". . . came from Sweden where summer is a bright delight to Indiana, where even Hoosiers admit it gets a little sticky. She's pictured with her hosts, the Steve Long family . . . Long, a marketing consultant with an international clientele . . . Mrs. Long and her daughter are on the left. They were photographed at a Kiwanis meeting at Poe's."

The four of us each smile at one other person, creating a circular, familiar newspaper-ready smile. Minna had been Dad's co–guest speaker at the lunchtime Kiwanis meeting, where he spoke about his business successes and his client, Minna's father. She provided color commentary.

I suppose four-year-old Adam would have been bored and didn't attend; he's not in the photo.

In August, all four of us accompanied Minna back home to her village, which gave Dad a chance to try to pitch his air freshener to the Swedish janitorial company, though he didn't seem to get much traction. Now that we were both ten, Minna's little brother and I might have had something closer to an attraction but for the braces Mom insisted I have installed the spring before.

Though my front four top teeth had grown in unimpeded thanks to the clear-cutting after the apple juice incident, they were still spaced apart a bit. "Gap-toothed," Mom called it, warning Dad and me both that a gap-toothed daughter would attract a gap-toothed hillbilly for a boyfriend, and that we had the means to do better. She drove me to the college town of Bloomington every four weeks to have my braces tightened.

I didn't exactly mind. In fact, I'd always admired the glamorous look of a teenage girl in braces. Headgear was ubiquitous in the '80s movies I watched, so it seemed actually rather chic to be a braces wearer, even though I was noticeably the only fourth grader who had them.

"No, no, that's the idea," Dad told me. "You need them now, before you're a teenager."

"You can't kiss with braces. You wouldn't be dateable," Mom said. The braces would go on when I was nine and come off before I was eleven, perfect timing for romance.

TWENTY-TWO

Without Heather, and with no more overseas trips scheduled, Dad sat in his office alone. He had an IBM computer he used to write documents and print them on a continuous strip of paper, perforated at each page with a row of perfectly round holes at the edges. A plaque behind his desk had a quote about success by Vince Lombardi: "The measure of who we are is what we do with what we have." Dad often spoke long-distance on one of the black plastic two-line phones to his partners in New York and to the Swedes, early in the morning.

I lingered there when I could, filing my nails like Heather had at the desk across from his.

"Why do you have that?" A piece of wood the size of a Scrabble tile rack held a golden plate carved with "Stephen F. Long" that sat at the front edge of the desk.

Sheets of paper with Dad's florid writing were all over the desk. He wrote with a gold Cross pen that twisted open and that I was not allowed to touch. Dad moved a stack of papers to sit beneath some air freshener prototypes and picked up his nameplate to explain it to me. The ringing phone interrupted us. He shooed me out.

It would be almost twenty years before I knew the details of the most harrowing call he received in that office. In 1987, I was completely unaware.

His New York partner, the other half of the valve brain trust and our soon-to-be ice cream empire partner, was on the line with Dad and a lawyer named Maurice. The news was bad, somehow. Maurice and the partner explained that there was no way forward for their project. The patent was rejected. It was over.

It was a body blow to Dad. Our profligate spending—from the braces on my teeth to the canopy bed I slept in—had hinged on his confidence in this valve, in the promise of a patent and the long-term wealth it would establish.

"Nothing we can do to save this?" Dad asked them.

"Nothing," the other men answered, definitively.

Dad placed the phone in its cradle and put his forehead in the cradle of his own hands. A moment later, ever the optimist, he had an idea to save the patent. He could pull in the Swedes. Half a minute after he'd hung it up, Dad picked up the phone again, to call Sweden.

"Fuck Long," he heard Maurice say.

"Exactly," the partner agreed. The phone call had continued without Dad, and the two-line phone had kept the other men's conversation active on line two. Dad silently listened to his partner betray him, to his plans for a patent be spun out around a complicated, lucrative plan that did not include him.

A decade after this call, McDonald's was serving McFlurries in its tens of thousands of locations. His partner had cashed out for an untold sum. Dad never held patent rights and didn't make a single Flurry dollar.

Adam and I knew the Flurry plan was dead, but we didn't hear about this phone call until around the time I was getting married in 2003. As kids, we carried on without this knowledge, consumed by scuttlebutt at our respective schools, obsessively watching a Louie Anderson movie called *The Wrong Guys* on VHS, and arguing over who got to be Mario and who got to be Luigi. As an adult, I frame this story the same way I have come to frame the story about Dad's first wife cheating on him. Who cheated first? Just because he got screwed doesn't mean he was the only one.

For Dad and Mom, this phone call was the beginning of the end of their financial success, which arrived about a year after our big move to luxury land. They had thought it would be forever.

TWENTY-THREE

Christmas in Martinsville had been reinvented, too. Our first year there, Mom declared that we'd be doing a Victorian Christmas and ordered all-new decor. The red, green, and gold tchotchkes we used to use were set aside. The new ornaments and decorations were all of a certain color family and aesthetic that could be generalized as pink and velveteen. Dad phoned in an order for Racine, Wisconsin, kringle, and three huge Os of it were delivered to our door Christmas Eve. Our living room had double-height ceilings, and we needed a nine- or ten-foot tree to be proportionally right. The fresh-cut tree was draped with lengths of velvet ribbon in mauve, bubblegum pink, and burgundy, the same colors as the ball ornaments and the little pre-tied bows whose green floral wire we wrapped around branches. Multicolored lights were trashy, so pure white lights illuminated it. Mom sewed a dusty-rose, lace tree skirt, which we only saw briefly; the gifts under the tree spilled out several feet around it in all directions.

Like a lot of parents, they took pride in Christmas being at least partly about over-the-top gift gluttony. In our case, we spent six or seven hours on present opening alone, an authentically exhausting start to the day. We went to church the night before, but never on Christmas morning. There was too much unwrapping to do. Mom filled a CorningWare with crumbled sausage, canned peaches, and Bisquick for our traditional holiday morning breakfast casserole, which kept us going for the marathon, along with wedges of kringle and mugs of sweet and creamy coffee for my parents.

Adam and I so loved the peach pancake bake that we improvised a dance of appreciation. In our pajamas, I instructed him on the hand and hip moves I'd seen Janet Jackson do. He did air guitar and said, "Mom, it's so so so good." We slid around the huge living room gobbling up Mom's delicious breakfast, smothered in a syrup made from the canned peaches' cloying liquid.

"It's sacrilegious," Dad told us, pointing to a card someone sent wishing us a *Merry X-mas*. Dad had a particular exasperation with removing the "Christ" from "Christmas" and made this point repeatedly every holiday season.

It was just the four of us for Christmas morning. I still had a stack of wrapped presents to open, but I was peeling the cardboard from a chemistry set I'd asked for and setting out beakers and droppers on the rug. I had most hoped for a dollhouse and had not seen it yet.

"These are the people trying to teach evolution in our schools. And giving out abortions." Dad's forehead was riven with three sharp lines across it, perhaps because he was so facially expressive. Three parallel lines were always there, even the rare times when his face was impassive.

Politics and religion were beginning to merge in Dad's frequent monologues, and his perspective was shifting ever rightward. The church in Martinsville just wasn't working for them any longer. Dad had met a conservative, traditional Lutheran pastor whose church was on the historic register and right in downtown Indianapolis. When Dad talked about meeting Reverend Mark, he also started talking about being a kid in Miami, going to Pinewood Church Camp, and the pastor there who told him, in 1951, that he'd become a pastor one day.

"We have all sinned and fall short of the glory of God," Dad continued, holding the offending X-mas card.

By early 1988, our family started attending the Indianapolis church every week, spending Sunday afternoons lingering with Reverend Mark and his family. Sometimes Dad would drive the forty-five minutes each way midweek to talk to Reverend Mark. On Good Friday that year,

Mom and Adam refused to go all the way to Indy when we'd be back again Sunday morning. Dad was sincerely hurt, the scar on his cheek now a deep pink. He quietly took his keys off the kitchen table but didn't say "*Llaves*" *en español* as usual. It was rare not to hear him provide a mini-sermon; I knew his feelings were genuinely wounded.

I chased after him. "I'll go." He was dressed in a shirt and tie as always. Adam and I had the day off school, so I was in a pretty standard fourth-grader outfit for 1988: stonewashed jeans and a sweatshirt with a bejeweled neon unicorn. He told me to change.

Each for their own reasons, my parents focused a lot on how we looked when we left the house. Mom came at her position as a true-blue clotheshorse who'd studied fashion in the only college classes she'd taken. She knew patterns and fabrics and trends and appointed herself our household authority on all of the above. Dad, whose insecurities quivered steadily beneath his confident speaking voice, was more focused on how we might appear to others. He carried with him a tiny part of the edge he'd developed as a Miami nightclub promoter, smoothing his duck's ass with Brylcreem, flicking lint from his narrow lapel.

I put on a black dress and chunky sweater.

Dad cleared out the cupholders, grumbling. Everywhere Mom went, she left in her trail a few plastic bottles of Diet Coke, capped and never touched again with about an inch of soda in the bottom. "Your mother is a 'never-finisher,'" Dad griped.

"Geez," I said, trying to match his annoyance, reflect his tone.

But Dad reversed back, protecting her. "It's hard for her," he told me. "She's just like this, and we love her. What do I care if she doesn't drink all her Coke?"

I loved rides with Dad. He talked. I listened. I could tell he was happy I'd come. We parked as we always did in the lot by the church, which sat in the shadow of the Eli Lilly drug company headquarters, and entered through the church's creaking, massive, wood door just before noon.

There were services at noon, one, and two, culminating in a dark ceremony around three in which the crucifix would be covered in a somber black cloth until its removal Easter morning. The hours there next to Dad felt both epically long and strangely fast, almost instantaneous. I watched him kneel and sing. I knelt and sang with him.

When we left, the medium-gray morning had turned nearly black only a few minutes after 3:00 p.m. Dad was quiet, reverent. I wondered if he'd remain silent like this all the way home—an anomaly I wasn't sure I could handle.

As soon as he turned the engine over in the Town Car, he was off and running. "Did you see that? Kneelers. This is why we go here." The church in Martinsville was more modern, and there was no means to kneel there. Reverend Mark's church had foldout padded benches to cushion our knees. Dad said that it meant more to God this way, to physically bow for prayer.

We spent the rest of the ride deep in theology. Dad's admiration of Martin Luther was boundless. He loved that Luther had publicly rejected the Roman Catholic Church while simultaneously embracing certain of their practices like making the sign of the cross and kneeling. These conversations enlivened Dad. He suddenly spoke far more about the church and religion than his business deals.

We pulled into the circular drive right around the time Della, our cleaning lady, was leaving. My Huffy was tossed on the grass sloppily. As soon as I saw it I reminded Dad that we'd left in a rush. He told me to move it.

Mom came charging into the foyer, looking for Della, who was gone.

"She stole my Chanel Number Five," Mom reported. She was ever so slightly breathless, having apparently searched her vanity the moment Della packed up. It was impossible for anyone to keep up with Mom's dizzying number of possessions, except Mom, who seemed to have a precise mental catalog. She always knew if something went missing. In this case, either her mental ledger had kicked in or she'd smelled Chanel No. 5 wafting about the vanity area.

Dad thought it was ludicrous. "She couldn't have." I knew Della, who I'd never seen wear any makeup at all, would be unlikely to take a bottle of perfume.

Mom and I sifted through the many items on the counter surrounding the mustard-yellow sink in her dressing room. We picked up each bottle to check; it simply was not there.

When Mom called to fire her, it was not a short conversation. Della provided a lengthy rebuttal, saying she'd accidentally knocked it over and spilled it into the sink. Embarrassed and worried for her job, she'd taken the broken, empty bottle home with her. Della told Mom she'd bring the broken glass back with her next week, to prove her innocence.

"Don't come back" was the final word. We were sitting in the carpeted area outside the master bath, the scene of the crime. Mom had pulled the spiral-corded phone from her bedside over to the vanity. Eye level with more than a hundred bottles and tubes and creams on the counter, I considered all the times I'd messed around with Mom's makeup and how difficult it was to avoid knocking something over amid all the little containers. I regularly tried on lipsticks and squirted Mom's bright white concealer onto a fingertip to paint my face during her sewing or shopping afternoons. I'd been lucky, I realized. Or blessed.

Mom turned to replace the phone in its base, and I made the sign of the cross over my heart, quickly so she wouldn't see me.

TWENTY-FOUR

I kept counting my own blessings. I felt I'd gotten away with so many things that year and was beginning to look over my shoulder and wonder if I'd be caught. No one had made an issue of the divorce story I told at The Club, but it felt like a close call, just as much as Della's firing did. I lay in my canopy bed considering how to avoid getting in any trouble whatsoever and came up empty except for the strategy to just keep quiet most of the time. This was already my status quo at home: listen more than you talk.

Dad and I went fishing many Saturday mornings that spring and summer. Adam was mostly content to watch a cartoon and enjoy a wedge of the Entenmann's Danish we always had on the kitchen counter, so he only joined now and then. I felt compelled to watch *Pee-wee's Playhouse* weekly, but it didn't come on until 11:00 a.m., so usually Dad and I had time to wake, visit the live bait shop, drive over to one of the lakes in our neighborhood, and fish for a good hour before coming home. I liked being outside and I loved Dad, although I didn't have much affection for the worm and fish part.

At 10:45 one morning, fishless and not unhappy about it, Adam and I packed the tackle box and made our way toward the car, parked across the road. Dad held the poles, and I had the rest, which I started to carry across the street when I noticed a black tire on its side in front of the Town Car. No car had passed all morning, and I was surprised a tire had just materialized there, at the edge of the pavement. I walked closer to it.

The tire pulsed and a long neck emerged. Glossy and black, a fat king snake was coiled there, its body making four stacked circles, tracing the size and shape of a tire. Now its head reared up.

All the neighbors must have heard my scream. I dropped the fishing gear in the road and wanted to run to the car, but the snake was between it and me. I was apoplectic from the dissonance of feeling trapped in a cage yet being outside in the world.

Dad picked up a hefty rock and threw it at the snake's head. He missed. The snake stared directly ahead, unmoving. He lobbed another one, this time grazing the side of its head, but it barely flinched. It was agony; I was revulsed looking at it but terrified to look away. I felt sure that if I took my eyes off the hideous snake, it would silently come closer. My heart pounded; I forgot Adam was there. Nine or ten rocks later, Dad hit the snake directly between the eyes, which didn't seem to hurt it but did startle it into retreat. I watched it unfold and slip its long body into the weeds.

At home, we agreed never to tell Mom, and didn't.

"Do you like Madonna?" Dad knew I was shaken and was maybe trying to distract me. "Her music, I mean? Not her lifestyle."

Of course I did. This was 1988. Years before, when I was in a dance class on Long Island, my class choreographed a number to "Material Girl," and Dad had said those were not our values and I should not listen to her music.

This might have been a trick question. "A little," I floated.

"Okay, well, I'd like you to get more familiar with her work. She's going to be here to do a business deal with me in the summer, and I think we'll need you to show her around," Dad explained.

Nineteen eighty-eight might have been the height of her fame, and it was unreal to me that she might know Dad or might come to our house. Our house? With its bags of groceries in the hall and dark mold in the showers' corners? No one had cleaned anything since Della left on the day of the Chanel No. 5 incident. "We'll have to clean up," I told Dad.

He explained we'd have some time to prepare. Madonna was interested in developing a fragrance of her own, and Dad's contact in the air freshener business had lined up some meetings. Once things were settled with her "people," Madonna would come and sleep in the lower-level suite where Minna had slept, and she and my father would be spending days together, sniffing samples of scents and combining them until her new fragrance was just right. "You can help," Dad promised.

I cleaned my bedroom in anticipation and checked in with Dad frequently about the plans, though I heard few concrete details.

Dad had his mind elsewhere. Early that year, I realized that Dad's trips to Indianapolis were not just for visits to the church. He was also going to something he called "night school" and would soon become a Realtor. On top of that, he was starting something new, as part of a company called SMI.

Although these career moves must have been acts of desperation, the *Martinsville Reporter* covered them with reverence. The announcement said he'd be joining a local real estate firm and that he remained president of REN Americas, Inc., which was noted as operating in Martinsville and New York City. His Swedish and other clients are mentioned, along with his business acumen and achievements. The April 1988 article goes on to say that he "has recently been appointed area distributor for SMI—Success Motivation Institute of Waco, Texas, and will be presenting seminars and consulting for individuals and companies in the field of human resource and personal growth development. SMI is the market leader in such programs with more than 28 years' experience in more than 50 countries."

Paul J. Meyer founded SMI in 1960 as a way to unite his Christian values and his business knowledge in one of the first-ever self-help, multilevel marketing programs. Their mission was "motivating people to their full potential," and their target audience was, essentially, Dad. Meyer's most famous quote is one Dad often muttered around that time: "Whatever you vividly imagine, ardently desire, sincerely believe, and enthusiastically act upon, MUST inevitably come to pass."

Dad listened to cassette tapes of Meyer's inspirational wisdom, and the announcement that he'd become a distributor meant that Dad paid for that privilege, probably at least $10,000. A 1990 Universal Press Syndicate article quotes several franchisees who lost between $20,000 and $60,000 on SMI programs or had other catastrophic outcomes, like being unable to keep up with their mortgages and losing their other employment.

"I mean, it works," Dad told us. The SMI tapes came in sets of twelve in vinyl binders. Each cassette had a molded slot, and a brochure was tucked in the middle. An aggressively positive arrow logo was repeated on every tape, along with its title. *The Magic of Thinking Big. Dynamics of Goal Setting. Psycho-Cybernetics. Advanced Selling. The Making of the Achiever. Winning Through Intimidation.* There were tapes for weight loss, for better sleep and stronger marriages. Dad's focus was the tapes on sales techniques, though we had tapes for every conceivable ailment or goal.

Heather's old desk was stacked with vinyl binders of cassette tapes. Dad had a clipboard with SMI order forms, the Cross pen slipped into the cavity up top. From outside his office door, I could hear the tapes playing, a man's careful, deep voice coming out of the tape deck and into the hall. "It is a self-evident fact that some people seem to attract success, wealth, attainment, recognition, and personal satisfaction, apparently with very little effort." I heard Dad clear his throat behind the door.

At dinner, Mom said how proud she was of Dad. He was running a successful international marketing business, selling houses in Martinsville as a Realtor, and now he was an SMI distributor, too. She bought him a new red tie.

TWENTY-FIVE

Dad said it would take a little time for the SMI roots he'd been planting to grow. In the meantime, he worked for one of Martinsville's Realtors in the spring of 1988. I don't remember him selling any houses, though he must have sold at least a few. He stopped mentioning the ice cream store we were supposed to open and Madonna.

I knew not to ask. That spring other concerns took hold. My grandma's health had never been strong but now was actively declining. Earl determined she would need to go to a nursing home and consulted my parents, hoping they could help bear the cost.

I was in my third summer as a winning backstroker. The country club pool—which I had not originally wanted to join—was the happiest place in my world. I had friends there and was successful at swimming. Most of all, I could forget about the clutter and strangeness at my own house. I was at the pool every day.

The dreams about destroying our house and how I felt inside it were relentless. My daydreams were sunnier. I had heard Dad's SMI mantra enough times to have started envisioning success, which for me had nothing to do with sales goals or weight loss. I started to think that one day I would be an adult, and I imagined having a home I could keep tidy. I had no idea how I'd do it, but I could picture it: a home with just-enough stuff and clean countertops and tabletops. Normal.

Dad and I got in the Town Car together. He flipped the air-conditioning to super freeze and said, "Whatever you vividly imagine, ardently desire, sincerely believe, and enthusiastically act upon, MUST inevitably come to pass." Dad's "MUST" was emphasized just as Paul J. Meyer himself would have, and we drove out of our subdivision and onto the freeway that connected Indianapolis to Bloomington. "Look at this," he told me, after a long few minutes on the road. He pulled over at a new-looking strip mall.

Dad had vividly imagined his next chapter—and his imagination landed him in this parking lot. He told me the plan. He'd be the proprietor of a new kind of company, where independent businesspeople could rent a desk or an office and share administrative services. The commercial tenants would cover the full rent, and Dad could move his REN Americas office there as well without any cost to us. Before Flurries and Blizzards, Dad had reimagined fast-food ice cream. Before Glade PlugIns, Dad had reimagined air fresheners. And decades before WeWork, Dad was bringing coworking to rural southern Indiana.

Dad signed a lease for office space and paid for it to be decked out in full 1988 corporate office style: mauve everything, like our Christmas tree. A wine-colored carpet met plum-colored baseboards and seashell pink walls. There were matching blond-wood desks, and a big photocopier and water cooler in the center room. Up front, a receptionist would answer the phones the way cousin Heather used to do in Dad's basement office. All Dad needed to do was recruit a few tenants.

He placed ads in the *Reporter* and in the *Indianapolis Star*. "Affordable offices. As low as $125/mo Why pay more? Inclds furniture, utilities, receptionist." No one replied.

Dad's world was closing in on him. As usual, I was unaware.

Arriving at The Club one afternoon that summer, I saw thirty or more people on the waffle-woven green lawn. Looking closer, I saw no one at all was inside the fence surrounding the aqua pool.

"What happened?" I asked Kimberly, who was a self-appointed authority in most situations.

"Snake in the pool," she replied coolly. I looked over her shoulder, gripped by fear. I hated the idea of seeing it, but I also had to see it. I had to keep it in my sights.

"It's pulled out *now*," she said in an annoyed tone. "They're back in the trees."

Above us was a tall tree whose branches stretched over the pool. Within the green leaves I saw dark movement. Two long, black snakes coiled against each other, drooping and looping themselves together, one of their bodies making a U-shape below the lowest limb. One of them, Kimberly explained, had slipped down and splashed into the pool a few minutes ago. Six feet of slick black interrupted the blue like the thickly painted lane-marking lines, except this one writhed and bucked when it hit the water. The pool was evacuated.

Looking closely at the tree's trunk, I now saw the corkscrew undulation of another one climbing up to the branches and leaves.

Inwardly, I made the sign of the cross over my chest. How had I been fortunate enough to miss this? What if I had been shooting across the backstroke lane when the snake fell in?

"Literally, they are always doing this." Kimberly said she often saw a snake or three, twisting above the pool like this. Today was the first time one had fallen in.

I'd spent two and half years on my back, looking up, but I'd missed this.

I got back on my Huffy and sped home, no longer interested in swimming.

I did return to the pool but not soon, and not often. Dad said I could help him run the new business, Morgan Executive Suites. I unwrapped new phone handsets from their Styrofoam and we worked together to run phone and fax lines into each room and staple cords next to the purple baseboards. I had my pick of empty offices, and I set up in various rooms with a steno pad, writing stories and pretending to interview people. Dad let me sit at the reception desk until he hired a woman to work there. Like Heather, she was primarily there to answer calls that never arrived.

When the ads went unanswered, Dad did some active recruiting of his own. He was the speaker at the Martinsville Chamber noon luncheon on July 7, 1988. The event took place at Poe's, and his talk was titled "The Motivation Station—Does Your Train Stop Here?" Dad's opening line was directly from Paul J. Meyer: "Everyone should explore their full potential." Four days after his talk at Poe's, the newspaper announced the opening of Dad's shared office venture, and his three tenants, including a family plumbing company recruited at the luncheon and Dad's own marketing businesses. The third tenant was the lawn care enterprise Dad had hired to care for our giant yard; he'd set up a barter. Dad was behind on paying the mowers, and the homeowners' association was hassling Dad about the ever-longer grass in our front and back yards and the ever-longer stretches of time between mowings. Dad's idea was to give free office space to the yard guys in exchange for free lawn care. They took him up on it.

That same summer, while Dad moved his home office to his new commercial space, Mom moved her mother to a nursing home in town. To afford her care, Earl and Grandma would have to sell the house they'd lived in since they were married in 1956. That house on the steep hill and whatever big black Doberman lived there at the time was as much of an identity as they had. And it was their home. To divest themselves of the asset in order to qualify for Medicaid funding for the nursing home, Earl signed the house over to my dad, for safekeeping.

TWENTY-SIX

No other tenants ever signed a sublease, but Dad went in every morning, waving to his receptionist on his way past her quiet desk. His golden nameplate sat on his own quiet desk, stacked with SMI tapes and brochures, where he theoretically met real estate clients. When Dad's first residential realty arrangement didn't bear fruit, he signed on with another agency.

"It's the next step on the ladder," Dad explained. He told us that he was going to advance his real estate career by becoming a broker, "where the money is."

Mom, recklessly tolerant most of the time, said, "But you're not selling very many houses as an agent." She questioned what another semester of night school in Indianapolis would do, other than pull Dad closer to the church there and more conversations with Reverend Mark. Given our financial situation, Mom's interest in theological conversations was waning.

"This is actually the exact thing I have to do. I'm exploring my full potential," he told us. As he always did, Dad had threaded together an involved plan. This time, it required something of Mom. While Dad was becoming a broker, Mom would become a real estate agent. They would work together and multiply their wealth. Even better, Dad had so recently taken the real estate agent course that his textbook was still up to date enough to pass muster. Ceremonially, he handed Mom the colorfully tabbed binder for real estate school and told her the schedule.

They'd be driving to Indy Tuesday nights, and their broker and agent classes would be concurrent, and across the hall from each other. They'd have time to pop in and see Reverend Mark afterward.

Adam and I would stay home alone those nights. I was ten, and he was almost five. My job was to microwave Hot Pockets for our dinner, and Adam's was to set up a Jell-O factory by the living room hearth. "Lime or cherry?" he called out across the expanse of Asian rugs and furniture. I found it very tedious having to be the customer, but I conceded that it was his turn to be the maker. "Vrrrrr," Adam rumbled the noises he thought belonged in this make-believe kitchen and pounded the keys on a beige adding machine standing in for our cash register. Whereas I was strapping and big for my age, Adam was small, frail. Younger. More trusting. He easily slipped into pretending this way, imagining we were other people. "Ninety-nine, ninety-nine and six cents. Or dollars," he told me, jamming down the button that made the spool of paper tape feed out wildly.

For extra protection on these nights alone, Dad announced a treat for us: we'd be getting our first dog. Our cats Ethel and Lucy had died before we left Long Island, so this dog would be our first pet in years. Adam and I were ecstatic.

"We have to get a cocker spaniel," I told everyone. My brother had some other breed in mind. Kimberly's family had a purebred Maltese, which she strongly suggested. Dad insisted on a mutt.

"Purebred dogs are so snooty. You can pick it out, any dog, but it has to be a mutt from the pound," Dad said.

Their lives must have been very stressful in the fall of 1988 with night school, financial troubles, Grandma in a nursing home, and everything else. They continually forgot about the promised dog. "We'll go next week," Dad said again and again, but we didn't. We were ardent with our reminders, but nothing happened. One afternoon he simply arrived home with a black-and-brown mutt in the back of the red-and-white pickup. She was smallish, a puppy, and had a crazed look in her eye. She was perfect.

Our house had a built-in doghouse about the size of my parents' luxe bathroom. It was in the side yard, where we installed her in an indoor-outdoor living situation. Her doggie door led directly into the backyard, where she could run free. The main entry to the doghouse was a Dutch door. I'd close the bottom half and stand inside, pretending to vend lemonade or books with her at my feet. This was the attention we paid the dog. None of us walked her or trained her; I didn't know those things were important. I named her Dolly, after Parton.

Mom's and Dad's real estate courses were complete by the end of the year. I'd been desperate for a dollhouse for more than a year now and felt sure that this Christmas I'd get one. The last package I opened that morning was flat and wide, about the size of a board game. Resigned to the idea that I would have to wait longer for a dollhouse, I was shocked to see that the rectangular box was indeed a kit for a Victorian dollhouse. A picture stuck to the front of the cardboard showed a pink, gingerbready house, scalloped trim dripping from the peaked roof. I wanted to wallpaper it and set up little beds and sinks in uncluttered splendor. Here was a house I could decorate and tend with precision. No piles. No mold. A house that would be just so. A dream in a box.

"I'll build it for you," Dad said. He sipped coffee in one of our blue armchairs from Hong Kong and wore the same ratty blue robe he'd had on Long Island. Mom had remade so much of our lives, but Dad's old clothes had been left untouched for the most part. "Actually, we'll build it together," he promised.

TWENTY-SEVEN

"I guess Martinsville isn't ready for this kind of thing," Dad told us. He was more than a little bitter about it.

The last detectable traces of Morgan Executive Suites are classified ads from January and February 1989, which add the word *luxury* to the description, list a higher price, and include a note of the urgency Dad must have been feeling. He moved his office back to the basement of our house that March.

My own attention was locked on fifth-grade matters: the Great Books club I'd been invited to join and a certain necklace Hallmark would be releasing that Valentine's Day. It was a 14k gold heart, and for some reason the girls in my class had our attention fixed on this piece of jewelry. It cost $10.99. It would only be available for a limited time. We imagined its delicate chain around our necks, considered how we might react if a fifth-grade boy gave us this Hallmark necklace during our classroom Valentine's Day party, thought about how we'd arrange the necklines of our shirts to emphasize it. Boys were not really a going concern for me; I still wore braces. I'd been asked to go together by a kid named Randy at my lunch table. He made his pitch over chocolate milk and chili hot lunch, and I declined on the spot, never telling Mom. I was afraid that if I told her, she'd encourage it. I didn't care for Randy. I did want the necklace.

I woke on Valentine's Day to find a card next to my breakfast cereal. Its envelope bulged unnaturally, and inside was the necklace, a gift from Mom.

"Thank you so much oh my gosh!" I felt like I'd won something on a game show.

Mom was pleased that I was pleased. She helped me drape the necklace in front of my Université de Sorbonne sweatshirt. I finished eating and grabbed my bag, tucking the necklace underneath the shirt, realizing it would be more humiliating to wear a necklace from my mom than to not have it at all. She stopped short on our way to the driveway.

"You have to show it. Pull it out, sweetheart."

I refused. I told her why.

"No, no, no," she told me. She'd already thought of this and had a script for me. "Tell them it's from 'someone special' and they'll be left guessing." To her, this was genius subterfuge. It sounded thin to me. "No. They won't know. The less you say, the more you'll cultivate an air of mystery, Amanda."

I relented. But really, had I been able to remove the necklace myself after she dropped me off, I would have. I couldn't manipulate the clasp very well so I just left it under my sweatshirt. No one noticed. I went to Kimberly's after school. We poured tall ice waters and retreated to her white-carpeted bedroom.

Kimberly pulled out the valentines she'd received earlier in the day and revealed that she'd come away with two—*two!*—Hallmark 14k gold necklaces. From two different boys. I tried to think of something to say as I computed the cash value of all that gold. There was really no reply that could convey my sincere shock without betraying how jealous I felt, how sad that no boys had thought of me. Instead of answering, I slyly flipped my own necklace outward, hoping the afternoon sun would glint across the heart shape now that it was outside of my sweatshirt.

"Who?!" she cried. She was fully delighted that we could share in having received necklaces and that she was the one with twice the suitors. "Who?" Kimberly held my necklace in her hand, looking at me with admiration. She was close enough that I could see her freckles.

"Someone special." An immediate mistake. A completely bald lie which, as I'd rightly predicted at breakfast, was six million times worse than being necklace-less.

"Your mom." Her delight evaporated and she pulled away from me. "Duh." Mom had not told me what would happen when my untruth was discovered. She had not developed the tale any further, and I surely had not either. I denied it, hotly. My brain raced through the names of boys who might possibly have given it to me. I wanted to just say a name—any name except my mother's—though I wondered how I'd get away with it at school the next day. I was too slow. "Just admit your mom gave it to you. It's grody if you don't just say it was her."

I went quiet. It was a new depth of embarrassment. A multilayered way to feel bad about myself that I had not thought possible. I walked home.

Adam and Dad were in the yard chasing Dolly, who'd caught a snake that was still arcing and snapping, alive, in her teeth. "Don't tell Mom!" Dad cried over his shoulder. Adam was in a sprint, exuberantly following Dad's lead, until he tumbled, grass-staining his white sweatpants. "Catch her, Dad!" he called. His blond hair was cut in an '80s flattop, and he rolled around the grass, laughing. He was not as afraid of snakes as I was.

There was no chance I was telling Mom about the snake. I was so furious that I barely could speak to her.

"You made me lie," I told her angrily. The same month, Mom, a Realtor, was listed in the *Reporter* as a new agent. She had not worked outside our home in more than ten years. She sat at our oak kitchen table with a stack of papers, listening to a Hall and Oates tape on the kitchen radio.

"You lied yourself," she said. "If you'd have just said 'someone special' and been coy like I told you, it would have worked." I stayed angry. I hated the necklace. I left her there, listening to "Maneater."

A month later, our house was listed for sale with Dad as the agent, though Adam and I had no idea. There was no "for sale" sign out front. Two days after the listing was in the *Reporter*, the paper printed a photo of Mom and me holding between us a handmade quilt I'd won at my elementary school's carnival. By then I must have socially recovered enough from the Valentine's Humiliation of 1989 to attend the event with Mom only. Dad and Adam would have stayed home to watch basketball. Having lost out on several spins around the cakewalk, it was very exciting to win the quilt, "one of the main prizes awarded," according to the *Reporter*. Mom and I came home triumphant. She suggested we hang the quilt on our family room wall—which was a strange suggestion given that the house was for sale and we'd be moving as soon as it sold, not hanging decor.

That spring, I don't know whether Dad mowed the front lawn himself or found enough to pay the lawn care people to do only that part. In the beginning of that spring, the front was trimmed often enough that its length was not noticeable. The back was left untouched, ragged.

Inside the house, our collective tension rose. Out the back windows of my bedroom, I could see Dolly running through the unkempt grass and decided to join her. I took my journal and a pen and walked out the front door. I wished I'd had a book, but when Adam and I aged out of the picture-book phase of life, nothing replaced them. We didn't go to libraries or bookstores. I only read when teachers assigned it or read aloud, as my third-grade teacher had done after lunch, splitting *The Rats of NIMH* into fifteen-minute reveries every afternoon. I loved books and stories, but they were not easily within reach on Longs Island.

I tromped outside. Recently, a twelve-inch-square chunk of one of the double front doors had been removed. Termites maybe, or something else. The doors were textured in a mod, linear pattern, their thick wood painted cadet blue. In the missing spot, Dad had tacked an unpainted chunk of plywood, which scratched my bare ankle as I walked out.

Dolly was out front now, barking. She'd grown into the kind of dog who barked constantly, somehow keeping her mouth in the same open position as she howled and woofed without end.

Enter the stately gates of our subdivision and you'd drive between two rows of tightly planted old oaks, such as you'd imagine in a Jane

Austen novel. On your right, thick woods. On your left, a world-class golf course. Directly ahead, the first house you'd encounter was the Longs' house, and the first creature you'd meet was Dolly. She greeted every car coming to our fancy enclave with her anguished woo-woo-woof, her black lips—parted to make her awful sounds—nearly touching the tires of every Mercedes and Jaguar that rolled through.

I grabbed Dolly gently and pulled her with me toward the backyard, careful not to touch her neck. Recently, we'd noticed two ticks had attached themselves there and every day they grew fatter. Dad said they were filled with blood, despite looking gray and stiff. One was as large and hard as the bowl of a tablespoon. I wanted to pull them off, but Dad told me that would be worse. "Just leave it. I'll do it." He didn't.

I opened my journal on the dock, where the wood was soft, damp. Dolly ran toward me and the water and when I lunged to catch her, the dock's rotten planks gave out. Both of us almost fell into the lake but managed to hang on to the tilted wood, afloat.

The homeowners' association sent Dad a letter about Dolly chasing cars.

The homeowners' association sent him another letter about the plywood on the front door.

Madonna released *Like a Prayer* that spring, the first-ever album infused with fragrance. She'd found a company—not Dad's—to embed patchouli and frankincense into the vinyl, to give listeners a church-like feeling. That turned out to be her fragrance project.

The red-and-white pickup was repossessed. Men came up the hill to Earl's house and took it away one night. In the morning, Earl phoned. The truck was in his name, and the repo was a ding on his credit. "Earl is always mad about something," Dad told Mom.

More ads ran in the *Reporter*, advertising our house for sale. "Golfer's Dream. Gorgeous elegance. Club-area spectacular. Brick contemporary in elegant golf area. Security system, 2 fireplaces, pegged oak floors, formal dining room, walk-in closets, Jenn-Air range, 6BR/6.5 baths, thermal glass, circular drive, hot tub, large view deck, dock, city utilities, guest quarters. PLUS pro landscaping, foyer."

Having both my parents as real estate professionals was part of a plan to make sure they didn't pay a commission on the sale. Nonetheless, no one made an offer.

TWENTY-EIGHT

The grass in the backyard was waist high. I knew it was full of snakes. I no longer went back there. I didn't go to the pool at all in the summer of 1989.

I joined Adam in his long-established indoor routines. Snacks. TV. The air-conditioning was always set to 60 degrees. We usually wore shorts in the summer, and we wrapped our freezing legs in afghans in the family room. We watched *Cheers*, *The Price Is Right*. There were more VHS tapes Mom had made of movies on TV: *Brewster's Millions* and *Teen Wolf*. We anesthetized ourselves all day long.

When I got bored of television, I went to my bedroom to work on the architectural plans I'd started. Dad had not yet built the dollhouse, so I had started penciling in plans to decorate it, giving each room a purpose. I drew other houses and buildings, too, imagining other places.

"Dad." I stood outside his basement office, hoping to be invited to come in. If he was in a good mood, I might ask again about building the dollhouse. He said I could come in, but I knew from the clip in his voice it was not a good time to ask. I stood next to him, lingering, still bored. The grass in the backyard swayed outside the sliding glass door.

Dad sat at the little table next to his desk that held his bulky computer. The screen glowed an electric blue, and he'd typed a long letter in white text. He pressed Page Up to highlight line after line. The text reversed out so the screen was white, and he deleted passage after passage of whatever he'd written. The systematic deletion, blocky white line by blocky white line, was so interesting to watch, so unlike anything I'd seen, that I couldn't take my eyes off the screen.

"Are you enjoying reading about my divorce?" he exploded, turning his head around at me, catching me looking over his shoulder at the monitor. Dad's lips set into a hard expression and his eyes emanated fury. I was scared and didn't answer. "Are you?" He hit my leg, a fast angry slap. Embarrassed and confused, I left the office. I went across the hall to the exercise room and rode Mom's stationary bike for a while. Then I got into our sauna, fully dressed.

Dad found me in the sauna and apologized. He explained that he was writing an application essay for the Lutheran seminary and because they usually didn't accept divorced people, he had to write an explanation of his divorce. It was upsetting to write. He thought I was being nosy. He was sorry.

I was just glad to have the fight behind us, so I agreed. I didn't know what a seminary was. I didn't care to know. I only wanted to be alone.

Upstairs, I met Mom entering the house on my way to my room. I hadn't realized she was not home. She carried a new-looking brown plastic briefcase into the foyer, hot summer sun baking the slate floor. Mom closed the plywood-patched door behind her. Excitedly, she opened the briefcase on one of the living room coffee tables for me. Inside were twenty-some rubber stamps that said things like RECEIVED and ORIGINAL and URGENT and PAID. They nested together in the case with exactly enough space to fit properly with an order notebook and three colored pads of ink. In the pocket side of the case were a few hundred emery boards that read 1-800-STAMP-ME and business cards with my mother's name.

"I have a new job." Her bubbly delivery was forced. When she finished the sentence by saying "selling stamps," all the animation in her voice was gone.

In our last weeks in Martinsville, our home was lonely and strange, my parents broke, actual snakes all around us, dread and uncertainty thrumming through every inch of the massive house, carried like the icy air-conditioning that enveloped our family that humid summer via every vent and chute in the house's bones.

I was sad and didn't know why. I stopped going out of the house the summer after fifth grade. In order to be accepted to middle school orchestra in the fall, I was taking viola lessons in my future sixth-grade classroom; some weeks my meeting with the gaunt, domineering, red-haired strings teacher was my only outing. I had no idea what was happening to our family or how to fix it. So I lay in our cool basement. Most of the summer I was inert, half-dressed, and watching VHS tapes—too old for toys and without any precedent for book reading outside of school. The basement carpet was beige on darker beige checkerboard and plush. The ceilings were low. The TV was always on.

One afternoon that July, a boy from my school dropped by—a shocking first—and Mom led him downstairs, where I was under an afghan watching *DuckTales*. By the time he was halfway down the steps it was too late to refuse the visit, but I was mortified. In three years, no one from school or my swim team had been inside my house and on this afternoon, depressed and purposeless, I wore no pants. Chris invited me to ride bikes, but I had to decline for fear of revealing my lack of pants. He decided to stay and watch *DuckTales* with me, and my mind raced, inventing excuses for why I'd be staying under the blanket after the show. The cartoon squawked on while I realized that Chris had walked past the bare plywood chunk holding our front door together and through our upstairs a few minutes ago, seeing the bagged groceries all over the floor, stink and mold in all the sinks. I couldn't imagine why he was there.

"Pool's open, you know," Chris suggested. He and I were both eleven. I thought of him as older, as my birthday had been only a few days before, but he'd been eleven for six or seven months. Chris had first met me in my blue-ribbon backstroke days a few summers before. I looked over his shoulder and through the glass door of the walkout basement. The lawn swayed like a field of wheat.

"Leave!" I shouted at him. "I didn't invite you." I had never spoken to anyone like that, ever. I was swallowed in shame and couldn't tolerate any witnesses.

Five minutes later, after he had left, Mom scooched over my afghan-wrapped feet and told me that alienating boys was going to cause a lot of social-life problems for me in middle school. I knew she was right—this might be the last time I saw Chris until we were both in the halls of our new school in sixth grade. I imagined him nonchalantly spinning the combination on his locker and whispering to my new classmates about what a freak I was. *I don't even think she was wearing pants,* he'd tell them. If it was possible to feel worse—more alone, more bewildered—I did.

"Well, maybe we'll just move so you don't have to go to that middle school," Mom said.

I cracked a smile. She did love me. She loved me enough to joke that we'd move away so that I could avoid a boy making fun of me in sixth grade. "I love you," I told her.

"I love you, too, but we really might move. Have you heard Dad talk about becoming a pastor?" she asked. I had not.

This conversation, sometime in the first few weeks of July 1989, was the first breath of a clue that we might not live forever and ever in the grand Martinsville estate. Yes, we were miserable and broke, but that did not signal moving house to me. Even as it surfaced as a possibility, I viewed these kinds of future plans through the Vaseline-smeared lens of *we might one day.* We might one day open an ice cream store, or we might one day bunk up with Madonna and invent a perfume. We might not.

This monumental move, from my parents' dream home and into a wholly unknown world, surely unfolded more gradually than I remember. There must have been years incrementally urging us toward church life, easing us out of living large in the mansion; there were, after all, the feelings about the church in Martinsville, the long diatribes about religion on family drives, and Dad's trips to Reverend Mark in Indianapolis.

When it was time to move, we did so quickly. Mom explained what a seminary was. What felt like a moment later, we were in the Town Car, following a truck that held many of the things we owned, but not all of them. We would have needed three or four trucks for all of it.

Of those last months in Martinsville, I remember very little. There is a single sharp memory of Mom and me, driving around in her car, scavenging for boxes to pack her fabric. We rode around Martinsville forlornly looking for cardboard at the back doors of stores, picking up clean boxes when we found them. Mom hopped out to grab some behind Marsh, and I sat in the car alone for a few minutes, the air conditioner chilling my skin. Mom's stamp briefcase was at my feet and I snapped open its latches. When she returned, I had the case open and was examining a stamp that said FAXED.

"Did you sell any stamps, Mom?" I asked with pure sincerity and curiosity. I had not heard that she'd sold any yet and I wondered.

Mom didn't answer, but a strangled cry started in her throat, and then she wailed and sobbed, putting her head down on the steering wheel. I joined her, and we cried for several minutes, never speaking any words, the stamp case still open on my lap.

Then we were gone.

PART THREE

Fort Wayne, Indiana

1989 to 1994

TWENTY-NINE

In Fort Wayne, our new house had one and a half bathrooms. We all showered in the same one upstairs, which Mom was trying unsuccessfully to fill with all the toiletries from the six and a half bathrooms we'd had in Martinsville.

A shower rack at eye level had spots for six bottles, and eleven teetered on it. Conditioners and body washes lined the tub edge. Some had but an inch or two of product, but releasing them into the garbage bin would have meant an uncomfortable sense of closure for Mom. Insignificant as it was, she could attach great and private meaning to our family's time with a pearlescent-blue bottle of Finesse and if she never used it up, that time could endure forever. A moldy loofah dangled on a hemp rope. Containers of Salon Selectives and Herbal Essences stood upright on the floor. You had to pick a spot to stand in the shower and stay there.

From the upstairs bathroom I heard a knock at the front door. I wrapped myself in a faded Smurfs towel, tipping over a few bottles standing sentinel on the linoleum as I tore toward safety, rushing across the hall to my room. I was terrified of being seen naked.

A Lutheran pastor stood at our threshold, talking to Mom. He wore a short-sleeved, black shirt with a square of white at his throat, wire-rimmed glasses on a ruddy face. I pressed play on my triple-cassette boombox so I wouldn't have to hear them.

He only stayed briefly. Mom's footsteps were on the stairs a moment later, then her voice was barbed as she entered the bathroom. "What a mess. Amanda. It's a pigsty." She asked me to pick up the bottles I'd toppled. I did.

"Pastor Francis came by to invite us to lunch after church tomorrow," Mom said. We hadn't been very regular churchgoers the first eight years of my life, and now men in clerical collars—penguin suits, Dad called them—arrived unannounced on weekend afternoons. And we had to eat meals with them. The Longs had made a swift transition from what we were before to a full-fledged church family. We ate pizza now and then, but it would have been absurd to suddenly open a pizzeria. Dad becoming a pastor felt about as normal as it would to see him tossing a pale round of dough over his head and chanting "*Buon appetito.*"

Dad was not yet admitted to the Lutheran seminary but already called himself a "Sem" and called Adam and me "PKs"—pastors' kids. We were bona fide members of a subculture we'd never heard of a month ago.

THIRTY

We lived in a town we'd never visited in a rented house of about 1,300 square feet in a shabby subdivision; Adam and I were enrolled in a Lutheran K–8 school on needs-based scholarships. Dad was enrolled in the seminary's Elementary Greek course as a pre-seminarian. His application to be a seminarian had not been approved and wasn't certain to be. An undergraduate degree—which he lacked—was necessary, and the school didn't seem especially eager to admit divorced people. They'd asked him to write a whole essay justifying the end of his first marriage.

Returning home from class, Dad pulled into the driveway of our new house and flicked the electric windows down. I raced to the yard to greet him. "*Theós eínai agápi,*" he said to me, his reddish face in the space between the tinted window and vinyl roof of the Town Car. Around this time, I heard the phrase "sticking out like a sore thumb" for the first time, and it perfectly suited the way our car looked parked on the cul-de-sac of other rentals.

He exited the car with a load of books and papers under his arm. On the top of the stack was a small book in cinnamon-colored leather, a Greek New Testament with a yellow ribbon marker.

I trailed him indoors. "My dogs are barking," he told us, weary from his day. Dad pulled out ragged sheets of paper covered in the triangles and loops of a new alphabet, some sections highlighted in neon yellow. Dad's previous Greek linguistic experience was limited to the fraternities of Gainesville, Florida, and now he was learning to read, write, and speak in this language just to better understand the Bible.

"*Kyrios*," I stumbled out the pronunciation from the first flashcard he handed me, and he replied, "Lord, Christ," immediately.

Mom came in, a Kroger bag in each hand. She put them on the kitchen floor; the cabinets were stuffed. I kept quizzing Dad at the dining table, helping him prep for a test. The oak table, which had taken up a minor portion of the vast Martinsville kitchen, now dwarfed our eating area, nearly touching the sliding glass door at the back of the house.

"Nominative or accusative?" I asked, reading from his worksheet. Dad used his Cross pen. He wore a silk tie and embroidered-cuff shirt. His brown eyes shone eagerly, kindly. We sat at the same table and wide, sturdy chairs we'd used for years. He was the same dad he'd always been. Simultaneously, he was now a forty-six-year-old college student, Man of God, student of ancient languages.

A *gong* erupted from the living room. In Martinsville, the quarter-hour chiming of our grandfather clock was swallowed up in the enormity of the house. Here, the clang was audible in every room; its church-like bells interrupted us midsentence every fifteen minutes, its golden weights and chains vibrating behind their glass.

THIRTY-ONE

At twilight, the long, heavy Town Car inched into the parking lot of Lee's Famous Recipe Chicken. Dad parked it between a Ford Focus and a jalopy of unknown provenance, its tailpipe held on with a bent coat hanger. Mom reviewed our instructions.

"Don't let on," she said for maybe the fourteenth time that day. "We can't let on."

Adam, reverting to his early childhood fascination with the military, saluted from the backseat.

Mom had a folded sheaf of printed pages in her hand and several pens in her other fist. She made to leave, and Dad stopped her, rolling his eyes.

"Sandie." He smiled. He loved her so very much. They had been married for fifteen years and thus were several years deep into the wordless communication of the long-married. Dad looked at the paperwork she held, emblazoned with the Lee's logo and the logo of the mystery shopper company that would be paying for our dinner. Tonight, we were their emissaries.

Dad reminded Mom that if we took the papers in, we'd give it away. Another pre-sem family had hipped us to this opportunity, warning Mom that the highest and most holy rule was secrecy. Let on, and the jig would be up. Keep your cover, and your family would eat a free meal at a restaurant once a week, plus earn an easy $25 for the extra time we'd spend researching conditions on the ground.

"When you entered, did an associate greet you within thirty seconds?" Mom read from one of the sheets, prompting us. "Did they smile?"

I made halfhearted attempts to memorize the question list. Adam's face turned determined, and he obediently recited our marching orders: "Is the food visually appealing? Served at the proper temperature?"

We were hungry and ready for espionage. Mom stuffed the papers in the padded console between the front seats, and we embarked across the parking lot, whispering the survey questions under our breath.

Everyone had to order something different so we could sample a variety from the menu. Both the men's and women's restrooms needed to be visited so we could be sure they were amply stocked with liquid soap, that the sink areas were tidy. *Did the cashier thank you at the end of your transaction? Was the parking lot free of debris?*

Adam's eyes darted side to side. If there was a double agent behind Lee's red Formica counter, Adam would be the one to root them out. He was too professional to say it aloud, but you could tell his mind was racing with the phrase *act casual*. Much of Adam's life up to this point had involved ingesting cartoons and almost all of them involved some kind of covert task force situation. Wearing stonewashed jeans and a Cosby-style sweater to fit his first-grade frame, no one could be more prepared for this mission than my brother.

At our booth, we tore into our barbecue and fried chicken sandwiches and scooped coleslaw and mashed potatoes out of little Styrofoam pots. Dessert was a choice of a chocolate pudding parfait or a strawberry creme version. Dad paid in cash.

We had to go to Lee's exactly once every ten-day period and never the same day of the week on consecutive weeks. In no time, we'd memorized the fifty-question survey due after each visit, and Adam and I could tick them off in the rote way we were now ticking off the Bible verses we were being asked to memorize in school. By Christmas, we were so conversant in the questions and in the menu that we were improvising (*Can I have gravy on the green beans?*). We had to work our way through the entire menu, which meant someone had to order something called Livers and Gizzards every fifth trip. We nominated Dad.

Dad was a superhero. Mom took every opportunity to tout his extraordinary powers, and she showed us, too, by deferring to him and listening during his long sermon-like speeches during our car rides. He was King. "Dad's smarter than me," she said if she didn't have an answer to one of my questions. "Let's ask him."

Back on Long Island, I'd had a phase of early elementary school skepticism, and my constant inquiries drove Mom crazy. A fabric softener ad showed a load of their folded towels fluffed twice as high as the competitor's, and I asked her about all the ways they might have faked the result for the ad. She deflected such queries to Dad whenever possible. Taste-test ads were my favorite to cast doubt upon. "How do you know those people were actually drinking Folgers Crystals?" I'd insist.

"Because they said so," Mom attempted. Dad was a sales guy, from janitorial supplies to Miami hotel rooms to motivational cassette tapes, and my reluctance to believe the pitches on TV must have cut a little close. "Don't be like this. Don't question everything. You'll be a miserable adult," she promised. I liked the idea that the secrets of the adult world were discoverable with just a bit of investigation.

My cynicism about TV ads coincided with a rigorous spell of *why* questions Mom found profoundly annoying. *Why is it that girls can wear pants but boys can't wear dresses? Why is there no school on Saturday? Why do we only brush our teeth with cold water instead of warm?*

As stubborn as me and exhausted by my interrogation, Mom answered, "That's not true. Dad brushes his teeth with hot water."

As she intended, I was frozen into silence.

"He's very manly and tough. He turns the water on as hot as it will go when he brushes his teeth. I've never met anyone else who does that, and it really shows how indestructible he is. How strong." Then and for at least fifteen more years, I imagined Dad swishing near-boiling water between his teeth twice a day, in awe of his fortitude.

THIRTY-TWO

Those of us on free and reduced lunch at school had to carry with us a sheet of little labels. One small white sticker was to be turned in each day in exchange for our meal, which was the same meal as the paying students received, except we were only allowed a cardboard pint of white milk, not chocolate. Starting at the new school was fine, if a little disappointing. I'd been gearing up for a full-on public middle school experience and was sorry to be attending a school that included both once-weekly chapel and younger kids (including my brother). Our English teacher had us doing book reports on Christian fiction, and the teachers took extra care with Adam and me, whom they also referred to as PKs.

PKs, as well as pastors' wives, were set apart. I don't remember any particularly special treatment of or expectations for the families of the various pastors I'd known before then, but in Fort Wayne there were so many Lutheran pastors and pastors in training that, long ago, their families had formed a formidable gang. Unwittingly, I was in it.

Our dads knew Greek. Our mothers wore modest clothes—often floral dresses with balloon sleeves—and gold-cross necklaces. Not crucifixes, which were more of a Catholic thing. The empty cross of the risen Savior was ours. We went to church every week, often both the early service and the late one with Bible study in between. Money was tight; we frequently ate at potlucks. We had all eaten some version of a carrot-raisin-pineapple salad and its fluffy competitor, mayonnaise-marshmallow-mixed-fruit ambrosia. Pastors' kids were expected not to swear or smoke and to derive genuine thrill and satisfaction from certain hymns. Ten percent of us PKs had gone entirely off the rails and into leather-jacket-wearing, godless rock-and-roll-listening, premarital-sex-having rebellion, and the other 90 percent of us were left to compensate for the wayward, demonstrating our unmitigated rectitude, even if we were teenagers.

It wasn't all bad. It was simply new. I could see that any disruptions in my academic performance would be forgiven on account of the pressures of being a PK. In sixth grade, perhaps because it had so long been suggested to me that I was a surly teen, I became one. I longed, always, to descend into a moody funk, despairing at how embarrassed my parents made me, how unfair life was. These sullen spells, during which I would stare flatly into space, occasionally scratching out an angry couplet in my diary, were promptly pardoned. I may not have been allowed to say the words *ass* or *hell*, but I had full license to be miserable. I had lots of practice and was good at it.

In the same way, my parents could no longer take jet-setting vacations or while away long, late evenings in New York City bars, but they were afforded a special status in our new community and plenty of unexpected delights. Being a clergy family opened as many doors as it closed.

Dad held forth on the importance of sports for health and socializing, telling Adam it was about time he got involved in basketball, football, or, ideally, both. Dad had played both in high school in Miami. "And let's get you a duck's ass," he said, reaching into the backseat and ruffling Adam's dark-blond flattop.

The forbidding Town Car nosed its way down a curvy drive through the manicured greenways of the seminary. Designed in 1955 by renowned Finnish architect Eero Saarinen, the property was an architecturally austere 191 acres anchored by a blue amoeba of a person-made lake and wide, grassy lawns. A twelve-foot-tall bronze Martin Luther statue presided at the entrance. Dad came here every day for Greek, but the whole family came only on Saturdays, our assigned day to shop at the food bank, a privilege allowed us because Mom volunteered once weekly at the clothing bank across the parking lot.

"With a duck's ass, you just literally smooth it back and the hair stays there. It's the grease." I imagined Adam, a first grader in 1989, with a rockabilly haircut.

"Okay," Adam said. He was six, and he knew what I did about agreeing.

Mom had managed to bring tons of dry goods—still packed in Marsh grocery bags—from Martinsville, but we also needed fresh things each week, and Mom never had the assured feeling that we had enough, no matter how much we had.

The shopping carts at the food bank were half-size. There wasn't exactly a limit on how much you could take, but the small carts discouraged big hauls. We were permitted one each of brand-name muffin mixes and cans of Campbell's soup, the regular-looking groceries, which were in short supply. Then we piled in the things that were plentiful: logs of processed cheese in white paper that read "USDA" in blocky blue letters. Cans of pears and corn with the same labels. Tin cans printed with austere black lettering: "PORK with natural juices, ready to eat." White boxes with black-lettered CORN FLAKE CEREAL.

More of a big room than a store and quiet as a library, it was a lot less interesting than a regular supermarket. Mom and Dad went around the corner and into a riveting conversation about the Ten Commandments with another pre-sem couple. A far cry from The Club, the seminary was our family's new social hangout. My parents took everything so seriously then, even socializing.

Bored, Adam and I chased each other through the basement, pushing and falling onto the flecked terrazzo floor. I showed him a squat can that said TUNA but nothing else. No mermaid. No cartoon fish. We had never seen so-called government food before this, and its plainness was one of many things that were disorienting and weird to us. We heaved with the hilarity of this squat, plain can, trying and failing to catch our breath. We held our midsections, gasping. We were not laughing maliciously, but in a way that felt outside of ourselves. Who were we, anyway? A couple of golf-course, country-club kids lying on the floor of a food bank, hysterical over canned fish.

Adam reached for me with both of his six-year-old hands, attempting to serve me what we called an Indian burn—a cruel counter-twist of the flesh of the forearm. I giggled and lifted the tuna higher. He cried out but was interrupted by an overly loud throat clearing—a seminarian's wife fulfilling her volunteer shift and looking askance at us.

Mom returned, furious. Her blond curls vibrated as she set her jaw into an angry scowl. The three of us loaded the Lincoln with our charity-provided groceries. Dad stayed on campus to study and play ping-pong in the student center with his new friends, the other middle-aged men who were also pastors-in-training.

On the drive home, Mom scolded us. First of all, we were not to embarrass her, or embarrass Dad, which could possibly end this precarious arrangement they'd maneuvered. Pastors' kids were well behaved. She knew we could do better.

And second, we were not to ever make fun of poor people. It was news to us that we'd been making fun of anyone, so Adam and I mounted a vehement defense. Mom explained that poor people were forced to eat free food from the government, with those plain white labels.

"I wasn't making fun," I protested, embarrassed now.

Mom was quiet.

I wanted to be absolved of my crime. "How can I be making fun of people if it's the same food we're eating?" I asked her.

"Are we going to be poor people now?" Adam wondered, as if we could try on this identity for a week or a year. The two-word phrase "poor people" was already shorthand in our household for a certain kind of family (not us). But this was a new glimpse at the term, from the inside. It was exciting; we could be anyone.

Adam investigated the bags at our feet, filled with plainly labeled cans and cardboard. Our butts scooched on the slick leather seats, and air whooshed out of the vents. Mom, silent, hot tears running down her cheeks, drove the heavy car to our new neighborhood.

THIRTY-THREE

In the fall of 1989, we had no money. Mom did not have a job, and Dad was a full-time student. There was no windfall from the sale of our Martinsville mansion, which never sold. We'd simply abandoned it for the greener pastures of Fort Wayne with its course in Greek and free government food and the dolorous hope that Dad would be accepted into the seminary program. Eventually the house went into foreclosure. In 2021, I learned that the real estate agent who listed it—who had briefly been Dad's boss—purchased it himself at a deep discount from the bank.

On September 20, 1989, about one month after we moved, Mom was pulled over for an expired license plate. She was scheduled to appear one week later, September 27 at 9:00 a.m. and, according to court records, "DEFENDANT FAILS TO APPEAR." The court certified a suspension of her driver's license and two days later, September 29, "THE DEFENDANT APPEARS AND ENTERS A PLEA OF GUILTY. THE COURT NOW FINDS THE DEFENDANT GUILTY AS CHARGED AND ASSESSES A FINE OF $10.00 + COSTS."

On October 20, 1989, exactly two months after we'd moved, the seminary registrar wrote to Dad informing him that the admissions committee had accepted his application. He would be a seminarian in the upcoming winter term, with a full load of courses. They included Biblical Hermeneutics, New Testament Greek, Lutheran Worship, Lutheran Confessions, one study group each on the Old and New Testaments, and a fieldwork placement at our local church, where Dad would do things like give scripture readings during service and assist the pastor with visits to sick congregation members. He'd hardly need his executive wardrobe and brassy nameplate for any of this, set to begin in the new year, 1990.

Even if money was tight, it was hard to imagine ourselves as poor. We were surrounded by the things we'd had in our mansion in southern Indiana, and we were never once hungry. When Dad was growing up in Miami in the '40s and '50s, their dining furniture was a redwood table and two picnic benches. Their sandwiches were sometimes mayonnaise-only. *That* was poor. We were something else.

My triple cassette deck in pastel colors was still my most-utilized possession, and it was set up on my dresser to facilitate near-constant use. I was a bit tired of my old tapes—Debbie Gibson and Rick Astley—but I played them sometimes. More frequently I played tapes I'd made myself, four different 30-minute live radio broadcasts from my favorite Indianapolis station (which didn't come in way up in Fort Wayne). We had no money for new tapes, and I was nostalgic for our old place anyway. Night and day I played the songs and morning-show banter I'd taped several months before in my Martinsville bedroom.

"Enough!" Dad roared into my bedroom and turned off the tape player, interrupting my umpteenth listen of *John and Jerry in the Morning*. He told me it was time to move on. "Long past time, actually," he said, shaking his head. "Get on with your life, for God's sake."

Adam and I kept ourselves focused on first and sixth grades, and Mom declared that she'd soon be working again to bring in income. I know she struggled with this. She'd recently become a licensed Realtor, but she never sold a house. She never sold a custom rubber stamp either. Mom would be getting a *real* job in Fort Wayne. Her identity as a stay-at-home mother defined her, and she and Dad had spent a lot of time over the years drawing a crisp line between families whose mothers worked and those whose didn't. In our house, there was a right side and a wrong one, and we were about to become turncoats.

"What kind of mother works while her children stay at home with no supervision?" she wondered aloud.

Dad took the opposite approach, an incomprehensible, guilt-induced declaration that turned the situation into a responsibility Adam and I should bear. "You're old enough now. You've really been indulged by having a stay-at-home mom all these years. Don't you think it's time you could look after yourselves a little?"

Tearfully, Mom asked what would become of Adam and me if we were neglected after school. In her estimation, the evenings we'd spent alone during their real estate school terms were more palatable than being alone in the dangerous late-afternoon latchkey hours. Two years before Hoosier Dan Quayle—the current vice president—went after Murphy Brown for "family values," the concept was already alive in the air, especially in the Christian Midwest. When Mom considered the term "working mother"—a phrase that has no linguistic opposite—she only heard "failure." She was proud to work for IBM as its only woman engineer in the '70s, but a decade later, she'd not only birthed two kids but also ingested films like *Baby Boom* and *Mr. Mom*—and two terms of President Reagan. She surmised that, motherless during the day, we'd rot our brains in front of the TV and eat junk food. She must not have noticed that we'd been doing just that, even when she was around.

Mom's fraught, shaky-voiced questions (*What will you do all on your own after school?*) were directed to us during a commercial break of *Matlock*, a show Adam had discovered and was smitten with. I hated the program and called it *Fatlock* to annoy him, but I watched it all the same, gaining leverage so I could make him watch a game show with me later. My brother and I were prone on the floor, and I was squirting canned American cheese directly into our mouths with a soft-serve-like swirl. Neither of us wanted to get up to fetch the crackers. Andy Griffith reappeared on-screen.

"Cheese me," Adam ordered, his jaw wide.

I told Mom not to worry about the junk food and TV thing. We'd be okay.

The Lincoln Town Car was repossessed.

"I turned it in," Dad told us. "It was too much car for our new lifestyle." The way he explained it, the transaction had been an act of sheer humility, nearly papal.

For several weeks in the fall of 1989, Dad got a ride to Greek from an Idahoan seminarian classmate—large-boned and tall like Dad—who drove a miniature, brown two-door Pinto. Jovial and bearded, godly in his kindness, the seminarian picked up Dad, Adam, and me and wedged us all into the tiny sedan. We were dropped at the Lutheran school before Dad was carried away to class.

Adam and I stood on the sidewalk outside our school, watching the two large men retreat in the wee car whose license plate slogan prominently said "World Famous Potatoes."

"It wasn't his idea," I muttered. I slung my bag over my shoulder and started walking toward the school's limestone entrance. I walked with indignant purpose, even though there was no rush. We were forty-five minutes early for school because that's when our ride was available.

Adam scampered to keep up. "What?" It was dark and frosty, and the building wasn't open yet. "Did you say something about Dad?"

I wanted to explain to my brother that, obviously, unlike what he'd told us, Dad had not *chosen* to get rid of the Town Car. We woke up one morning and it was no longer in our driveway. Dad had not paid the lease payments. I was eleven, not stupid. A few months ago, the same thing had happened to the red-and-white pickup truck. The truck lease was in Dad's name, but Dad didn't keep up with the monthly payments as promised. The pickup was Earl's only mode of transportation between the hilltop house in the woods and everywhere else, and it had been repossessed. That's why Earl had been so mad.

We both had to ride to school in the potato-mobile, but Adam was small enough not to see everything I could see. I wondered what I owed him, what he ought to know. I'd never told him about Dad's divorce. Keeping Dad and Mom our unblemished King and Queen was the vertebral column of the magical beast that was the Long family—ever optimistic, always ready to land on our feet. I remembered that besmirching Dad would be the worst of all outcomes, frightening in its dark uncertainty.

"Nothing," I told Adam. We zipped our coats against the wind, looking through the clear top panes of the metal front doors to try to see what teachers did in the before-school hour.

THIRTY-FOUR

"Livers and gizzards, and one extra biscuit," Dad told the teenager behind the counter.

We came to Lee's a lot these days, now that we had a new-to-us Oldsmobile station wagon and could drive ourselves there. I sensed that the $25 we earned per visit was most of the reason why. Adam and I took up residence in a booth and began squirting barbecue sauce on the mashed potatoes, part of our strategy to liven up a meal we were eating more than twice a week in the early days of 1990.

We could afford the car because our parents now had jobs.

Mom worked for the headquarters of a regional hardware store chain as a typesetter—a job she'd done eons ago at *Camping* magazine in southern Indiana and also at her job at the brokerage firm in the World Trade Center. The *Fort Wayne News-Sentinel* has an employment ad from November 1989 that is likely the one she answered. "Typing speed of 40 WPM is necessary in addition to good clerical and communication skills . . . starting wage of $6.79 per hour." It was twice minimum wage.

Dad had harkened back to his Johnson Wax days and teamed up with another seminarian, Mr. Padilla, to be a two-man, night floor-waxing team for a forklift dealer's showroom. Dad had recently shaved his mustache, but Mr. Padilla had a lush, dark caterpillar on his top lip. Dad liked to practice his Miami Spanglish with him.

Friday nights, Dad and Mr. Padilla went in and moved all the heavy equipment to the factory floor, swept the main retail area, then laid down a sticky coat of gloss over the already-shiny floorboards. "*Que pasa, cabrón,*" Dad cried into the cavernous space, looking for Mr. Padilla to emerge from behind a loaded pallet jack. The men came home late Friday and returned Sunday after their respective church services for a brief afternoon rendezvous to restore the forklifts and other gear to their original positions after the wax had dried. Adam was often conscripted to tag along to help. "Let's do this, Dad," he'd say, although he always left the house with a bunch of Legos in a Kroger plastic bag so probably helped only minimally with the floors. I don't know what Dad and Mr. Padilla were paid.

My father once told me that he earned $265,000 in 1986, the year we moved to Martinsville. In 1990, our main household income, from Mom's job, was just above $14,000. The Lee's checks, and Dad's floor-waxing money, and the work-study stipend the seminary provided in exchange for Dad's ten hours a week in the school's development office were our other income. The annual household total was certainly under $25,000.

That spring, our school banned Bart Simpson T-shirts. Mom heard about one of the shirts on the news. It said "I'm Bart Simpson. Who the hell are you?" She pronounced it sad and wrong. "You're better than that garbage," she said. It was a moot point. We had not gotten new clothes anywhere except the seminary clothing bank in a year, and we hadn't seen the show.

On March 7, 1990, Dad ran a red light, and the court documents of that incident are the only records I've found of that spring. Perhaps learning from Mom's failure to appear for her ticket, Dad did show up in traffic court, on his forty-seventh birthday in late April. He was issued a notice for $25, which he didn't pay. The judge moved to suspend his driver's license on May 25, and then he paid.

"Those crooks!" Dad cried out, slamming the door of our little house, shaking its frame. Dad tossed a handful of mail on the dining table where Mom had set up a cardboard-box-packing operation. We were moving in a month.

"What crooks, honey?" Mom agreed with Dad that, unfortunately, many people were "after us" because they were jealous of our good fortune. Crooks seemed to seek us out. It was our lot in life.

"Lee's, the ungrateful bastards." The mystery shopper company had sent a letter dismissing us from further service as secret-agent fast-food eaters. We'd disregarded our assigned schedule for visits and otherwise taken advantage of the opportunity. Our family was supposed to visit once every ten days, but we were there every three or four days. Mom would order more food than we needed and would microwave the extra biscuits for breakfast or pull out a tub of Lee's coleslaw with dinner on a stay-home night. The letter, enclosed with a reimbursement check for our last meal, discharged us, permanently.

"We've done so much for them," Mom spoke in the sharp tone of a woman wronged. "We practically kept that place open."

Dad agreed. "And this is how they repay us."

THIRTY-FIVE

The Longs' money situation meant it was all-hands-on-deck that summer.

"She used to be a lifeguard," Dad told Mrs. Evans. He meant me.

Dad and I stood in the tidy kitchen of a woman whose hair was confidently cut the mannish length of Princess Di's. Mrs. Evans's pitchy brown curls were moussed into oblivion. Her eyes were lined darkly. She wore azure mascara. On the drive over, Dad had called her a *yuppie*.

The Evanses lived in a subdivision whose houses' backyards were laced together with paved walking trails. "Well, the pool is a very short walk, and all the sidewalks connect here." She gestured out the window above the sink, and Dad and I looked out to see a bike and a trike tossed down near the concrete freeway that snaked through green lawns.

I was not anything close to a lifeguard, and Dad knew it.

"She knows CPR, how to rescue people, whatever you need. You should see her kick. Hell of a swimmer," he concluded. Mrs. Evans had placed an employment ad in the seminary's newsletter, distributed five days per week via photocopy on the cafeteria lunch tables. She sought a teen babysitter for her two children and would pay $2 per hour to supervise them this summer three days a week, including daily trips to the subdivision's pool. Mrs. Evans worked at the Fort Wayne Convention and Visitors Bureau, and she had two children, five-year-old Jessica and two-year-old Skyler.

"Anyone who names their kid Skyler . . ." Dad had said earlier, defending his yuppie assessment.

I stayed quiet in the Evanses' kitchen, in part because I was excited that I'd been deemed grown-up enough for this sophisticated job, and in part because I was terrified. I was neither a certified lifeguard nor a teenager. Dad owned up to this, obliquely.

"I have to say, she's twelve," he said. I was eleven. Dad looked at Mrs. Evans with his sincere brown eyes. "She's a very mature twelve, takes care of her brother. She's been like a little junior adult her whole life."

It occurred to me in Mrs. Evans's kitchen that Dad could lie easily and plainly. It also seemed possible that he might not have remembered my age. Maybe he actually thought I was twelve. It really could have gone either way.

"I was like that," she said. She looked up at my tall dad, enchanted. "Responsible." Mrs. Evans tightened the belt on her shirtdress and smiled at me. "Sky! Jess!" she cried out.

Skyler's spiky, white-blond hair appeared first as he peeked around the corner. His sullen sister followed him. Their house, like all the houses in their subdivision, was newer and beige. Every room was extremely clean, and the Evanses' possessions were all stacked and arranged with intention inside the house's cabinets and drawers. I met the children, stiffly, and Mrs. Evans showed me where to find their swimsuits and how to make their lunches. I was hired.

Sixth grade was ending in a matter of days, and we were moving again. Every minute Mom and Dad were packing, or taking advanced courses in Lutheran pastoring, or working at the hardware store headquarters. Adam's summer had been planned for him; he'd be playing baseball in a free municipal youth league that met every day, all day.

Summer mornings, Adam wore slim jeans with a ringer T-shirt that said "Wildcat League." He carried his brown mitt and a granola bar and Mom left him off at Jury Park for the day.

Dad dropped me off before 8:00 at Sky and Jessica's. I was to feed them breakfast, play with them in the morning in the house or outside, then pack a lunch and walk to the pool with them. Mrs. Evans was due back at 2:45 p.m.

The other two days of the week, Mom often dropped me at the Allen County Public Library downtown, on the way to her job. We didn't have library cards, but I thought it seemed smart, or at least interesting, to hang out at a library. I had nothing else to do, so I spent many of Mom's workdays in their fluorescently lit stacks. I was too shy to ask for help finding something to read; I paced between the shelves, picking up anything that struck me or that sounded familiar. I read. When I needed a break, I sat on the carpet and looked out the library's skinny, tinted windows at cars driving down the busy road below. Mom always sent me with quarters for the vending machine and was never late to pick me up at four.

THIRTY-SIX

Our new house, where we arrived in the summer of 1990, shared space with only a few other homes. Somewhat cheaper than the first Fort Wayne place, the house was situated within an expanse of tan-colored farmland outside Fort Wayne, immediately surrounded by cornfields with trailer homes two long blocks to the west, another trailer park two blocks to the north, an auto-parts junkyard a quarter mile south, and, next to that, our county's largest waste management complex. In a return to form for us, the rental house had a hot tub on its rear indoor porch, though the house was the most run-down one we ever lived in.

"It's a dump, basically?" I was in seventh grade, the argumentative aspect of my personality flourishing.

"No, it's a waste management complex," Mom told me.

We could smell it, whatever it was.

Mom stacked papers on the foam-and-vinyl cover of the hot tub. We hadn't used it yet, except as a mail-sorting area. The hot tub shared an enclosed porch with the side door, our main entrance.

When we moved, we'd schlepped the boxes that had been packed and taped a year ago in Martinsville and were as yet unopened. This house was even smaller and all on one level. The detached garage was full of still-packed boxes and other articles that needed no carton—the not-yet-built dollhouse, Mom's suitcase of custom rubber stamp samples, a spool of Kleen Kids soap dispenser labels.

The previous renters of this brown, low house had a teen girl, and I was given her bedroom, a long, wooden-floored space with low built-in cabinets along one wall. Maybe her family was like ours and did their moves in a hurry; the cabinets were filled with issues of a magazine I'd never seen before, *Sassy*. I'd just turned twelve, and when I opened an issue at random, my childhood was instantly pulverized. I rocketed forth into feminism, music, cool clothes, thrift stores, black nail polish, Manic Panic–dyed hair, and caring about boys without caring what they think of you. Nothing in *Sassy* was like anything I'd ever seen or heard, and no other PK was reading it. When we moved into that hot-tub house in the country, the '90s began and so did my teens.

I was a despicable babysitter. After Dad dropped me off, I'd greet the kids in their bedrooms, dump some Legos on Sky's floor, and tell them to play while I helped myself to a second breakfast of cherry Pop-Tarts, which Mrs. Evans kept in ample supply, stacked in the cabinet at neat 90-degree angles. Most days I ate between three and five Pop-Tarts and frittered a solid hour downstairs by myself while the kids played, fought, and tore apart the upper floor of their house. A sense of obligation kicked in around 10:00 a.m. I'd reluctantly tidy the upstairs and then bring them downstairs to play and get ready for the pool. I enjoyed the pool because I was a kid and I liked swimming. I don't remember ever watching the two- and five-year-old in my care or ensuring their safety. Sky wore water wings, and Jess had taken swimming lessons last summer, both of which tempered any sense of accountability that I may have inferred from the payment and the title of babysitter.

Post-pool we wove our way back to their house via the sidewalk network, then collapsed in front of the TV, sunbaked.

When Mrs. Evans's minivan pulled into the driveway, Jess and Sky ran to her open arms.

THIRTY-SEVEN

Replaced by our new dog Pete, Dolly had been left behind in Martinsville, like a lot of our stuff. We were not allowed to ask about anything there—our old school, the grand Asian dining room set we left in situ, our friends or relatives. We didn't see Earl and Grandma at Christmas or call Uncle Steve and Aunt Sandy anymore. That door was closed.

Adam was heavily into baseball by now. He spent summer days with the Wildcats at the park, and on rainy afternoons he retired to his friend Ryan's apartment and the boys hung out with Ryan's mom. Ryan didn't come to our house; the no-friends-over rule was firm.

Early that summer on one of my library days, the distinctive striped spines of John Updike's Rabbit novels had caught my attention, and their titles were the definition of innocuous. What could be more harmless than a book called *Rabbit Is Rich*? We still didn't have library cards, so I read on-site, working my way through Rabbit Angstrom's midlife crises during my final preteen summer, stretched out in the air-conditioning on the Berber carpet of a municipal building. The novels' protagonist resented his family, had an affair with a prostitute, arranged for her abortion, and made sexual overtures to a preacher's wife. Rabbit Angstrom thought about sex a lot of the time, but I didn't. I just devoured the novels, page after page. I didn't understand that my own family was rocketing between echelons of class and wealth, but I dove in, with abandon, to the WASP world Updike served me.

"Am I still supposed to write your dad's name on this?" Mrs. Evans pulled out her checkbook, and we stood together at her white Formica counter.

"Yes, Stephen F. Long." In June, Dad had told Mrs. Evans that he'd be getting me a bank account, and that she could make the checks out to him in the meantime. He could deposit them and give me cash. I had not gotten a bank account. Dad had not paid me either.

"Oh god, we'll remember this day forever, won't we?" She wrote *Aug. 2, 1990* in blue ink on the check above Dad's name.

"Why?" I asked.

"A war started today. Iraq invaded Kuwait. I suppose you wouldn't have heard about it at the pool." In fact, we had not been to the pool. That morning Jess wanted to watch *The Little Mermaid* on VHS, which the three of us had been watching weekly all summer. When the movie ended at 9:45 a.m., she asked if we could watch it again, and we did. Skyler declared it Little Mermaid Day and we'd decided to just watch it again and again until their mom came home. Our eyes were only off the screen during the minutes it took me to rewind the tape and begin it again. We'd eaten Pop-Tarts and green grapes on the white carpet. The sun shone outside, but we weren't in it.

"I'll tell you something, even if you don't realize it. Many years from now, when you're an adult, you'll remember where you were today. You might think about me and my kids in this kitchen. A war started today." Mrs. Evans handed me the patterned blue check. Her nails were glossy pink. I thanked her and walked out to Dad's car, waiting for me.

THIRTY-EIGHT

My seventh-grade year I woke up early to crimp my hair with a zigzagged hot iron, and I wore flowing pants in the style of MC Hammer.

Girls in my class and in the year above me had a special responsibility. Lunchroom staffing was short, and the school filled the gap by conscripting seventh- and eighth-grade girls to stay after lunch and load the industrial dishwasher with the lunch ladies. It took about half an hour, and they gave me a quarter afterward. I scooped other kids' gloppy uneaten chili and meatloaf into the sink and rinsed the orange polypropylene trays with a showerhead nozzle. Hot steam bathed my face and hair. I picked up my twenty-five cents and hauled ass to my classroom; I was missing math, my once-crimped hair puffed from the humidity of the dish room.

Tight as funds were, I was more than willing to sacrifice the quarter, but I couldn't get the teachers to budge. This is the way it was: the girls had to do the dishes and figure out a way to keep up with classes at the same time.

Now almost a year into being a "working mother," Mom made a monumental decision: she would become a nurse. Already borrowing significantly for Dad's graduate-level education, they took out student loans for Mom to join an evening and weekend RN program at a Purdue University extension program that began in January of 1991. Both my parents were going to be college students.

Christmas in 1990 was expectedly modest, especially compared to our '80s holidays. No kringle. A humbly sized tree. All I wanted, which I not-so-subtly hinted at, was for Dad to build that dollhouse from a few Christmases ago. I was, at twelve, easing toward being too old for it.

"It'll be better now," Dad reminded me. "You're older and you have a steady hand, so when you paint it and wallpaper it, it will look much better than it would have if you'd done it when you were younger." I admitted he was right, though I quietly doubted that this had been his plan all along. "All it needs is some glue, clamps, a few nails . . ."

"We'll build it together," I suggested.

"No, I'll do it. It's a dad thing," he explained, contradicting what he'd been saying for years. His word was final, as was his assessment that he'd intentionally waited to build it. When the dollhouse didn't appear Christmas morning, I put on my coat and took Pete outside. He lifted his leg to pee in the winter air, and I peeked into the glass pane of the garage door. The dollhouse, in its unopened box, sat in the spot where it had been since we moved in. I was too old for it anyway.

I began to pull away from Mom and Dad. Like any kid, I was straining and bursting against what I knew, which didn't line up with where I was headed. I hoped whatever was next for me looked less like Longs Island and more like what I saw in *Sassy* magazine or some moderately happier version of John Updike's adulthood. I still awoke about once a week from disturbing dreams about destroying the entire contents of our house.

A second version of this story is that I pulled away from my parents because they were busy; they worked and attended school and put meals on the table for us and kept us in school. What time did they have left for Adam and me?

And with the Longs, there's always more than one story. The Lincoln was "too much car" for us, or it was repossessed. The babysitting money would never have been mine, or Dad needed it more than I did.

There's yet another story, and it's about these stories themselves. As I approached thirteen, even having missed several pre-algebra lessons, I was ever more sure that the stories my parents were telling me were not adding up.

THIRTY-NINE

In February 1991, Dad was cited for "exceeding lawful speeds," for which he appeared in court and paid $40.

On April 15, 1991, my parents had an argument of epic proportions related to filing their income taxes, which Dad was scheduled to do that evening by dropping their return in the post office box at 11:59 p.m. Cutting it close was his idea of a good time. The shape and particulars of that exact verbal altercation have merged into twenty-odd other fights they had on Tax Days for the rest of their marriage. They may have begun this tradition in 1975, but I don't remember it until they screamed at each other across our tiny, dingy house that year.

"Well, why didn't you choose withholding?"

"We don't have a goddamn dollar, and we owe a lot more than that."

"Where is the money?"

"Why do you even have a job if the money disappears?"

"It's not my fault!"

It was never anyone's fault, but April 15 was ugly.

Now in nursing school, Mom quit the hardware store and took various low-level jobs at Fort Wayne hospitals in order to learn her new profession, and, crucially, to earn some much-needed cash. Hospital jobs are not like office jobs; their hours are all hours, and Mom worked the weirdest shifts. One week she'd be up at dawn and off to the hospital before school started. Other times she'd be on afternoons, and we wouldn't be awake at the same time as her for days. When we did see her, Mom's face revealed a new sense of purpose in her life, an accomplishment of her own that was taking shape, and a realm of doctors, nurses, and medical jargon that was all hers. She was happy.

None of us ever knew whether Mom's hoarding, and the related compulsive shopping for food and fabric and clothes, resulted from her happy times or her miserable times. Her need to buy things and stockpile them in our home was far-reaching and profound. It didn't seem to abate when times were easier, nor did it ease when material necessities like food and shelter were in jeopardy. Her hoarding was steady and constant, now justified by a higher per-hour paycheck than she'd ever earned before.

The house filled. We never called it hoarding. It was clutter. Our first couple of years in Fort Wayne were sparsely populated compared to Martinsville, but Mom's schedule and her income meant she'd swing by Kroger on her way home for a few things or stop by a dress shop around the corner from the seminary. She rarely ventured to that part of town without coming home with a garment bag.

The hot tub in the indoor porch had not yet been used, and it was hard to imagine doing so now. Mom's grocery runs had filled every kitchen cabinet, and much of the kitchen floor was covered in bags of canned goods and boxed dinners, including some from the food bank we still visited. Overflow food was stacked inaccessibly onto the hot tub cover and, when new bags arrived—they always did—older ones were pushed toward the center of the hot tub where they were impossible to reach. In time, the nucleus of this food mound smelled of rotting broccoli, eggs purchased four months earlier, once-frozen chicken TV dinners gone soft and pungent.

Mom got another job, at the dress shop she liked, reasoning that we could use some extra income, and, if she worked there weekend afternoons, she'd enjoy a discount. In the end the net was not in our favor. Between nursing school, her hospital shifts, and the store, she was never home. When she was, she lay flat on the couch, elevating her aching feet. She stood all day at both the hospital and in the shop, and when her discounted purchases were subtracted from her dress shop paycheck, we sometimes owed the store.

Mom's schedule was generally incompatible with her making dinner. We had heaps of food aging in all corners of our house, but neither she nor Dad ever felt like cooking it. The situation gave me that hollow, ill feeling I had in my troubled dreams, when I had to empty our house of its weighty possessions. I had an aversion to the waste, for one thing, but expressing it never ended well. "When did you become so judgmental?" Mom would ask when I indicated we could cook up some of the food in the house instead of getting Arby's or Olive Garden. I could see the money drain we'd been in since Martinsville, could remember the screaming Tax Day fight. I saw the bills arrive in the mail and get stacked on the hot tub unopened. I wanted to help us avoid more problems.

Maybe it was because I carried the self-righteousness of all preteens, but our conversations about these things were perpetually unsuccessful. It was never clear which of these stories was the real one. Instead of understanding whatever complex storm had gotten us here, hungry in a house stuffed with food, I just cooked it.

One evening, Dad was out of the house, scheduled to play air hockey with another sem and then do what he called a "ride-along" with a seminarian whose student-worker job was for campus security. They rode around the campus environs in a snub-nosed Ford minivan emblazoned with the seminary logo: a circle containing a cross, a serpent, a globe, and some Greek letters. Nothing happened on these patrols, but they were decidedly more adventurous than Dad's student-worker job as a fundraiser in the school's development office.

Mom walked in the door by the hot tub to the smell of chlorine and a tail-wagging Pete. But this evening, there was more: the scent of chicken-flavored Rice-A-Roni and frozen corn simmering in butter on the stovetop. I'd made dinner. She was elated.

I didn't mind. I enjoyed the creative challenge, and it felt genuinely good to please my mother so deeply. I kept doing it.

In eighth grade, girls in my Lutheran school were taking home ec, so I was building my culinary skills anyway. We swapped with the boys and took one two-week section of wood shop while they stumbled around the classroom kitchen trying to boil water. The girls had baked hams and trussed birds, peeled potatoes in a timed competition, and taken quizzes that asked us to define sauté, boil, broil, fry, bake, roast, and julienne. Boys knocking around the fake homestead for a few weeks was a little joke, but for us, it was deadly serious, preparation for our futures.

"Amanda Long, tell us about your family budget." My home ec teacher was a frizzy-haired, lifelong Lutheran, and she was keen that she got to teach us the family finance unit with a bona fide PK in her class. I sat stunned. As far as I could tell, our chaotic financial situation was not budget-based.

"Pastors' families live month to month, paycheck to paycheck." Now she was addressing everyone in the class. "They don't earn extravagantly and so they have to watch every penny. Don't they, Amanda?"

It was embarrassing. Though I knew I wasn't responsible for my parents' messy financial reality, I still felt I was. I didn't say anything. The teacher, whose first name was Jewell, continued on. "First, we list all of the household expenses on one side of the page. Then, we mark the family income on the other. Some expenses are monthly; others are weekly." I wondered if Mom and Dad had ever sketched their fiscal needs on graph paper this way.

Jewell underlined something on the board. Before she set us to work on our own budgets, she laid out some grim reality for us twelve- and thirteen-year-old girls. "Some of you," she suggested, "imagine that you'll marry rich and bring in loads of money and not have to fuss around with paper and pencil like this. That's not going to be true for most of you. You'll marry who you marry and have to figure it out with what you've got.

"Miss Long," she referred to me this way, having been rebuffed by my shyness earlier, when she used my first name. "You're a PK, and chances are, you're going to be a pastor's wife one day. That's usually how it works." The way she emphasized *usually* and the way some of the other girls tittered made me uncomfortable. I confidently decided there, in the linoleum-floored home economics lab of a Lutheran grade school in 1991, that I would be so many things in my life, but a pastor's wife was not one of them.

At home I grew more adventurous, trying recipes from scratch out of Mom's cookbooks instead of relying on the boxes and cans. I didn't have transportation, or money, so I used what we had and made what I could, like my home ec teacher had suggested I'd need to do. I became an old-fashioned Midwestern mom swiftly, declaring Wednesdays Cheeseburger Pie night and writing out lists of ingredients for Mom to shop for. She happily obliged.

FORTY

"Can you go over to the hot tub and see if there's cottage cheese in one of the bags?" I didn't make dinner every night, and when Mom did, sometimes I helped.

The hot tub was covered in mail and groceries and random touches of decor from our old life. A Chinese-carved cork diorama in a black lacquer frame sat next to a case of Diet Coke and a stack of thickly filled, unopened white envelopes from a law firm.

I delivered the room-temperature tub of cottage cheese, which Mom scooped onto canned pear halves and topped with cheddar cheese and mayonnaise, our salad. She stirred whatever was in the Crock-Pot and probed me more about whether I liked any boys in eighth grade.

I told her no, though what I was thinking was that none of them would like me. I was tall and clunky, and I felt left out of the group that I considered popular at school. To Mom's disappointment, I was getting really into being a disaffected teen, having recently set aside Paula Abdul for R.E.M. and my hair crimper for a dramatic chocolate-brown lipstick. I had read every *Sassy* in the house and even gotten Mom to send in a check for a subscription so I could devour the issues as soon as they were released. They may have kept my babysitting money, but they were never stingy with giving me things I wanted, like magazines or lipstick.

Dad was so successful at his student-worker fundraising job that he was offered a full-time, real-life job in the development office, which he juggled around his class schedule.

In October, Dad's request for a delayed vicarage was granted. Normally, a seminarian's third year was spent in the field—suburban Oklahoma, or a farm town in Minnesota or Queens, NYC, wherever a congregation in need called you. The idea was to test your chops at pastoring in an unfamiliar place. It was a bit like medical residency, a short-term placement fully out of our control. Dad asked to stay in Fort Wayne and do his fourth-year coursework while working in development, then take off for a vicarage in parts unknown in year four. It was a gesture to Adam and me to keep our schooling and our lives a bit more orderly.

Dad had an appointment in Indianapolis, and we all rode along. On our way home, the flat expanse of Indiana agriculture spooled out forever in front of us. Adam and I tried playing the alphabet game with signs, but even billboards were sparse on this monotonous drive.

"Limo!" Dad cried. He was very excited. I sat directly behind him and turned to see a long, dark car next to us, its windows impenetrable. Dad suggested it was one of the Indianapolis Colts or maybe a movie star.

I gaped out the window. Mom and Adam looked, too. Limos were uncommon in our part of the world, and this one looked a lot like our old Town Car, just fancier and with blackened glass.

The car immediately behind the limo was an older hatchback, into which was stuffed a very tall man, a long-haired man drumming the dashboard, and a drum kit.

"Nirvana!" I screamed. I was heart-stoppingly sure. No one was more famous than Nirvana was at that moment. But Dad said that no super-famous band would be driving through Indiana in a hatchback with their gear, looking, as these men did, unkempt.

"Their style is to be dirty," Adam explained. Even he knew this.

The long-haired man headbanged a little, his brown hair swinging, both of them smiling. As it was happening, I was aware of it ending, their car moving faster than ours, ahead of us toward more cornfields. I wished Dad would keep up.

I didn't have an ounce of doubt. "No, it has to be. It is," I stood my ground.

Dad, exaggerator and wishful thinker extraordinaire, shut me down. "You're going to have to admit you're wrong on this one, Amanda."

Confounding both of my parents, I became interested in tofu. I didn't know I was destined to become a vegetarian, but fiddling in the kitchen was sparking my interest. I had discovered that the way Mom dealt with food was not the only way. To date, my non-American food experiences had been forays into variations on pasta marinara and the occasional hard-shell taco. International food seemed exotic and appealing, and so did vegetables, which were an afterthought at home. I'd not yet heard of straight-edge vegans, but I was allured by the idea of a slightly punk-rock kitchen, turning the last generation's housewife fantasies on their head and connecting more to real food rather than packaged food. Most of all, I was captivated by the uncomplicated idea of one day being out on my own. I didn't have a way to articulate any of that, so I simply asked Mom to buy tofu.

She didn't, and I reminded her, several times. Finally, to her credit, she delivered. None of us had any idea what to do with it. Mom and Dad gave me such a hard time about it, and I was deeply stubborn. It wasn't even really tofu they were making fun of; it was the idea of trying something different. For me, that was the point.

It was silken tofu. Defiantly, I sliced open the Tetra Pak with a steak knife and carved a gooey, wet, white slab of it, put it between two pieces of white bread with Hellmann's mayonnaise, and proclaimed it "delicious" and "perfect." Which it was not.

Dad made a retching noise. Mom rolled her eyes.

"You'll get over it one day," Dad said, looking at Adam for encouragement.

Our days in that country house were limited. Dad had negotiated to have a special perk as part of his new job in the development office: campus housing. This was a revolutionary pivot point in the story of the Longs and how we lived. Once we tipped into territory in which a place to live, gratis, was possible, there was really no going back.

Without ever having so much as a toe in the hot tub, we packed and moved.

FORTY-ONE

Years earlier, when they were no longer able to afford the Martinsville house—or when they were called to the ministry, depending on which story you favor—the Longs did not declare bankruptcy. When we first moved in 1989, I heard them talk about "losing the house." I heard them say "The bank took the house," that dirty crooks had taken what was ours. Perhaps they were hanging on to a hope that the right buyer would come along and pay their asking price. Perhaps they didn't know how to declare bankruptcy or what to do about the mess they were in. I don't know what they knew, but I know what they did: nothing.

The massive house sat for many months, uninhabited except for the furnishings that wouldn't fit into our helter-skelter move. In the Longs' time with the house, things had deteriorated. The furnaces and air-conditioning units (two each) needed to be replaced. The carpets were stained. The wooden decks' boards were greenish, rotting, and sagging like the dock to the lake. Our front door was partially torn off, and the lawn was long and tattered. Maintaining the house was an expensive proposition.

When eventually Dad's old boss at the real estate firm bought it from the bank, he was shocked to learn he'd not only bought one big ostentatious house on a golf course but also another one, high up on a wooded hill. Earl's home was tied up in the same transaction. After Grandma's nursing home paperwork was settled and the old hilltop house was put in Dad's name, he had quietly used Earl's house as an asset against the massive house-related debts piling up.

The new owners got two houses, one of which was still stuffed with black lacquered Asian furniture, fast-food restaurant glassware, lamps and beds and sets of Laura Ashley sheets and other Longs' detritus. Three entire rooms were stuffed to the ceiling with fabric. The other one was Earl's.

In the fall of 1991, when we were moving to seminary campus housing, Earl would be moving, too. The new owner delivered the eviction news in person, as Earl sat in his easy chair next to a Doberman with a German girl's name. To avoid homelessness, Earl moved into a fixed-income apartment in town where no dogs were permitted. He was heartbroken to adopt out Heidi, and he never spoke to either of my parents again.

I heard my parents, particularly Dad, talking all the time. They talked about church and the seminary and nursing school. They talked, and fought, about money. About the war in Iraq. About TV shows they loved and Adam's baseball games. Dad was in constant monologue mode. He processed everything verbally, sermonizing. In 2013, the summer before he died, Dad wrote an 18,000-word autobiography peppered with clip art, which he emailed to me. In this Word document, which is uncharacteristically self-aware in many sections, he confessed, "One lesson I never learned: how to shut up. Just call me 'motor-mouth.' I admit it; I have a severe case of oral diarrhea . . . which continues to this day. Ask my wife, Sandie. She can hardly 'get a word in edgewise.' I'm not joking."

For all their talking, I never once heard about the fate of our Martinsville house or how Earl's house and Earl himself were tied up in it. They knew much more than I did, but I don't know how much. Did Mom know everything that Dad knew? Did they know his old boss moved in? Did they know Earl was forced out of his wooded refuge, forced to give up his beloved dog and live in a ragged apartment alone? These are among thousands of unknowable things about my parents, not covered in Dad's autobiography or any other record, and not something I knew to ask them about during their lives.

FORTY-TWO

The seminary house in Fort Wayne was the smallest house we'd ever lived in. In Dad's mind it was also the sweetest: we didn't pay a penny. A low ranch in pastel yellow, the house was spartan. We crammed in all the stuff we possibly could, including Mom's briefcase of custom rubber stamp samples, the unbuilt Victorian dollhouse, lots of garment bags, Adam's sports equipment, several trays of motivational tapes from Success Motivation Institute, fabric, and bags and bags of food. We retained many Oriental furnishings and all the *Sassy* magazines. We left behind an untold number of other items in the country hot tub house for the incoming tenants to inherit.

In 1992, I began high school and started fresh with my new persona, which fit under a broad umbrella I called "alternative." It was a Lutheran high school, and I attended on scholarship. Fort Wayne is brimming with so many Lutherans that the high school was large and diverse. I immediately felt at home, built deep and true friendships, and joined the yearbook staff because I'd decided I wanted to be a magazine writer.

Our new home and its environs were surreal. We'd been visiting the campus on and off the last few years, but now we lived there. Swarms of clerical-collared men would emerge from classroom buildings every 90 minutes at class dismissals. The enormous and imposing chapel clanged its bell on the hour, approximately in synch with our grandfather clock. The entire place was built with deep intention. The pitch of every roofline on campus is exactly 23.5 degrees, and each roof runs precisely east to west.

Every structure is designed around a 5'4" module and length and widths are multiples of that core structure. Every brick is diamond-shaped and was laid vertically, except the chapel bricks, which were laid horizontally to set it apart as sacred. A massive gym with the aesthetics of a Wes Anderson film set, spraying water fountains, stone benches for contemplation, and a Scandinavian-modern cafeteria are anchors of the campus, which was all arranged to functionally resemble a 1300s Finnish village. The landscaping is serene and maintained with rigor. Every tree planted on the property was selected for its ancient appearance.

Inside the cleanly rectangular house where we lived, it was lowbrow chaos. Outside, it was all Eero Saarinen.

There was no school bus service between the seminary campus and our schools, and Mom was immersed in nursing school and pre–nursing career jobs, so Dad was our designated driver. Mornings were fun. Dad, who now wore a black clerical collared shirt every day, slapped Aqua Velva on his cheeks and started our day. He pulled together eggs mixed with toast, or we'd make mugs of powdered instant oatmeal and hop in our used Buick.

"*This is the feast of victory for our Lord,*" Dad sang out in the car, stretching "feast" into "fe-ea-ea-st" as it was done in the Lutheran hymnal. His fingers played imaginary piano keys in the air. "*Hallelujah,*" he sang out happily. Not so long ago, Dad drove around with us singing '50s doo-wop—"Lollipop, lollipop" or "Sha-na-na-na, get a job." Now it was hymns, or liturgy.

He explained the controversy over the "old" and "new" hymnals in our version of Lutheranism. He held forth on minor theological points, quoting verses to back up his opinion. "Saved by faith through grace in Christ," he repeated, warning us that "being good" was a trap. Virtuousness was no way to get to heaven, and it sure as hell would not be ours.

Adam and I didn't talk during these rides. Dad did, and we listened. He occasionally moralized. Opinions he may have held loosely earlier in his life congealed into solid stone. Abortion: unequivocally wrong.

Marital indiscretions, cheating of any kind, gossiping: never okay. Being gay: sinful.

Less than ten years earlier, his business partner was a "fairy," and less than twenty years earlier, my research and Dad's own tall tales about himself indicate a moral compass whose needle spun wildly. But that was then, and this was the '90s.

FORTY-THREE

Dad was late. He was never on time, but this afternoon he was late for the late time I expected him. He liked driving us to and from school, said that it was special Dad-and-kid time. The high school was only a six- or seven-minute drive from the seminary, but he got wrapped up in his work in the afternoons.

"Maybe someone else can drive me home," I suggested. For the first time in my life, I had several good friends, offbeat teenagers like me who were into music. We wore raggy flannel shirts and wide-legged denim. I no longer crimped my hair or fluffed my bangs but wore my brown hair straight and plain, with a dramatic middle part. I owned several striped T-shirts, bought in thrift-store boys' departments.

Dad shook his head. "I'll get you. Don't insult me by saying I can't remember to come pick you up." I clicked my seat belt on and reached to turn down the radio. Rush Limbaugh was overloud, talking the way Dad did, about American families.

"And this Feminazi," Rush caterwauled. Dad warned my hand away from the dial.

"Just listen," Dad told me. Rush continued on about Gloria Steinem, suggesting she'd do well to seek an MRS degree. Dad laughed. He thumped the dashboard for emphasis.

"But if you can't get me after school, I can find someone else . . ." my words trailed off. Sometimes I'd wait an hour on the brick half wall outside the school after the bell rang. If the school secretary was leaving before I got picked up, she'd turn me around and have me call the seminary development office on her off-white desk phone.

"Yes, I'll be there in two minutes," Dad would answer from his own desk phone.

Now, in the car, I tried to make my point, but Rush was on to something else that had Dad's attention: *Murphy Brown* and fatherless heads of households.

With his version of extreme kindness, Dad reminded me that staying after school allowed me to socialize. Never mind that my friends' rides came five or ten minutes after school, or that he could plainly see I was the sole kid sitting outside the high school every afternoon when he eventually came. "You like getting picked up late," he said. I quietly agreed.

We had one and a half bathrooms in the seminary house, and before school I brushed my teeth in the hall half bath. As I rinsed cool water between my teeth, I thought about Dad who I imagined had just done the same, but with piping-hot water. Dad was invincible.

I spit roughly and emerged to see Dad buttering toast held in the flat palm of his hand. Our kitchen counters were so stuffed with food packages and dirty dishes that there was no room to butter toast there. Our dining table was laid like a dressmaker's shop with a cardboard sewing mat under an in-progress garment rife with straight pins. The other end of the table was stacked with drug manuals for Mom's nursing courses.

Dad held the dark slice of toast in his hand, scratching its surface with a heavily buttered knife. That was another thing about Dad—he liked his toast darker than anyone I'd ever met. "A little carbon puts hair on your chest," he'd remind Adam, winking at me.

Not today.

November 4, 1992, Dad held his charred bread in the slumped posture of defeat. Adam and I sped around the house, grabbing our book bags from under the Chinese table inlaid with a pagoda design. Dad seemed annoyed that we didn't share his malaise.

"Clinton won. That scumbag."

Like most Gen X high schoolers, I was apathetic about politics. Even so, I hadn't escaped the Rock the Vote campaign, and when Dad told me Clinton won, I felt a bit happy, felt a sense of new possibilities. The man who'd played saxophone on Arsenio Hall's show a few months ago would be our president in a few months. Cool.

"The world is ending," Dad declared. Adam and I were strapped into the Buick, having made our own breakfasts; Dad was too upset to do it. "You have no idea what's coming." He went on and on, his voice quavering, and his raw despair evident at the idea that liberals would now be taking over. I was fourteen and had no idea what that meant. Dad began to cry as he pulled into the high school parking lot. I'd seen Dad yell and argue. I'd seen him laugh and celebrate. But I'd never seen him cry.

FORTY-FOUR

From what I could tell, none of Dad's dire predictions materialized.

In 1993, all of us had almost exactly what we wanted.

Dad was officially a vicar. He'd finished his coursework and had only the one-year practicum of vicarage to check off the list. Then, he'd be a pastor.

Mom was midway through her nursing program. That year she'd finished her associate's degree and was pushing through to finish her bachelor's—the first in our nuclear family or in either of my parents' families of origin to do so. Both my parents attended college when they were eighteen, and neither went beyond their second year. Mom must have felt a little flutter of the independence and accomplishment she'd felt when she worked for IBM back in the '70s. She was the happiest I'd ever known her to be. She infused daily conversation with her new lingo, like "med-surg" and "pain scale."

"Then I told the person on the peds desk, I'm not your charge nurse, and I took the sharps with me," she might say, aiming to confuse Dad and impress us. It worked.

Adam and I had lived for four years in Fort Wayne, and while we'd been through some weird times, we felt at home and liked it well enough. We had friends. In our austere house, there was one special perk I'd not had before: a phone jack in my bedroom. My phone was clear plastic, with all the primary- and neon-color inner components visible; a coiled, yellow cord connected the handset to the base, and I spoke on it all the time.

Adam beat on my bedroom door, asking me to come outside. I covered the mouthpiece; "Just a sec-ond!" I told him. I was tall and strong but not as athletic as him. On the other side of the door I could hear him pounding his baseball mitt with his fist. He wanted to play catch as often as I wanted to be on the phone.

I ended my call and joined him, reluctantly. There were only three short cul-de-sacs of single-family homes on the seminary grounds. Dad often reminded us that we were in faculty housing even though he wasn't faculty—hadn't even graduated yet. The streets were named after theologians, and all the houses had single-digit addresses because there were so few. No other kids lived there, as most of the theology professors were too old to have school-aged kids. We exited the house, leaving the door wide open next to the 4 by our porchlight.

The most noticeable landscaping feature of the grounds were the enormous green lawns. Acres and acres of unadulterated mowed grass surrounded us, and because there was so little else, anyone or anything on those emerald expanses was noticeable. The gigantic Luther statue shot up boldly amid one of these green acres, purposeful and unmistakable. An eccentric semiretired professor neighbor of ours, who marched the lawns wearing a dark cape and muttering Luther's ninety-five theses to himself, was a conspicuous presence. And when Adam and I tossed his baseball on a Saturday afternoon, every seminarian, faculty member, or anyone else on the quiet campus watched and took note. "Go deep!" Adam's voice echoed across the verdurous swath. The sense of having an audience was so vivid that when we finished playing catch, I was inclined to take a curtsy.

We were not in a money crisis in 1993. My parents still argued about it occasionally, Tax Day was unpleasant, but Dad's work situation meant that our worries had receded, and we had grown used to living a slightly more moderate lifestyle.

"I'll take a Big Hot, an olive burger, four orders of fries . . . Amanda, what do you want?" This was our ritual. Dad's vicarage assignment was to an ultra-small congregation in rural Michigan, about an hour and a half north of Fort Wayne. Dad worked his office job at the seminary all week, then on Sundays we drove up and spent most of the day in a church surrounded by cornfields. Adam and I were compensated for our efforts with a morning visit to a place called Dutch Uncle Donuts and an afternoon visit to Hot 'n Now. "We can't afford McDonald's," Dad told us, "but Hot 'n Now is better." Hot 'n Now was a Michigan-based burger chain whose prices were astonishingly low, enough so that suspicion was cast on the quality of the food by most everyone, but not Dad.

Dad was a devotee of their olive burger, and Mom and Adam got their knockoff Big Mac, the Big Hot. I was grudging but found my way to a chicken sandwich or two orders of fries.

To make it to the church before early service, we woke in the dark and piled together in the minivan. Mom worked or went to school night and day, but Sunday she had to reserve for these trips, as Adam and I did. In dresses and sport coats, we rode north while Dad delivered a practice version of his sermon.

Arranging the pomp and presentation of a church service, without a senior pastor to guide him, must have reminded Dad of his Miami nightclub days. He was curating a sensory experience—the right look, the best music, message, and people. He carefully selected a high-quality alb and ornate chasuble from the Fort Wayne church garment store. Hymns were chosen for each service after research, planning, and a quick noodle of the melody on his electronic keyboard in the car. Sermons were written with precision and passion. He intended to blow their minds.

"Grace, mercy, and peace to you," Dad began, driving and trying to recall the thirty-five-minute talk from memory. He wouldn't let Mom drive. It was odd to see him nervous, especially because he was a nonstop and confident talker in daily life. In these first months of pastoring, he needed us to listen and be thoughtful, to help him hone his craft. His vicarage assignment had been a boon in two ways: first, it was commutable and we didn't have to move, and second, there was no permanent pastor in the Michigan congregation for Dad to answer to. He was all on his own, in his first-ever church.

"The Great Shepherd who wipes away every tear," Dad enunciated in the van as we tooled through Michigan farmland. His speaking voice for his sermons was direct and over-clear, an evolution of the voice he heard and sometimes used in the days he was selling the Paul J. Meyer Success Motivation Institute tapes. "Paul warns the Corinthians not to associate with sexually immoral people." Dad pronounced "sexually" with the same slur of syllables as Rush Limbaugh's pronunciation of "homosexuals" on his radio program, the second part of the word rushed out with derision. Dad was talking about Biblical truths, but if you only listened to the Paul J. Meyer–like cadence and timing, he may as well have been saying "Whatever you vividly imagine, ardently desire, sincerely believe, and enthusiastically act upon, MUST inevitably come to pass."

His strident sermons had begun to remind me of our Long Island neighbor, the fundamentalist preacher with the raging rottweilers. We thought he was crazy and annoying.

"What in the actual goddamn hell, Amanda?" Dad's rich, even voice slipped. He looked at me angrily in the rearview mirror. I had been listening to his sermon with one ear and reading *The Catcher in the Rye* with the other. I rolled my eyes toward Adam and put in a bookmark. I couldn't wait to be back home in my bedroom with my clear, coil-corded phone.

Living at the seminary was a version of our very best Longs life. Not only did we have free rent, but we also were absolved of house and yard maintenance. The Lutheran church had fully embraced us. Like Dad said, we were living in the palm of God's hand. My parents were proud we lived on those tidy grounds, and they began experimenting with socializing—at our house.

In late April 1993, my father turned fifty, and we hosted a rousing party with pastors, seminarians, PKs, nursing students and faculty, and assorted others. Adam and I kept the coolers in the yard filled with Cokes, and he orchestrated a big game of catch with some boys who attended.

Dad was the gregarious center of attention. We all ate on black-and-white paper plates that said "Over the Hill."

It was not only extremely out of the ordinary—our first actual party at home—it was fun. We took two entire rolls of film of happy, middle-aged people lounging on our Oriental furniture and eating spinach dip on torn pieces of King's Hawaiian bread from a spread on our patio.

That spring, Mom shocked us again. One of her nursing school classmates had a line on black-market *Simpsons* T-shirts, the ones that had been banned from our school three years ago. Mom got Adam and me each a shirt. Both were printed slightly crooked, and mine was, oddly, a mock turtleneck. They were clearly homemade, and still none of us had yet seen a single episode of the show. I don't know whether *Simpsons* shirts were actually hard to find by 1993, but Mom took enormous pleasure in bestowing these forbidden fruits to us.

"I know you've always wanted these," she told us. I wore mine to sleep in, and I never saw Adam's again after she gave it to him. I have tried to understand why she thought we wanted the shirts this much and can only conclude that she decided we would want whatever she forbade.

The April party was such a success that they followed it up with a ten-person, "murder mystery in a box" game and dinner that they hosted with some other seminary families. As a high school freshman, I couldn't imagine a scenario more eye-roll-inducing than my parents dressing up to playact the game of Clue in a 1950s-style sock-hop milieu. But they could have their fun, and I could have mine.

By then, my best friend was not only legally allowed to drive but also had a turquoise Honda Civic. She drove me home every school day, often via Dairy Queen. We took our treats to the seminary grounds and wandered, dangling our bare legs in the spurting water features, sprawling over benches on manicured greens. She never came inside the house, even though I slept over at her house across town most Friday nights.

"I'll take two lime Mr. Misties," my friend called out the car window and into the drive-through speaker. We laughed. Golden sun glinted off the iridescent paint on the car, and the speaker barked back, asking us to repeat the order.

We didn't know how to make Mr. Misty plural, and we didn't know what we would do or be after our first year of high school. Laughter rolled up and through us both. She couldn't catch her breath to answer the question. We gulped air, trying to put together the words "Mr. Misty" as well as the coins to pay $1.03 for each of us. On days we were short on money, we split it. It always felt like enough.

FORTY-FIVE

My parents' financial problems that final year in Fort Wayne were entirely invisible to me. I made mixtapes. I fantasized about being brave enough to dye my hair with Manic Panic. I rode around in friends' cars, music loud, windows down in all seasons, imagining what life would be like for me in a few years, when I'd be out of the house. I couldn't say why I wanted that so badly; I just knew that I did. Only in my twenty-first-century research did I learn more about the currents swirling beneath my awareness.

On July 30, 1993, a collection agency sued both of my parents in a small-claims suit. They owed more, but the agency was willing to accept $1,056.73, which could be garnished from wages they earned at the seminary and the hospital. Both of my parents' employers were named in the suit.

On October 18, 1993, the defendants in the small-claims case—my parents—failed to appear. They'd been mailed documents and visited twice each by a process server in the matter but didn't appear or pay. By December, their employers were ordered to begin garnishing their wages.

On November 19, 1993, a different collection agency sued my parents for $452.17. On May 27, 1994, a collection agency sued them for $150.70, and on June 28, a collection agency, on behalf of a dentist, sued them for $1,091.61. They did not pay, respond in writing, appear in court, or take any other action in any of these cases.

It was noticeable but not weird that they never opened their mail.

In the old house, the hot tub had been stacked with unopened lawyers' office envelopes, and mail at our new house was being stuffed into crevices everywhere, but unless it looked like a check, they would examine it but never open it. I think this was part of a strategy in which they could claim, to themselves or to each other, ignorance. Sealed white envelopes were fanned and stacked in the living room, kitchen, and bathroom. They sat atop Mom's sewing projects on the big dining table and under my parents' king-sized bed. The mail wasn't my concern, so I ignored it, too.

"These sons of bitches," Dad said, holding an envelope with the name of a dental practice in the return address area. He lifted it to the light coming through our living room window, looking to rule out the textured pattern of a check. Finding none, he tossed the envelope on the black lacquer Chinese secretary desk whose surface was already cluttered with mail. Dad had needed a crown a few months ago. "Is it wrong to try to get my teeth fixed? These people are killing me."

At the time, my parents were both employed with full-time jobs, and we had minimal housing expenses. They weren't paying down debts on the Martinsville house; we'd just walked away from that. Seminary and nursing school tuition were both being paid for with grants and loans, which had not yet come due. I don't know what their income was or where it was going. The debts they were accruing were mostly small to moderate—things that might have been a stretch to afford all at once or by surprise but that could have probably been dealt with on a payment plan. They favored this entirely hands-off method of managing their money; it was an inherent and absolute part of who they were.

Also noticeable but normal for us was the food situation in the house. For years, Mom had stacked and stuffed our cabinets beyond their bursting point and jammed our fridge. This was not new. Nor was it unusual to have excess food—shelf stable and perishable alike—sitting around in non-kitchen parts of the house. We had been eating spoiled food for years, but I didn't truly notice it until around the time I was fifteen, in our last months in that seminary house.

"It's still good," Mom told me. She pulled the foil back from a CorningWare dish on the counter that held brisket from three nights ago, sitting in a puddle of brown water, the flesh gray. "Get a plate."

Leftovers were plentiful at home because when Mom cooked, she usually made a quantity much larger than the four of us could eat in one sitting. The fridge, perpetually overflowing, never had room for leftovers, so they often sat on the counter and were tossed away untouched several days or a week later. Flies flocked to the kitchen. The sense of waste nagged at me, yet I still couldn't bring myself to eat the old, unrefrigerated meals. In my mid-teens, I was old enough to see the massive waste of food and money—I'd pretty much aced home ec a few years ago—but I was too young to do anything about it except work on the issue in my troubled dreams. I continued to dream of fully destroying our house, dumping all the food and mail and sewing projects into a black hole. Lately, the dream had a new aspect—a second home that was prim and tidy. A place where there was just enough of everything but not too much of anything.

Food aged everywhere in the house. Our garage now held some dry goods, many bags holdovers from the Martinsville days. The hall to the bedrooms was where we stored soda. The front layer of the fridge was relatively recent. Behind it, milk curdled in its jug. Behind that, frosty green mold bloomed on sliced cheese, and cucumbers rotted to pulp. The deeper you went, the worse it got.

Mention this to Mom, or try to address it yourself, and you were in for a terrific talking-to.

"Well, okay, *Martha*," Mom huffed. Earlier that year, Martha Stewart had debuted her first TV show, and Mom enjoyed saying how absurdly fussy and unrealistic Martha was about cooking and cleaning and entertaining—all the things Mom did in her very own Mom way.

I offered to help clean the fridge so we'd have room for leftovers or make shopping lists to help reduce the volume. Naïvely, I thought Mom was buying doubles and triples of things we already had in dozens because she'd forgotten we were already stocked. She refused my help.

I tried to keep cooking meals, but it was harder in that small house. The limited counter space was packed and so was the table. It was impossible to work in there the way it was, and impossible to tidy it up without Mom getting next-level mad. I had high school friends and evening plans. So, despite grocery trips that were reminiscent of apocalypse planning missions, we often got takeout from House of Hunan or sandwiches from Arby's for dinner. When Mom did cook, I grew more and more suspicious that the food was edible. Hot dogs were served with five-sixths of a bun. "I pulled off the moldy part," Mom explained. The Minute Rice was shot through with weevils, but Mom would just scoop out the part that "looked bad" and serve the rest, which was probably teeming with invisible eggs. I once opened a Yoplait for my breakfast whose expiration date was four years prior. "By definition, it's spoiled milk. It's supposed to be fermented," Mom told me. The yogurt had been stored on its side and the goopy blueberry and milky part was separated entirely from a strong-smelling clear liquid. "Just stir it and eat it, Amanda. You don't have to be Little Miss Prissy about it."

In addition to the rural church where Dad was vicaring, another Michigan church in Detroit's crusty, working-class suburb of Taylor was interested in Dad. When I learned this and put the pieces together that we might move in the summer of 1994, I was surprised. I thought Dad had taken the development office job in order to let us stay settled in Fort Wayne. Maybe he could play to his strengths with this office job in service to the church and still serve the rural Michiganders on Sundays, and we'd stay put, I thought.

"It's time to be a real pastor," he explained, telling us that we'd be moving at the end of the school year. He would be the senior pastor at the church in Taylor. Effective immediately, he'd be driving up now and then to begin to get to know the congregants, preach the occasional sermon, and start our new lives there, all balanced with his finishing up the vicarage and winding down his office job. By now, he owned clerical collared shirts in long- and short-sleeved versions and wore almost nothing else outside of the house. He was beloved by the church members at the small, rural church, who respected his views, relied on him for Christian leadership, and were attracted to the charisma that Dad had been deploying his whole life, from the mornings begging for breakfast in his grandparents' Miami apartment building until now. Dad was ready to move on and have a big, thriving congregation of his own.

The March 1994 issue of Fort Wayne's *Senior Life* newspaper ran a feature on Dad titled "Steve Long Has Discovered True Happiness" about his late-in-life transition to clergyhood and our impending move to Detroit. In his interview answers, Dad casts the changes in our lives as his choice to walk away from a thriving and lucrative business career. He gives credit to the faithless Swedes he met in the '80s for inspiring him to engage in church life. "I found that when the holy spirit calls—it's time to go," he told the reporter. "I found this the hard way because my family was hit hard financially and I found myself starting over at the age of 46. But in doing this I have found more happiness and joy than I have in all my life. It is true that Christ promises us peace beyond understanding."

Piqued that I'd have to leave my friends mid–high school, I mounted a vicious, if silent, revolution. Openly rebelling or contradicting them would get me nowhere. Above all else, Adam and I knew that agreeing was our number one job. We could not defy them. It was like asking for a cataclysm. Silenced into submission, I carried out my deep unhappiness about the move with two actions, both as bold as possible given they would have to be fully unknown to my parents.

First, my best friend and I wrote lyrics by the Cure on one of the seminary's stone benches. For two years now, she and I had held our Mr. Misty cups and roamed the campus, imagining the intrigue of our sophisticated future lives. I had never had a boyfriend or anything close, and she had decided my first kiss would happen on that particular bench, under a weeping willow. As the time for us to move to the Detroit suburbs approached with no kissing candidates emerging, we took a Sharpie and a flashlight out one night and wrote "Kiss Me, Kiss Me, Kiss Me" onto the pebbled stone in blocky, black letters meant to last forever.

Second, I made a decision. The last few years I'd spent a significant amount of my time trying to figure out my parents and, most of all, to try to make our household more peaceful and less weird. With so little to show for it, I had begun to ask myself why. I decided that when we moved to Michigan, I could focus more on myself. I was interested in drawing and writing. I loved music. I pictured myself, one day, in a home of my own without Mom's stuff piled everywhere. I imagined having the confidence of the creative women in music I'd started to idolize: Kim Deal of the Breeders, Kim Gordon of Sonic Youth, and Kristin Hersh of Throwing Muses. Maybe my parents would always be like this. Maybe I would have to let them deal with the consequences of whatever they were doing without feeling like I had to help them fix it so we could be normal. We weren't.

PART FOUR

Suburban Detroit

1994 to 1996

FORTY-SIX

A Michigan left is a disorienting driving maneuver in which you pass your destination then loop backward and eventually turn right. Every suburb in Detroit is ribbed with thoroughfares split with these U-turn opportunities, and Telegraph Road—perpetually gray and loud, always audible from inside our new house—offered these turnarounds every half mile. Liquor stores, called "party stores" in local parlance, are situated two or three per corner. Buildings are low, no more than three stories. Our city was an arbitrary square of six miles by four miles amid a limitless wash of grunge. Blockbuster Video. Dunkin' Donuts. Dialysis centers. UAW meeting halls. Mobile home parks and fast-food outlets. The jewelry stores were pawnshops. Colonial-looking insurance agencies. A movie theater and a mall. And Dad's new church, a tan brick castle in suburbia with a crenelated roofline and stained glass, lancet windows. The congregation was founded by farmers in 1878 when that intersection was surrounded by agricultural land. By 1994 when we arrived, most church members were auto industry workers. On the other three corners were a party store, a White Castle, and an A&W Root Beer drive-in.

Our house sat in the middle of it all, half a mile from the church.

We moved early in the summer of 1994. Dad was installed as the senior pastor of St. John's Lutheran, Mom graduated with her associate's degree in nursing and became an RN, Adam was enrolled in the elementary school attached to St. John's, and I would be turning sixteen in a few weeks.

My sweet-sixteen summer calendar had just two engagements: Lollapalooza and a summer school course in civics.

In order to graduate high school on time with Michigan's requirements, I'd need an extra social studies course. The public high school nearby accepted me for a four-week intensive; my classmates would be kids who'd failed it the year before. Lollapalooza was going to be much more fun.

It was 87 degrees all day long. Four days after I turned sixteen in our little brick house in Michigan, my friend drove her turquoise Honda up from Indiana so we could attend Lollapalooza '94 together at a massive parklike venue north of Detroit, where my parents dropped us off. The sun roasted us for twelve solid hours except for the occasional minutes we'd dart into a tent fitted with sprinklers. Misted and cooler, we'd emerge, take in another band on one of the stages, roll our eyes at the clusters of people playing hacky sack, browse the vendors of natural juices and drug rugs, and marvel at our outrageous fortune.

"This is real," she said to me at least two dozen times. "Us. Here. Everyone."

"Everyone" was underselling it. Beastie Boys, L7, George Clinton and the P-Funk All-Stars, the Flaming Lips, the Breeders, Verve, Nick Cave and the Bad Seeds, A Tribe Called Quest, Guided by Voices, Palace Songs, Luscious Jackson, and the headliners, Smashing Pumpkins, who berated us all as frat-boy sellouts. The headliner was supposed to have been Nirvana, but Kurt Cobain had died three months before. Nirvana would have berated us, too.

We only cared that we were there, wandering between the safe-sex tent and something called an Electric Carnival—christened by Lollapalooza's own magazine "a phreaky cyber sideshow"—where we could try out computers and play a piano keyboard hooked up to a video mixer. Slam poets shouted and raved in their own tent. Vendors sold Thai and Indian food, whose spices hung in the humidity. Big, loud juicers ground carrots into syrupy orange tonics and bald, barefoot, and robed Tibetan monks drifted through the crowd alongside us.

We always hoped this world existed and today, finally, we plunged into its depths.

Sunburned and barely able to hold our teenage selves upright by eleven that night, we prowled the parking lot for my parents' Ford Aerostar. They were due to pick us up.

"What if we, like, don't get in the car?" my friend asked. We entertained the idea of always living on the craggy hill of Pine Knob Amphitheater, but the van eventually rolled up, my tired parents in the front seat.

They let us play a Smashing Pumpkins cassette on the dark drive home. We barely heard it or spoke. Our ears were still fuzzy and thumping from our day of amplified sound, and I was realizing that when my friend left in the morning, I'd again be officially marooned in my parents' world. I had no local friends my age, no way to find my own place in the exotically grubby place we'd landed, and no way to stop the hurricane that was the Longs.

"Forgive the clutter!" Mom declared as we pulled into the gravel driveway after midnight. We slept among still-packed moving boxes, and deeply.

FORTY-SEVEN

Politely, during her visit, my friend didn't remark on my new surroundings. The house was just fine, a 1920s bungalow the church had owned for many years as a rental income property and had recently lightly renovated for our family to live in rent-free. But the buildings and land around it were very different from the bucolic seminary grounds. Directly across the street was a vacant lot, thick with weeds and used by a construction site nearby for their cement trucks to reload. All day, their cylindrical bellies turned and engines idled. On either side were a UPS sorting facility and a cardboard manufacturer. A sign whose paint had flaked off in large chunks was meant to read FOR LEASE but was no longer legible.

Our side of the street was a bit more residential, and our house sat among five others separated by half-acre cornfields, run-down garages, open lots of dirt, and a few industrial buildings. Half a mile down was the White Castle across from the church.

Not all Detroit suburbs were like this. We quickly learned that the southern part where we lived, Downriver, was the working-class part where autoworkers had migrated from Kentucky and Alabama a generation before. Our neighbors had been—or still were—poor white people. Union wages and benefits bought many people an almost middle-class lifestyle in 850-square-foot, tract-home subdivisions, though pickup truck culture and the occasional Confederate flag lingered. The suburbs to the north and west of Detroit each had their own characteristics, the west being several notches more respectable, normal, and middle American than Downriver, and the north and east being downright chichi. "The armpit of Detroit, Amanda," Mom described Downriver to me. "And Detroit's the armpit of America."

Drive twelve minutes from our house, past the Marathon Oil refinery—an amber-lit fairyland at night—and the always-running Mill Steel, and you'd hit the city limits of Detroit.

I was so bored early that summer. I asked Mom to take us to the Taylor library. I loaded up several novels and books of poetry. Adam browsed the Lego books, and Mom hit the jackpot. She'd sewn all her life but never done any quilting, which she aspired to try. It seemed like a perfect pastor's wife pastime. Mom got more than twenty how-to books on quilting and checked them out with our new library card, along with my stack. "This is free. Like a free bookstore," Mom explained. I already knew how I felt about libraries; I'd practically lived in the Fort Wayne public library during the summer of 1990.

Throughout our time in Fort Wayne, my parents had been spending money they didn't have, on everything from abundant groceries and clothes to medical costs to patio furniture. They navigated an erratic boundary known only to themselves between what we could and could not afford. Cable TV was for "rich people"—not us. We usually never had more than four channels. But we spun through baffling amounts of food waste and never-worn clothing, took hours-long, gas-guzzling car rides for entertainment, and generally didn't openly show any concern whatsoever about finances, even as tall piles of windowed envelopes accumulated on the kitchen counter. "It's only money," Dad said. As far as I can tell, 1993 was the last year my parents filed state or federal income taxes. In 1994, they quit.

Before we moved to Taylor, their wages were already being garnished because of old dental bills and traffic tickets. When they stopped paying taxes, the court declared that their wages would be garnished by the IRS, and papers were filed with the seminary and with the hospital where Mom worked. These papers were filed right around the time they stopped drawing an income from both of those sources; the wage garnishing was too late to matter. If they ever opened the formal white envelopes mailed to our last Fort Wayne house that conveyed this news, they didn't betray it. We just moved.

The urge I had to separate myself from them flourished that summer, in part because it felt mutual.

I was sent to the public high school for my civics make-up course filled with delinquents. Being poor and moving around had thrust me into some interesting situations, but this setting was by far the roughest exposure I'd had to the grit of the real world. My fellow students smoked cigarettes during class, daring the harried and balding social studies teacher in charge of us to care. He didn't. He must have known that several students got high in the parking lot on our midmorning break, which I experienced as a prolonged stretch of fifteen minutes in the July sun, longing to remain unnoticed by my classmates. I slumped against the wall of the school, seeking shade while the kids with cars sat in their backseats passing joints, sometimes needles. A kid named Jarrod with a pockmarked face often wore a T-shirt that declared "I ♥ LSD." The classwork was very easy. My parents, deep in their own malaise and the transition to this new life, never asked me about it, and I never told them. I got an A.

Afternoons that summer, to avoid stupor, I decided to help Mom unpack all the food we'd brought in the move. Our unfinished basement had a built-in workbench and wall shelving, and the dozens of boxes of canned and other nonperishables were stacked on the cement floor down there. Yet Mom was grocery shopping all the time, filling our kitchen and leaving all this perfectly good food untouched. At sixteen, the lonely feeling of having no friends locally felt deeper because I spent my mornings as a reviled nerd in a jaded '90s version of *Welcome Back, Kotter* in which the teacher didn't give a rip. The prospect of spending untold hours with a purpose—that would help our household—was alluring.

I unpacked all the food, filling the built-in shelves and then building another crude set of plywood shelves along one wall. Everything was organized. Need marinara sauce? We have twenty-three jars of it, and now they're all on the same shelf. Water chestnuts? Yes, there's a section for those. Instant gravy. Canned beans. Dehydrated potatoes. I made a mini supermarket, almost like the seminary food bank, just for us. I felt sure this would help Mom and help keep our expenses down.

"I don't know why you think you know everything, Amanda." Mom's tone was sharp, accusatory. She knew that for more than two weeks I'd been unpacking the food and setting up the basement while Adam lounged in the living room watching *Matlock* in a Detroit Lions jersey. Mom hadn't said anything at all about my project until I finished. Then she was angry.

"Now we'll never find anything," she said.

Her anger lasted years and years. On principle, because I had organized it, she wouldn't use any of the food on those basement shelves. My family lived in that house for eleven years, and when I helped them move out of it in 2005, I found a thick, ashy dust on the cans and boxes, undisturbed since 1994.

Just like in the Martinsville mansion, Adam's bedroom was immediately next to my parents' bedroom upstairs, and mine was as far away as physically possible, steps away from our back door on the main floor. Adam and I grew up in the same household but were treated as entirely different people, either because I was the oldest, or the daughter, or just because my parents were who they were. He was forced to be their forever-baby, sleeping nearby them nursery-style while I was responsible for so much in our household and exiled to my grown-up-style quarters far away. I had so frustrated them with my independent streak that they doubled down on coaching Adam to grow up in their image, priming him for life as a businessman even as they watched me devolve into

Feminazism. The pursuits my brother and I undertook when we moved to Detroit reflected this, alternately aggravating our parents—my interest in going out to punk shows—and delighting them—Adam's newfound fascination with golf.

I wasn't yet in the habit of sneaking out; I had no friends. But I began a life, like my mornings in the civics class, that my parents could not have ever imagined and that was conducted under their roof but nearly entirely in parallel, outside of their awareness.

I got my driver's license and was allowed to use one of the cars to drive to my new school, a private Catholic high school twenty minutes away, where I would attend on scholarship. Even my parents could see that the local public high school was too coarse for my sensibilities, and Dad had somehow wrangled this free ride for me, setting aside the ideology of his years of seminary training. The catalyst for Lutheranism itself was disgust for the Catholic Church and rebellion against it. October 31 is not only Halloween but also Reformation Day, and Dad had been threatening for years to dress in an alb with a rope belt and carry a hammer, emulating Martin Luther nailing his theses to the cathedral door. But this was 1994, not 1517, and I'd be attending eleventh grade under the full reign of Roman Catholic culture.

My parents must have come to the school a few times, but I don't recall it. Dad may have been sheepish about showing up in his black clerical collar amid all the Fathers and Brothers who were part of the faculty. It was also a twenty-minute drive each way, and no one thought that Mom and Dad would do this, much less regularly. I drove Dad's fifteen-year-old, new-to-us Oldsmobile Cutlass to school first thing in the morning and returned the car promptly to his church's parking lot after school. He saved parishioner visits for afternoons and evenings. I was left to navigate the Catholic kids on my own.

The academics were rigorous, and in fact the Advanced Placement classes I enrolled in demanded most all of my energy, especially that first semester. The differences between my Lutheran high school in Fort Wayne and the Catholic one outside of Detroit were vast in other ways, too. My burgeoning dedication to nonconformist culture—from Walt Whitman to L7—strained against everything and everyone at this new school. In September 1994, the first episode of *Friends* aired, and I think I was the only girl at my school not smitten with the show. In the interest of making friends, I tried to hide that I found it painfully banal, but I was terrible at concealing it, especially because I'd made this verdict without ever having seen the show. That same year, I managed to become a member of an activist group, TV-Free America, that I'd found advertised in a suburban record store. Beginning that fall, along with the *Sassy*-esque Delia's catalog, strident photocopied newsletters arrived monthly at our house. Folded and sealed with a round sticker, you could make out the skull and crossbones on a clip art TV monitor and have a pretty solid idea that the membership believed TV was for the intellectually lazy and the brainless. My parents correctly assumed that my membership was a haughty teenage judgment of their screen-soaked lifestyle.

I found blue nail polish and wore it to school, an outright pedestrian move today that seemed, in my early-'90s Catholic school, nearly Satanic.

Without consulting me, Mom and Dad set up a date for me with a teenager from the new church. "This will never happen for you if you don't work at it, Amanda. You're *sixteen*," Mom moaned. It was horrifying to her that I hadn't dated or kissed anyone yet, so she arranged this root beer get-together with a tall boy who was visibly disturbed by my vintage men's clothing and azure fingernails. I wanted desperately to tell Mom I'd kissed someone so she'd get off my back, but without a viable warm body to attach to that lie, I knew I'd get caught.

I got the idea that I wanted to ironically wear corporate branded T-shirts and had heard that companies would give you a free shirt if you asked. "Free advertising for them," Mom agreed. I wrote a letter to the address on the side of a jar of Hellmann's mayonnaise, hoping to get a T-shirt to covertly declare affection for the Smashing Pumpkins song "Mayonnaise." Hellmann's didn't respond, but several others did. I wore T-shirts touting Vlasic pickles, tubbed margarine, a chain of gas stations, and the pièce de résistance, a Reddi-Wip whipped cream shirt with an illustrated slice of pie that boldly said "Reddi for anything."

Writing on clothing was disallowed by the school dress code, and I wore these T-shirts under code-authorized button-ups with non-jean navy or khaki pants. We were allowed to wear jeans once a month if we paid a dollar to a Catholic charity, and I so vehemently opposed every part of that scenario that I was always the only kid wearing khakis those days.

I did finally make friends. All three of them were boys.

I was increasingly interested in reading and books and wanted to go back to the library to get more. I had been just twice—once in the first week we'd moved there and then again to return my books a few weeks later. At the time, Mom said she wasn't done with her quilting books yet. "How can I be expected to make a quilt in two weeks?" She laughed. Months passed and when I asked, she said, "Are you crazy? Can you imagine the late fees those crooks are going to charge me?"

Mom and Dad were firmly in their own worlds of a hospital nursing career and the head of a bustling Lutheran congregation, neither of which were mine. At night, to relax, they watched TV with the lights on so Mom could paint her nails. Adam was lost, consumed in the culture of the Lutheran school attached to the church with its half-baked sports teams and twelve-person classrooms. The togetherness we had as the Longs at that time was mostly around the perplexing features of local culture that were new to us. None of us had ever thought for more than a moment about the auto industry until Dad provided counseling for a family who'd purchased a Japanese car, only to be exiled by their factory worker siblings and cousins. The favored plant was Ford's, always with an apostrophe and *s*—never Ford. Same with Kroger's and Meijer's, a store open twenty-four hours every single day except Christmas and carrying everything from apricots to snow shovels to negligees. We drank in this new world with collective astonishment and simultaneously left one another all alone to navigate it.

FORTY-EIGHT

In 1989, when Earl lost his house thanks to Dad, I'd had no idea. Our new lives in Fort Wayne had so fully enveloped us that the crisis of Earl, the foreclosure, and the Doberman weren't even a shadow hanging over my middle school years. I was oblivious.

I wonder now if my parents whispered about their culpability at night in their bedroom, always so far away from mine. Or if they proceeded on as they did with so many other things, heads held high, with a warped story about it all being Earl's fault. If they reacted in any way, I never was witness.

In 1994, another cataclysmic event happened completely out of my view. I didn't learn about it until long after both Mom and Dad were gone, and I have no evidence that they ever discovered all of what I know now. Dad told me a portion of it during a difficult conversation we had in 2012, but I don't believe he ever knew the whole story about what happened to his son, Tim, from his first marriage.

In 1972, when Dad was unceremoniously dumped in Indianapolis by what he referred to as the Jewish Mafia, his young children were told he was dead. Clearly, his wife knew the truth. She and Dad both signed the certificate of divorce in August of that year. His children, who at the time were seven, five, and one and a half, may have later learned or suspected more, but I'm not in touch with them. I imagine they grew up believing their mother was widowed; I know that she swiftly remarried, and her new husband adopted all three of them and gave them a new last name. The youngest, Tim, almost certainly had no memories of our father.

Two days before Thanksgiving 1994, twenty-four-year-old Tim finished his classes at Miami Dade Community College and his route delivering pizzas for a local Italian restaurant. He returned to the high-rise apartment he shared with his sister—our sister—passing his pal the doorman on the way up. The doorman, nicknamed Red just like my grandfather, was a frequent visitor in the siblings' apartment. Tim and the doorman regularly hung out after Red's shift ended, eating sandwiches, drinking beer, and watching TV until three in the morning.

That night, Red asked Tim to join him in the building's meter room to see a motorcycle he was thinking of buying. Tim went up to his apartment first, then returned to the lobby of their apartment building where Red and Red's girlfriend were waiting to walk him out to the meter room. Tim was never seen alive again.

Red attended the wake. He threw dirt on Tim's casket during the service and later spent time cleaning and packing up the apartment with our sister.

In July 1995, Red was arrested. After a sordid trial, he was convicted of brutally murdering Tim and hiding the body in blankets and garbage bags, for which Red is presently serving a life sentence. Red's girlfriend ratted him out after they broke up the next summer. Until her confession, for seven months, my half brother's murder was an unsolved case.

When I first learned all of this, in 2020, I found a long news article with a mugshot of Red next to a smiling photo of Tim. His face glows—white teeth, thick brown hair. He is distinctly of my father. His photo is startlingly similar to other photos I have found from the same newspaper of Dad as a high school football star in the early '60s. I have never seen anyone, including Adam, who looks more like Dad. From what I learned from the criminal court records, Tim's personality was quite like Dad's, too.

The motive for the murder was money. Tim had saved $2,100 in cash to purchase a Jet Ski, which he planned to buy that Thanksgiving week. In a deposition from the trial, a friend remembered Red saying he knew "a kid with a lot of money" and if he could get it, he'd "never have to work and retire and live a life of splendor, riches, and travel everywhere." Red lured Tim, cash in hand, around midnight. In the meter room Tim was shot five times, three in the head, twice in the torso. According to court documents, everyone who knew Tim knew he had this money. Tim couldn't stop talking about the wad of cash in his bedroom and what he was going to do with it. My father would have behaved the very same way.

Local news reported thoroughly on the story, going into almost unimaginable detail. Red's public defender tried to discredit the girlfriend by mentioning her work as a "phone actress" for 1–900 sex lines. The lawyer also described her 1994 appearance on *The Phil Donahue Show* in which she dressed in KKK regalia and said she'd pulled her children out of school during Black History Month. She later said she did it for show. "It was an act, a performance," Red's lawyer told jurors, suggesting her propensity toward falsehood. The various documents of that time tell me how many bullets went into Tim's body, which causeway Red and his girlfriend took to dispose of the body next to a dumpster, and the fact that Tim loved in-line skating and street hockey—"typical Generation X," the reporter wrote.

I don't know whether my father knew any of these things about his son or if he knew how Tim died. In 2012, Dad tearfully told me that he'd discovered on Ancestry.com that one of his kids, Tim, was dead and had been since 1994. "One of my kids," Dad said. Not, "your half brother." Dad may have been sparing me the details, but more likely he only knew what Ancestry seemed to report at the time, a lifespan of 1970–1994.

I believe that if he'd seen these brutal details, he could not have held on to them quietly. Like his son, if Dad ever came into some cash, or some mind-boggling information, he would have been compelled to run his "motor mouth," as he called his compulsion to spin stories. Dad also had a special disdain for Phil Donahue, whom he called a *bleeding heart*.

If Dad had known of any connection, he would have again regaled me with a story he told us annually, about an encounter with Donahue in the '80s in a LaGuardia men's room. At the urinal, Dad said, "I've always wanted to have it out with Phil Donahue." According to Dad, the talk show host didn't reply.

In addition to knowing that Tim was dead, I know that Dad knew other things, much more than he ever told me and much more than the contents of the pirate's chest jewelry box whose contents I inherited. Researching their lives is my way of exploring what can be known and what will always be unknown about my parents. When I consider my own life, I see the shadow of Tim's unknown parallel life overlaid with mine like a sheet of cellophane. His life means something else, and so does mine, when they are examined together, like two colors overlapping to create a third. For every question my research answers, others emerge and multiply.

When I think about Tim, I think about the first Thanksgiving the Longs spent in our Michigan house, which was the week Tim was killed. In under six months there, our dining table had been subsumed in piles of fabric and white plastic shopping bags. We normally ate meals in front of the TV, plates on knees, undoubtedly laying the groundwork for my joining TV-Free America. On Thanksgiving, Mom had gone to Kroger and bought sixteen plastic trays of Stouffer's side dishes: mashed sweet potatoes, mushroom-souped green beans, one or two of every option in the freezer case. She roasted a turkey. The four of us sat at our extra-large dining table from Martinsville, which squeezed the limits of the modestly sized dining room here. Mom's cardboard pattern board was spread across it and bags and pinned fabric pieces were stacked on two-thirds of the surface. We found room for four plates and maybe two-thirds of the microwaved black Stouffer's trays. The turkey sat on the stove in the kitchen, and the stuffing and gravy and creamed spinach we put on the carpet by our feet. In an oblique acknowledgment of the mess, Mom suggested we dine with the lights out.

"By candlelight?" Dad and I agreed that this would add a touch of something elegant to the proceedings. We couldn't find candles. Mom turned off the dining room light and turned on a light in my bedroom around the corner instead.

"This is the same as candlelight," she told us.

FORTY-NINE

Less than a year into our Michigan lives, Mom had worked at four different nursing jobs. We were in a vastly larger metropolitan area than anywhere we'd lived before, and the options—and the higher than ever pay—were intoxicating.

"The ad says eighteen," Mom told us, shuffling the classifieds. She drove to the party store on our corner to get a *Detroit Free Press* most Sundays after church. Often, she'd circle ads that enticed her and spend the late afternoon back at the church, using the inkjet in Dad's office to print letters and resumes.

"No one would pay eighteen dollars an hour, Sandie." Dad made around $30,000 and had a hard time believing his wife could outearn him, but there it was in black and white.

Mom had worked in a few hospitals already, their locations in a ring around the city limits of Detroit, which both my parents had declared a no-go zone. "Crime," they said.

Mom bounced from RN job to RN job, seeking the highest pay rate available, quitting with little to no notice to work somewhere with slightly higher pay. Would she work afternoons and evenings for another dollar an hour? Yes. Would she work as far away as Dearborn or Bloomfield, or work with the most challenging patients on the most understaffed units? For the right price.

In the financial upheaval of the mid-'90s, Mom and Dad had closed their joint account and now each had their own haphazard financial system, with accounts at separate banks. Mom told me her National City PIN (1186) and asked me to memorize it because I'd be the only other person to know it; Dad was not allowed. They'd also agreed on a division of fiscal responsibilities. Mom would pay for our family's food and clothes. Dad would pay for everything else. Mom was always the spender and the shopper, so having her making regular purchases at the grocery store and TJ Maxx and JC Penney made sense. Dad would cover insurance, utilities, and other bills. Each would pay for their own gas, and there was no rent or mortgage. The church owned the house.

A parsonage is a home provided gratis for clergy, which we had. To sweeten that deal, Dad had pored over IRS documents to determine the maximum possible portion of his salary that the church could make a "housing allowance" meant to cover clergy's mortgage or rent payments, as well as maintenance and other household costs. More than half of his salary was designated as an untaxed "housing allowance" even though the house was also provided to us. Money matters were murky, but it felt like, with Mom's new earning potential and a "free" place to live, what could go wrong?

I have tried to determine how many different medical institutions employed Mom between 1994 and 2013. I will never know the answer to this very tangible question whose mystery is lost in thousands of paper pages—paystubs, health insurance documents, State of Michigan licensure, applications, resumes, offer letters, termination letters, human resources complaints (to Mom and from her), and other records. At least thirty hospitals, nursing homes, hospice agencies, insurance companies, and other organizations hired and paid her in those years. I can't determine the number of jobs she had any more precisely.

In 1994, when Dad spent $800 on a boxy, maroon 1984 Impala for me, it was so that I could work an after-school job he arranged for me. One church member had a family business, Lang Feed, that could use some phone-answering help. Their regular receptionist, the ironically named Joy, had broken her foot and couldn't do the filing on crutches. I was to arrive immediately after school and provide Joy a smoke break by answering the phone for fifteen minutes. When she came inside afterward, much friendlier, she set her plaster-cast foot on an open drawer of the green metal desk we shared and told me where various papers should be filed.

Joy thrust a carbon-copied yellow invoice at me. "Freight. Tall cabinet over there. Third drawer."

"Slaughterhouse, Eastern Market. Down there. Take the damn staples out first." The office space was very small, but she shouted every directive, aiming to be heard over the *thunk thunk* of the machinery and stoves in the vast back area.

Joy wanted me to get all the filing put away before our only visitor, the UPS man, came, around 4:30 in the afternoon. When the door opened, Joy sat taller in the wheeled office chair and fussed with her cardigan. "Maybe Taco needs you," she'd suggest, implying I should go to the factory floor. Taco was her generic name for any of the Latino men who worked in the back.

The smell in Lang Feed was heavy and wet, a blend of cooked and raw meat. At least weekly, the glue machine would act up, adding a burnt and artificial note to the usual organ meat aroma. I worked at Lang Feed shortly before becoming vegetarian. I was afraid to go in the back and ask "Taco" anything, so I usually stayed in the office, encroaching on Joy's coveted time with the UPS man.

The *Detroit Free Press* reported on a scene from inside Langs in 1984: "'All our meat we buy from slaughterhouses,' Lang said as he made his way around a tub of chopped kidneys headed for a second-story vat that looks like a small boiler. Inside the vat, more than a ton of dog food is cooked for 45 minutes then funneled into a filler machine with rotary pistons that squirt the murky mixture into cans." These were the scenes I was avoiding as I lingered by the file cabinets.

I kept my earnings from this job, which were paid in cash and which I used for gas money to drive to school.

FIFTY

The dream of destroying our house bit by bit never stopped. It was a kind of comfort to return overnight to this psychedelic landscape I'd made, where I could enact every demented and destructive thing I wished to do in my regular teenage life: get rid of all that weighed us down, escape.

I installed three-inch fringe along the roofline in the Impala's interior, and my new friends—the boys—called my car the hooptie. Joy's foot emerged from its cast, and I applied for a new job, waitressing at Java Joe's, an urbane coffeehouse two suburbs over.

It didn't seem like we were in the precarious financial situation we used to be in, but the equilibrium was uncomfortable. Mom was buying, buying, buying and working, working, working. Dad was learning how to be a church leader. In all of his business and leadership experience, he'd almost always been a lone wolf, answering to no one. Now he was leading a dynamic group of several hundred parishioners, helping them carry their varied burdens of sin and sadness, and shepherding them toward being a harmonious, financially sustainable congregation. He was constantly stretched thin, pulled into certain groups' allegiances or swayed by other groups' gossip. As my parents always had, Dad stood out as unusual: extra tall, quick with a semi-rude joke, a Midwestern Lutheran pastor who sprinkled in favorite phrases from Miami and Lawn-GUYland, an accent he turned on for effect now and then. In any given week, he was visiting the housebound, offering counseling sessions, attending committee meetings, marrying and burying as needed, and of course preparing a sermon and selecting music for each week's worship. "Oy vey," he'd grouse, loosening his tight, black-and-white clerical collar as he returned home. "I gotta pee like a racehorse." With the church secretary's help he was also in charge of the church finances; she was sworn to secrecy that the IRS was garnishing his wages directly from the church bank account, but she didn't take that vow as seriously as Dad hoped she would. I know Dad's life at the church was not easy, and I know that he could have been prepared for only a small fraction of what he faced. Holy Week in particular was always murder.

"Spot me," Dad said, his elbow propped on the wooden doorframe at the threshold of my bedroom. The question mark at the end of his statement was missing but implied. We'd been talking about ordering pizza. All agreed that nothing was edible or appealing in the house, and it would be a Jet's night. I handed him a $20 from my coffee can of Java Joe's tips, and he asked if I had five more. "It's usually $22 with tip."

Thursdays were traditionally days when there was no money in our home. Dad was paid every other Friday. Mom never told us when she was paid, but we understood that she didn't have any capacity or interest in paying for pizza any day of the week. Dad's cash was kept in a lidded casserole dish in the dining room. It was white with blue faux-sponge-painted geese along the side. I had half a mind to walk to the dining room and check there before handing him more of my tip money, but he was blocking the door. "I'll pay you tomorrow," he said. The scar on his cheek burned red. I handed him a ten.

Other Thursdays, Dad would sometimes come home arms aloft with a free pizza. He'd made good friends with the Chaldeans who ran one of the party stores on the corner. ("They're Middle Eastern but Christian," Dad told us, fascinated.) The Chaldeans had an ingrained reverence for the clerical collar, and if Dad ever came asking for a pizza or falafel, they must have felt spiritually compelled to offer alms to our not-really-poor clergy family.

Adam was trapped in the school attached to our church, a nearly neglected place with very few students whose academic standards were clearly lacking. Sending Adam to a different elementary school would have been tantamount to driving a Japanese car, a credibility death sentence. In 2021, I learned from archived *Free Press* clippings that one of the reasons the building and people exuded such empty sadness is that the school community was healing from a horrific child sex abuse scandal in 1977. The perpetrator was a repeat offender who had previously been fired from Lutheran schools in Missouri and Wisconsin and whose various trials stretched into the '80s. He pleaded guilty to abusing three third graders under his desk during class time and served three years in state prison; the victims were awarded $1.3 million each in 1980, with the school and principal also found negligent in a civil suit that year. The predator returned to our church and was the organist when we arrived in 1994. I have tried to determine what portions of this Dad knew, and when he knew them, but I have not succeeded.

The car, and the regular paycheck and tips I was earning, nudged me further into my own semi-adult world. Unconsciously following Mom's lead, I began working until ten on school nights several nights a week, later on weekends. I wonder if Mom hated to be at home the same way I did.

I'd bonded with my new friends over music, and we'd just begun to go to shows in Detroit at St. Andrew's Hall or the bar beneath it. My parents knew how badly I wanted to go out and see music, but they rarely allowed it. I was still sixteen. They cited crime, along with their concerns that I'd be staying out too late or not driving safely. They established some rules whose specificity strained against logic but which I took very seriously. I'd been living on Longs Island my whole life, and the stakes of defying my parents were truly unimaginable. I could not and would not disappoint them. But I would go see live music.

Rule #1: Do not drive on the freeway.

This rule was developed with an eye toward keeping me in the suburbs, outside the city of Detroit. However, Detroit and its live music and late-night parties were readily accessible via streets with stoplights; it just took longer. They were not wrong that the late '90s was a high-crime period in Detroit, and that was why it was infinitely more foolish for a lone teenage girl (no such thing as a cell phone, six dollars in the pocket of her vintage dress) to drive slowly through the city, stopping at long red lights with no one around. Twice I saw a would-be carjacker approach, but only one of those times I saw a gun.

Another easy workaround was to tell my parents, "I'm going to Scott's," whose house was twelve minutes away on the highway and sixteen minutes on the surface streets. What's four minutes? I drove the long way, then hopped in his car, or he got behind the wheel of the hooptie, and we'd go to Detroit. When asked where I'd been, I found it easy to report I'd gone to Scott's, a factual statement, and to omit that together we'd driven to Detroit to see Majesty Crush or Sonic Youth. I thought the Foo Fighters were stupid but fondly remembered my imagined-or-real Dave Grohl sighting, so I went to see them, too. I saw PJ Harvey and Fugazi. I took late shifts at Java Joe's, vacuuming and putting chairs up on tables long past closing, tooling my large car toward home only when I had no other options and always on the side streets. In the dark and quiet lateness, I'd turn the heat to its highest setting, sending a ripple through the faux-leather fringe in the car, my mixtape turned up ultraloud to compensate.

Rule #2: Do not lose your virginity.

The most confusing of all the Longs' rules, it may have been the one most important to them: preserving me. The boundary was official.

"You can never come back. It's permanent," they warned. "Don't give away something that's meant for your future husband."

But as official as it was, the line felt pliable. With only one single awkward date to my name, Mom continued to pelt me with information.

"Hand jobs are crucial," she explained, winding her way toward an out for me, purely as a technicality. "If you leave one young man with blue balls—just one time—you absolutely won't live that down." She took a breath. Her hazel eyes looked into my hazel eyes. "Permanent damage."

Could I possibly pull off the Herculean feat of being the kind of good girl who was bad enough to keep a man? In teenage agony, I covered my ears but couldn't unhear it.

Mom said, "You can be dramatic about it, but it's true." Both of my parents spent time worrying that my mannish style of no makeup, slouchy old-man pants, and cardigans would leave me lonely. Or that my strident equal-rights, TV-free, women's lib bullshit would scare off any prospects. I was bookish, aloof, and weird enough to be obliquely cool to some of my peers but hopelessly unappealing to my parents.

I once heard Dad ask Mom, "Would it kill her to come home with a hickey once in her life?"

Rule #3: Never lie.

Self-explanatory.

The back door's lock was flimsy. Even if I'd forgotten my key, I could slip in unheard with a strategic shake of the golden knob. The screen door in front of it, on the other hand, was steel and prone to loudly smacking closed. I handled it with gentlest care, easing it open and closed in a smooth, silent motion. Inside, the smell was not unlike Lang Feed—a bit wet. Our basement had flooded in a spring storm in 1995, and my parents adopted a firm position on the matter. "It's not our house," Dad explained. Neither he nor Mom would clean up the flooded area or do any repairs to prevent future water damage. The house was a parsonage, and therefore officially the church's responsibility. "If the church elders want to improve their property, they are welcome to do that," Mom huffed. Everything on the floor sat ruined, emanating mildew. The massive food store had been saved by my shelving project the summer prior, but the rest was weeping cardboard and piles of Mom's soggy, hangered, never-worn clothes. Mold crept up the cinderblock walls.

The moisture had also loosed the linoleum on the four stairs between the back door and my bedroom door. It curled upward, its adhesive barely gripping the wood stair below. On each stair there was only a single flat spot for my foot.

After midnight, I parked the Impala at the far end of our large yard, the always-loud thoroughfare masking any noise. I tiptoed up toward my room, the handrail attached to the particleboard wall in one spot, loose at two others. I was never caught. I may never have been noticed at all.

FIFTY-ONE

Mom instructed me on what to get from her car. "In the backseat, there's a Kroger bag with frozen biscuits and some shredded cheese." It was Christmas Eve 1995, and we had a new tradition of hosting some of the church leadership between the early- and late-evening services. Having finally come around to hosting guests in middle age, she took to it rabidly, making enough food for roughly seven times the number of people in attendance. Her dogged preparation was limited to food and did not include cleaning the bathroom or moving the piles of fabric and bags. The piles were invisible to her, flagrant to me. By the Christmas of my senior year in high school, it was all I could see.

In the driveway, I opened her unlocked car and tried to recall what she wanted. Only "Kroger bag" had stuck in my memory, but there were more than twenty Kroger bags. They were piled among medical supplies for her weekend traveling nurse gig. Medical forms with patients' personal and health information were stacked under bags of our household food, which were squeezed next to packs of adult diapers, syringes, and small vials of various medications. In winter in Michigan, the climate allowed for groceries to chill indefinitely in the car (never mind 48-degree sunny days or blasting the car heater when she was driving it). By December, the car grocery stash was ample. I rooted through a few—half-and-half, bagged pasta—and couldn't remember. She'd be unhappy if I brought in something different than what she wanted.

I took a few steps around the corner and called up to her. The rear kitchen window had broken over the summer, and a triangle the size of a pizza slice was open to the elements. "Mom!" She could hear me and shouted back to get the bag with the tube of biscuits. Mom's memory for some things was uncanny. I'd witness her "forgetting" monumentally important things like deadlines for the AP tests I was supposed to take at school, but her mental inventory of groceries was razor sharp. She knew the Pillsbury Grands! were in a bag with cheese and a jar of cinnamon. She could have told me the precise contents of the other bags if I'd asked.

When the window broke a few months prior, I wondered how we'd fix it. The glass had cracked and split, just over the kitchen sink, and the raw edge of the remaining glass hung ominously, a bit horror movie–like as our portal to view the backyard.

"It's not our house," Dad said smugly when I'd asked. He said this with a wrinkled expression, conveying his annoyance at being asked, and at the situation. "It's not our house, and I won't fix it. St. John's should." Like the curled vinyl on the rear stairs, the broken window was part of the decade-long standoff between the church—whose position was that we got a free house and a mostly tax-free salary meant to repair and maintain the house—and Dad—whose position was that we didn't own the house and were being robbed of prospective equity and therefore should not be responsible for any repairs.

Neither side gave in. The house aged and deteriorated around us.

To remedy the triangle of air allowing us to commune directly with the outdoors at all times, we turned up the air-conditioning in summer, the heat in winter. They were never shy about cranking it down to 60 or so, and if the AC had to work a little harder to combat the summer air roaring into the kitchen, so be it. The same was true of the furnace, which they asked to put in a little more effort to offset the icy winter winds that flew through the kitchen.

Mom banged around between the stove and countertops, filling Crock-Pots with little meatballs, melting Velveeta for a dip. I couldn't face the piles, but I had a sense of shame about guests seeing our house in its natural state. I set to work on the bathroom. The trick, always, was to find a way to clean without moving all of Mom's stuff. You couldn't. There was nowhere else to put it, but also, moving her stuff was the surest way to tap into a primal rage she concealed most of the time. On other occasions, in frustration, I'd find an empty cardboard box and wipe my arm across the vanity in that bathroom, packing up dozens of nail polish bottles and scented soaps and conditioners. I liked to see the counter's surface sometimes, feel a moment of serenity in that flat, empty surface.

The consequences of such a move were never worthwhile in the end. So, while she popped open her biscuits, a spoon's edge pressed tight to the foil, I sprayed 409 in the bathroom sink and wiped at the toothpaste blobs in it. I ran the vacuum over the small area of the living room that didn't have furniture or piles of bags in it. I left the nail polish on the bathroom counter, and the towels on the floor, where Mom wanted them.

Everyone noticed the piles no matter how much I tried to prepare the house. I often overheard church members talking about our messes between early and late service.

The evening's guests included the choir director and its members, the head elder, various other church workers and musicians, including the organist who was the perpetrator in the sexual abuse case at the school in 1977 and had served three years' prison time for his crimes with children.

The next morning, my final "childhood" Christmas, we opened gifts for hours and ate Mom's special peach and sausage and pancake bake, as we did every year. My snobby music and fashion tastes must have intimidated Mom in her pursuit of fitting gifts for me. Midmorning, in front of my brother, dad, and mom, I unwrapped a vibrator, which Mom had tucked under the tree among the other gifts.

"Let me know if you want help figuring out how to use it," she said.

FIFTY-TWO

"Martha," Mom called to me. Then louder, more sharply, "Martha!" I couldn't hear her over the vacuum cleaner and finally turned it off when I saw her frantic waving. "Are you working at Java's tonight?"

I was on a quick housekeeping and homework mission for a few hours between school and work, and then, yes, I was heading to the coffeehouse. In 1995, Ms. Stewart was a fifty-four-year-old media mogul whose empire was built on home-keeping ideals. I was a high school student who had taken a vow to only wear my electric-blue Doc Martens for the entire '95–'96 school year and who regularly wrote fragmented, anguished poetry and mailed it to a pirate radio station I'd discovered. To Mom, we were basically the same.

She wanted a dinner plan, as Dad would be out all afternoon. After officiating a number of church members' funerals at a parlor down the street, he'd gotten to be pals with the funeral directors, who tossed him work whenever someone died and was without a spiritual leader. "The unchurched," Dad called them. Most clergy had qualms about this, or busy schedules, but Dad told the brothers who ran the funeral home, "Call me anytime." They did. His usual fee for officiating was $100, but the unchurched were charged $125 with a finder's fee going to the brothers, who had our landline on speed dial.

I told Mom I'd eat a sandwich at Java Joe's and she and Adam could get Arby's. I'd sworn off meat in much the same way I'd sworn off television. I was young enough to be beholden to others' schedules and meals, so I occasionally ate meat my junior year of high school, just like I saw TV now and then, when it was unavoidable at home or when my friends wanted to watch Monty Python VHS tapes. Like the TV thing, there was a note of judgment and rebellion in vegetarianism, too. By the middle of my senior year, I ate at home infrequently and was 98 percent vegetarian, flummoxing my parents.

When he realized I was serious about this no-meat thing, Dad smiled and said, "Do what you like. Have fun. This will last until some hunk asks you to make him a steak, and your resolve will CRUMBLE." He laughed. "You will never find a man that can live like that," Dad predicted. "If you're not a Democrat when you're young, you don't have a heart. And if you're not a Republican by the time you're thirty, you don't have a brain. Same thing!" He bumped my shoulder. "Let's see."

At Java Joe's, much like at Lollapalooza, I found vegetarian food along with a whole cast of offbeat people who felt a lot more like who I wanted to be than the Longs did. Tino worked at the airport handling luggage all day, and all evening he drank black coffee and smoked Camels and talked about punk music with us. Ami was a raver who wore glitter eye shadow, impossibly tall platform shoes, and a septum piercing. There was a poet who wrote in a leather journal and drank Darjeeling by the pot. A frustrated cartoonist. A frustrated actress. A singer-songwriter with an artificial leg. Often, a harmless gang of local pseudo-punks would walk out on their bill or heckle the folksinger who played some Friday nights. They wore navy mechanics' jackets bedazzled with safety pins and called themselves the Pukes.

After all the pressure I'd felt to pair up with a boy, to be kissed, to be attached to someone and validated, I finally found someone at Java Joe's. Gilbert—the manager—was an artist, ten years older than me, with hair longer than mine and a house of his own in Dearborn. During lulls, Gil would draw pictures of me on the backs of concert fliers at the cash register, slipping them onto my tray with customers' raspberry iced teas and our signature drink, the Crunchy Frog. I liked how he smiled at unexpected moments and how easily he would stand at the counter and draw with confidence, unembarrassed.

Gil drew a cartoon version of me winking, and he tucked it under a lavash sandwich I was carrying to a table of four tortured-looking high school students debating a Jean-Paul Sartre play. An ice-cold wind rushed into Java Joe's ahead of three bombastic young men in blue jackets, their hair gelled upward haphazardly.

"No, no, no." Gil tightened his apron as he came from behind the counter to chase them out.

"You can't kick us out," one said.

"It's a free country," the tall one said.

I put the sandwich and the coffees on the table I was serving, careful to hang on to Gil's Sharpie-drawn picture.

"Fine," Gil said. "But Pukes pay first." He wasn't about to have the Pukes pull their usual move. He demanded a $20 deposit before letting them past the threshold. Everyone in the café quieted their conversations and lowered their ashy cigarettes, waiting to see what this three Pukes versus one coffeehouse manager confrontation would produce.

"Empty your pockets," he instructed.

The Pukes were somehow young or naïve enough to comply. For a gang, they weren't that tough. Gil was twenty-seven and wearing an apron, which lent authority to the situation. Between them, the three Pukes had under a dollar in coins and were therefore denied entry. "Cheapest thing is black coffee for a dollar, which you can't afford," Gil told them. He shuffled them out into the winter night and locked the door behind them, declaring the rest of the night Puke-free and making Java Joe's a private party cave for the rest of us who would stay until closing time. No one would go in or out the rest of the evening. The Elastica CD on the sound system behind the counter was turned up a click. *Is it just that I'm much too much for you?* The mood was jubilant.

At the next table, I wrote their drink choices on my order pad and then on Gil's drawing I wrote, "I need your help in mop room." I delivered both slips of paper to the counter.

A few minutes later, he and I were alone in the fluorescently lit janitorial closet. At seventeen, I had spent many years passively being dragged here and there by my parents' choices and had rarely seen an opportunity to make a choice of my own. Asserting myself felt both dangerous and long overdue. I considered inventing a mop- or broom-related question for Gil, but my head had gone fuzzy quiet, despite the increasingly loud, Puke-free party just outside the door. Even over a blaring version of Portishead's "Glory Box" now playing in the café, we both heard a glass shatter on the tile floor around the corner. Neither of us moved toward the kitchen. Our uniform was jeans with a men's dress shirt and thrift-store necktie. Gil reached for the bottom of my tie and gently pulled. I thought *I'm finally kissing someone and Mom will get off my back*. I anticipated the relief of ending a conversation I'd been having with her for a decade about why no boys ever seemed to want me.

I smelled Gil's hair, felt his hands on each of my shoulders. His lips trembled as they approached mine. I forgot about my mother.

"How was work?" Mom asked the next morning, performing a Jenga-style operation on our fridge, which was jammed. She was trying to find eggs for breakfast. I reminded her that we kept eggs on the counter now, to save space. Midway through my junior year, I'd taken up the ad hoc role of household manager in Taylor. I made fewer meals than I'd made in Fort Wayne, but I did more of the cleaning than anyone else, was the authority on the family schedule, and the go-to person when anyone had a question like "Why are the eggs not in the fridge?"

The night before was rich with stories, but I couldn't find the words. Mom might have liked the Pukes story. She really would have liked to know about the kiss even if she would have disapproved of the man behind it. I didn't answer her.

"Where is the strip steak?" She looked at me as if I would know. Mom had a pack of bacon in her armpit and a tub of cottage cheese in her hand. "For dinner, I was going to defrost it." Since I'd become a vegetarian, my parents had increased their meat consumption to compensate. Most days they found a way to eat an extra portion in my honor.

Dad walked in, dressed in his penguin getup. "I couldn't fit the ice cream back in there last night so I moved the steak to the outdoor freezer," he told us. The "outdoor freezer" was a seasonal phenomenon. When the fridge/freezer/cars were full, and when it was winter, they would store cold food on top of the air-conditioning unit by the back door, under my bedroom window. Enter our house in winter and you were likely to find the surface of the AC covered in leftovers and groceries: a partially eaten Jell-O salad with foil over it, a jug of milk, the inner basin of the Crock-Pot that had cooked a chicken and potato dish a few nights ago.

Dad marched down the steps to retrieve the steak, but we only heard "Goddamn it. Those no-good crooks." We had a problem with the outdoor freezer. Down-on-their-luck locals had discovered our food storage habit and apparently came by in the night. Dad insisted it was "some homeless guy." It had already been established that packaged meat was the first to be nabbed. Other times, we could tell that someone had come by in a shopping mindset but had turned their nose up at what was on offer. We'd find containers shifted around, Saran Wrap peeled back.

In the '90s, when I knew no other way to live than the way I had lived on Longs Island for all those years, I did not ask myself or my parents these questions: *Is the food still good when it sits outside all day and the afternoon temperature is warm? Do people ever eat bites out of the food and then leave the rest? Do animals poke their snouts into our leftovers? And should we find it dangerous that "some homeless guy" was food shopping just below my first-floor bedroom window?*

I stood at the kitchen door, unable to focus on Mom and her questions. I was remembering Gil's hands on my shoulders. One of his hands had slipped inside my shirt while his thumb gently worked a spot on my collarbone, under my bra's elastic strap. Several hours later, I could still feel the pressure of the thumb, the scratchy sensation of my shirt returning to the skin on my shoulder when he finally pulled his hand away.

Mom rolled her eyes at how mad Dad was getting. "I'll just go to Kroger," she shouted down to him, regarding the steak. "How was work? You never answered." She looked at me, wearing scrubs, getting ready for a hospital day.

"Fine," I told her. Work was fine.

FIFTY-THREE

My days were numbered. Senior year was almost over. I'd gotten into a Lutheran college in Chicago, the perfect balance between getting far away from the Longs and remaining in the orbit of the church and the world I'd come to know. Plus, PKs got $1,000 off tuition.

Like all of my parents' financial decisions, this one, to take on $14,000 per year in tuition because we were getting $1,000 off, did not add up. I was so unaware that I didn't participate at all in the FAFSA paperwork and all that my parents did to secure loans and grants so I could attend. Financially, I was very inexperienced. I knew only that the coffee can on my radiator where I'd been keeping Java Joe's tips had a little more than $800 in it, my freshman year spending money.

I was in the kitchen looking for a snack on the counter when the phone rang. By now, Dad had used electrical tape to attach part of a garbage bag to the broken window. I stretched the coiled cord and answered. "Privacy Manager has identified a caller for you," a robotic voice announced. To avoid what Dad called "lowlife bill collectors," we had this service installed on our phone that provided a caller ID function—unheard of among my friends' parents then—and a first step for any caller: instructions to announce yourself and your intentions before the Longs would entertain the idea of speaking to you. Debt collectors were persistent and unscrupulous. My parents' debts were many. By now, any mail that looked anything like a bill was tossed in the kitchen garbage can unopened. You'd find a stack of white envelopes under the remnants of someone's sloppy joe sandwich or cracked eggshells or a plastic cheese wrapper. The calls were endless.

For this reason, Adam simply never answered the phone. It would ring and ring on the kitchen wall, and Adam rarely seemed to register it as an interruption to the show or sports game he had on. My parents answered around half the time. If I was home, I always picked up.

I believe that all the calls coming into the house were legitimate requests for expenses my parents had accrued and never paid. Some people may have dealt with the problem by beginning to pay off the bills. Instead, the Longs paid a monthly fee for these phone blockers, which got everyone at St. John's clucking with gossip, and then they further paid for a second unlisted phone line to be installed in my bedroom. There was a profound fear that perhaps a male classmate of mine would phone me to ask for a date and be discouraged by the Privacy Manager robot voice. "We can't let that happen," Dad told me.

"Funeral home," I said, passing the phone to Dad, who already had a hundred-dollar bill in his eyes.

"YELL-o," he said cheerfully.

The summer before departing for college, I had two missions to accomplish: dealing with my wisdom teeth, which had to be removed, and consummating a yearslong flirtation with one of my three male high school friends. Having gained a little kissing confidence at Java Joe's and realizing that I was about to dash off into the wide world, I wanted to attempt something romantic with someone my own age. Subconsciously, I think I also wanted something to tether me to home, to Michigan. I'd spent so long plotting my escape from the Longs that it was terrifying to consider that in just a few weeks I'd be out from under the strictures they'd built for me, away from the mess. On my own.

It occurred to me at some point that summer of 1996 when I turned eighteen that my parents, like me, were adults. Why hadn't I considered this before? Why had I spent so much time worrying about their money problems? Cooking their dinners? Vacuuming their floors? Trying to make things right? A little mantra began to click into my thoughts. *It's not my problem*, I said in my head. It was a riff, and I began experimenting with it. Spoiled food outside? Black mold infesting our basement for years? *These are not actually my responsibility*, I reminded myself. Perpetually unpaid bills, unclean house? *These are obligations my parents—two adults— have. I don't have to fix it. In fact, I can't.*

The freedom of starting to articulate these thoughts in my head was intoxicating. *They got themselves into this mess. I guess they'll have to find a way out.* The only tug on my heart was Adam. Five years younger than me, he'd be stuck that many more years in their bizarro world, and I hated that he had no other choice. At the same time, I couldn't have lasted another day myself.

I accomplished mission number one easily—making a move on my friend on his mom's couch during an *X-Files* episode. After slipping up the back stairs late that night, I caught sight of a yellow-purple mark on my neck. *There*, I thought. *Six more weeks left living in this house and I finally have a hickey.* I didn't bother covering it the next morning. Dad saw it and was livid.

He had been building a bookshelf in the living room and threw a wrench at the wall when he saw the mottled bruises on my neck. I reminded him, in the self-righteous tone only available to someone who has just turned eighteen and has spent several hours necking the night before, that he'd *wanted* me to have a boyfriend. He'd even wanted me to have a hickey! He was too mad to answer me, but I heard him mutter as I left, "I never said you should be slutty."

Having given my parents exactly what I thought they wanted and still fallen short, I was in a tough spot for the rest of the summer, especially because my wisdom teeth still needed to come out. Bitterly angry at me though he was, Dad had a plan.

Throughout the course of his life, Dad hated to pay for anything. He was especially loath to pay for services. Goods, he could understand. But the use of one's professional skills or a particular facility? Why should he have to pay for something like dry cleaning, a car wash, or snow shoveling? It was a fascinating perspective given his funereal side hustle in which he was paid for his own time and expertise. It wasn't hard to talk him into buying a new TV or ordering in Pizza Hut. But the bills he always neglected were for the intangibles: parking tickets, plumbing, dental work.

Sometime in 1995, a dentist named Dr. Alan Allen walked into Dad's office in need of counseling for a personal and spiritual matter. It was complicated, but Dr. Allen had nowhere else to go, and he'd so often passed the gothic-looking church in the middle of fast-food land and he wondered if the pastor there could lend an ear. Dad never refused anyone. They sat together and talked and prayed, and at the end of the session, Dr. Allen asked, "How much?" And Dad, perhaps lacking peers or non-church friends, suggested they barter instead.

"The next time I need my teeth cleaned, how about I come by?" Dad put forth. "And maybe we play a round of golf in the meantime." They shook on it.

Dad and Alan, as he called him, became friends, a salvation for my very social Dad who really didn't have other friends in that era of our lives. He knew many people at church but was their pastor, not their friend. He didn't keep in touch with anyone from our previous lives. Dad and Adam had been getting their teeth cleaned gratis at Dr. Allen's office for a year and a half. Mom hated dentists so never went. They didn't make an appointment for me because they said I was so young it didn't matter. Then why did Adam go? This was Longs' logic on full display.

Dr. Allen agreed to see me regarding the wisdom teeth. He was a dentist, not an oral surgeon, but who's keeping score? Painfully, four teeth were extracted from my mouth, stitches were sewn, and I was sent home in Dad's care with a bottle of Vicodin. Dad took mercy on me and said he'd make me eggs mixed with toast or coffeebread, whatever I wanted. My mouth throbbed and I couldn't even speak an answer. I pulled out a box of Cream of Wheat and handed it to him. Ten minutes later, Dad cleared the sewing things from a spot at the table and put in front of me a low, wide bowl of hot cereal, swimming in half-and-half and white sugar. I was starving, having fasted the night and morning before the tooth-pulling. I sat in front of it and when my numb mouth opened, several tablespoons of blood splashed into the all-white bowl. No eating. At least until I was more healed.

I spent two days on the couch, consuming Vicodin and not much else. My mouth continued to ooze blood. Having never had my wisdom teeth pulled, it was hard to say if "excruciating" was the norm, but I figured it must be. Near the end of day two, I could no longer pretend I was any version of okay. "Take me to Alan," I grumbled through bloody gauze.

"You should really call him Dr. Allen. I mean, *I* call him Alan . . ." Dad explained. I put my shoes on and walked to the car without looking to see if he'd follow me.

Dr. Allen was seeing someone else when we arrived, so the dental assistants agreed to examine me and see what was happening and why I felt so much worse this long after a routine procedure. Tentatively, I lowered my jaw to let them look.

"Shelly, come look at this," the woman in floral scrubs said.

Shelly got a penlight and approached. "Oh my god," she said.

"Oh my GOD," floral scrubs said.

"It's sewn to her cheek," Shelly said. They exchanged several looks communicating the horrifying crimes that had been committed inside my mouth by Dr. Allen, who seemed to have stitched my gums to my inner cheek in at least two spots.

Shelly *snip snipped* a thread, and I felt an immediate release of the painful pressure that I'd had the last few days. My mouth was pulp. I was deeply unlikely to be giving or receiving hickeys in the coming days, but I was going to college 280 miles away in less than two weeks.

PART FIVE

Chicago, Illinois

Milwaukee, Wisconsin

Ann Arbor and Suburban Detroit, Michigan

1996 to 2005

FIFTY-FOUR

Escaping Longs Island was a fantasy scenario so deeply embedded in my psyche by now that actually doing it should have felt triumphant. Instead, it took a little time to sink in. Who was I if not Amanda Long?

The dreams stopped. Having more or less the same dream—of obliterating my parents' house and all their possessions—at least once weekly for eight years or so, it felt uncomfortably sudden when this very specific dream disappeared from my life. My dorm room sleep was so thick and full that my clock radio alarm at maximum volume didn't wake me at all the first week. The annoyed other women on the fourth floor did, pounding on my door, then opening it and shaking me. *Can't you hear your alarm? We can.* Having been released into independence, I was sleeping with abandon.

I lived with abandon, too.

Chicago in 1996 offered me so much of what I'd always wanted, alongside things I never dared to want until I found them, a short El ride away from my dorm. I scoured *The Reader* for live music to see, weird films scheduled for a single screening in a crusty art theater, plays performed in basements. For a $3 roundtrip, I rode the train into the city, memorizing the colored web of lines on the CTA map and comparing it to the places I longed to go. If the green line could take me there, I went. I ate the spiciest Thai noodles. I discovered tostadas in Pilsen and Vietnamese lemongrass broth in Lincoln Park. I drank black coffee on overstuffed, ratty couches where there were free refills and 11:00 p.m. poetry recitations. I paid the student rate, or went on the free day, at the Art Institute and other museums. At the UIC library I saw Stuart Dybek read "Pet Milk," a story whose opening image reminded me of the way Dad's dad made coffeebread. In Boystown, I found thrift stores with outrageous vintage fashions and incredible lamps and ashtrays and coffee tables I had nowhere to store and could not afford. I browsed records and chapbooks in Wicker Park and sat for hours in Earwax Café, reading Rick Bass short stories and starting conversations with other earnest young people. No one had a cell phone to distract them. Greek diners were open twenty-four hours, and after classes and homework were complete on campus, I'd plunk myself in a diner booth with a cinnamony cup of rice pudding with raisins, a bottomless coffee, and my notebook. I'd draw and write until 3:00 a.m. before making my way home on the El to tuck in for a few hours before my alarm buzzed for my 8:00 a.m. class (Philosophy: A Primer). At my roommate's request, the alarm was now set to buzz—not radio—and was tucked into the covers by my pillow—not on the shelf beside it. I may have never been happier.

Three times in my life I have been flooded with a singular glorious feeling, an exhilarating uncertainty in which the eager question interrupting every other thought and breath is: *What will happen next?* Not knowing gave me life. This may be ham-fistedly described as "hope" or "optimism," but I experienced it much more deeply, a severance with the way I used to live and an outrageous leap into whatever is next. I had lived eighteen years locked in the Longs' ways, unable to control very much at all about how I lived. I felt ashamed of how my parents kept their house, how they treated other people. I felt envious of people whose parents were standard-issue Midwesterners with nothing to hide. I looked over my shoulder constantly, knowing that if my parents were not caught for their misdeeds and held to account, I would be. Now I'd found an all-new place where their influence was absent. I could imagine something else ahead.

My dorm room had an ecru, two-line phone, where we regularly received voicemails with campus instructions. ("Attention students. The cafeteria will close one hour early on Halloween night.") I received voicemails from my boyfriend—the high school friend who had provided my hickeys and was attending college in Kalamazoo. Long distance was expensive, so we limited calls and stuck to letters and voicemails delivered when the other person was known to not be home. My parents called the landline regularly. They missed me. Oddly, I reciprocated this feeling, even in my haze of furious and beautiful independence.

On September 23, 1996, I wrote to Mom, "NEWS: I just got a message that the school newspaper is assigning me the new music reviews which entitles me to 3 new free CDs per month from brand new (or new to the corporate world) artists from SONY, free music posters, and discounted concert tickets, all under the scenario of my being a college journalist. Does anything sound more perfect for me? I love & miss everybody. See you/talk to you/e-mail you soon."

In an October letter, I reported, "I am seeing your e-mail messages, which is good." As far as I can tell, I was writing letters home, Mom and Dad were sending occasional emails whose green letters on a black screen I saw on periodic visits to the computer lab, and Mom was sending me greeting cards. I have crates of letters I saved from friends writing me in those years. I can't find any letters from my parents, just a few cards "To the World's Best Daughter" and "I Miss You, Daughter" that were mailed to my campus PO box and signed by Mom.

In a September 30, 1996, letter I wrote, "Dear Family, Here is a copy of <u>my first real printed in a newspaper article</u>." The byline read "Amanda Long, A&E Correspondent."

"Finally!" Mom said. She'd been trying me for a few days, but my days in college were always so full. I tugged the coiled cord across the carpet to my twin bed. Classes, assignments, and friends I'd made on campus consumed much of my daytimes. I found that many of my new friends were happiest inside the bubble of our Lutheran college. I liked it fine, but after sharing a food-service dinner with my friends, they most often wanted to do something like take pillows and blankets to the campus screening of *Gremlins* in the gym, and I wanted to fly into the night and discover something or someone new. I was indeed rarely reachable on my phone.

I told Mom about all I'd been doing—a Degas exhibition at the Art Institute of Chicago and lunch of pilfered cafeteria bread and oranges at Buckingham Fountain, Sebadoh at the Vic.

"Who went with you?" Mom asked. She had made it clear I should dump Mr. Kalamazoo soon and take up with a Lutheran boy, which I had not gotten around to doing.

When I admitted that both of these activities were undertaken alone—in fact, in glorious self-sovereignty—she was disappointed. "But you should make friends. You can't be all alone." Now that the dating pressure coming from Mom had been released, the marriage and children pressure had begun.

I changed the subject. The rush of good feelings my new Chicago life gave me could scarcely be dampened, but Mom knew precisely how. She failed to understand that I did have friends, and I was making friends, out in the wide world that demanded I explore it. But she somehow needed to lecture me about being a loner, a sort of loser without friends or a real romance. Mr. Kalamazoo was faulted for being raised Catholic, lacking ambition, playing guitar in a noise-rock band, and most of all for skipping the courtship phase and blurring a friendship into a romance. To Mom, this didn't count.

Mom and I agreed to talk next weekend. I'd plan to be home Sunday afternoon and they could all call me. I missed Adam, too.

FIFTY-FIVE

"Amanda!" I shouted into the phone. I'd said my name three times now, but Privacy Manager was blocking my call home. "State your name," a robot said again. I hung up.

At my desk, I made Adam a card and wrote a short letter. He was in high school now. I felt sad for him that he was alone in our parents' house. I wondered if he felt reluctant, as I had, to bring friends home. I had no words to explain why the house I lived in was stacked and stuffed with bags of food and piles of clothing and fabric and hundreds of bottles of shampoo. Two of my three best high school friends report being in my house a total of twice in the two years we were schoolmates.

The last time Dad had reached me on the phone he was home alone and took the opportunity to tell me two things: "Mom has a new job, and Adam is a homosexual."

Mom always had a new job. She was working at different hospitals, nursing homes, and other medical facilities and institutions all the time. Sometimes she was chasing better pay or hours when she switched. Sometimes, she'd have a dustup with another nurse or supervisor and was either asked to leave or passively not scheduled for any hours, an uncomfortable but clear message from HR. The second news item surprised me.

"He's not gay, Dad." I hadn't been gone *that* long, and in my new life I was beginning to know many more gay men than I'd ever known before. My brother was not gay.

Dad protested, saying he wasn't certain but was feeling increasingly sure. His evidence involved the fact that Adam played video games on our shared desktop computer in the family room and had not had a serious girlfriend. He was thirteen. Even though I was unable to see then that Mom was projecting all of her own fears and insecurities onto me, it was dead obvious that Dad was simply terrified of the prospect of gayness in Adam. He had nothing to go on, and he was wrong.

I was sure that Adam was not secretly gay, but I did worry he was lonely. I had precious few updates on what was actually happening back on Longs Island, and Mom and Dad had proven to be unreliable narrators. In researching them for this project twenty-five years later, it's incredible to me how small an imprint they left on the world in those years, how little there may have been to know. In Martinsville, some of their most mundane moves were documented in the *Reporter*. Nary a *Detroit Free Press* or other media mention has revealed a clue of their public life in the late '90s.

Now that I was a first-year college student, it was clearer to me than ever before: these two were adults. As grown people—who had, by the way, done tons of responsible-seeming things like get married, hold jobs, and procreate—they simply had to be aware of the consequences of their actions. Once I let go of the idea that their responsibilities were mine or that the results of their actions would be mine to clean up or solve or answer for, I relaxed a bit. I felt silly for trying to fix their problems or help them. I felt glad that I could simply love them and live my life and write off their quirks (from homophobic alarmism to Mom's career circus) as quirks.

Dad had agreed to pick me up on the Wednesday before Thanksgiving at a Chili's parking lot near an interstate exchange in Ann Arbor. An upperclassman from Lansing was driving me most of the way home for my first visit. In the rainy dark, we sketched in our plans for riding back to Chicago together Sunday, and I switched into Dad's car. I was filled with stories from my time away, bursting to tell him about my new gig writing music reviews for the school newspaper, my student worker job at the on-campus video producer, my truly fascinating classes and of course, my exploits in the city. But Dad fell into our old habits from the old days. He drove and talked; I listened. He kept talking.

"Can you believe it?" Dad turned to me in the car thirty minutes into a soliloquy, waiting for me to agree, to disbelieve. I hadn't been closely following, but he was regaling me with stories of his church members and their interpersonal dramas, their backstabbing between committee meetings, the little details of his life that I'd missed.

We walked in the back door, passing the AC unit, stacked with half-filled CorningWare pots of leftovers. The back stairs' linoleum curled up to greet me. Just like home.

Mom hugged me hard. Her eyes were damp, sad and happy at the same time. I squeezed her back, my chin atop her head. I'd been taller than Mom for years, but it was disorienting to feel bigger than her in this moment when I'd missed her so deeply. Adam and I caught up for a minute, but it was late. We all went to bed.

In the morning I saw my room, perhaps in the way my high school friends would have seen it, as a stranger. The Hole and R.E.M. posters. The teal phone—my parents were still paying for the second line. The backyard view of the food storage/air-conditioning unit and side yard view of a massive maple tree. Mixtapes I deemed B-list and hadn't packed for college. On the top of my tall chest, emblazoned with dusky roses from Mom's North Carolina furniture shopping spree a decade earlier, was a neat stack of envelopes.

Several window envelopes with my name in dot-matrix printer type on them and my college's logo top left. An illustrated letter from Gilbert. The new TV-Free America brochure. I returned under the covers to read Gil's letter and then tucked it in a deep part of my suitcase. The rest of the stack I carried across the hall to the kitchen.

"Happy Thanksgiving," I told Mom. She was portioning cereal into bowls, and I saw no sign whatsoever of frozen Stouffer's trays, a turkey, or anything else holiday-esque.

"You're old enough now that we can go to a restaurant for Thanksgiving," she told me before I could ask. "Okay, Martha?" She had been working, hard, and she didn't want to be judged. I did not judge. She still had to work some of the weekend and understandably it just wasn't feasible to cook a holiday meal. I surveyed the scene and wondered if anyone even could have cooked in there. The piles were stacked higher than I'd ever seen. On one twelve-inch section of the counter, a bag of dinner rolls was on top of a once-frozen pizza was on top of a stack of clean and folded dishtowels was on top of a bag of ziti was on top of a flat of twenty-four eggs. The rest of the counter was more of the same.

"Cereal or eggs?" Mom offered, gesturing toward a carton of eggs on top of the fridge. I didn't know if those were newer or older than the eggs on the counter. An open bag of white bread was a chartreuse sponge at one end, halfway given over to mold, the other half designated for breakfast, The milk was outside.

I took my bowl of dry cereal toward the dining and living rooms, and the house—fully alive with everything in it—came to greet me. When I lived in the house, I was in constant conflict with Mom. ("Martha, where did you put those eggs? They were perfectly fine." "Mom, just use up ONE of the bottles in the bathroom and throw it away. We'll have more room to stand in the shower.") The harmony of my leaving came with the consequence of utter disrepair in this house. And I'd only been gone two and a half months.

I bit my tongue. I could talk to her about this, or I could just fix it. I was born to fix this. I'd clean up before returning to school. "Mom, this mail is for you." I handed her the college envelopes between bites of dry Raisin Bran.

"It's yours." She rolled her eyes. "I didn't sign up for a club that wants to destroy televisions."

"No, these." I pulled the envelopes out and told her they couldn't be grades yet. It was too early in the term. "They're financial papers, I think."

Mom reminded me that they'd taken care of it all with grants and loans. I'd had no understanding of FAFSA or anything else, and I'd let them take on all of that during the application process. There was nothing we needed to do, and nothing we could learn from these financial aid office papers, she said. Mom wouldn't take them or open them. "They're yours anyway."

The Friday after Thanksgiving, Mom told me to keep out of the kitchen. She was at work on a surprise. Fine by me. I was spending the afternoon deep cleaning the bathroom, living room, and dining room. Trash: discarded. Piles: consolidated. I was unsuccessful in getting Mom to discard the moldy bread loaf ("Half is still just fine") but chalked that up to a minor loss in the battle, not the war. I stacked Mom's tower of public library books on quilting out of sight beneath the dining table. ("We own them now," she'd rationalized. "Once you owe that much in fines, you might as well just say they're yours now.") Wood surfaces were Pledged, glass surfaces were Windexed, and every inch of the moldy and hairy bathroom was Fantastiked.

"Don't work so hard!" Mom cried from around the corner. I could smell simmering onions on the stove. "It's your vacation. Rest."

I didn't mind. I felt useful. It was clear my parents could not do this and that I could. I didn't know why. I also had no cleaning supplies at school, or really any use for them living in a dorm with housekeepers. Embracing my true Martha nature, I enjoyed the satisfaction of wiping things clean. Mom joked that I'd get more use of her cleaning supplies than she would, even though I lived two states away.

When I finished, the house was cluttered but almost unrecognizably improved. The smell—of our dog, the moldy basement aroma—had been replaced with the pungent sting of the spray disinfectants I'd showered around the house. Some surfaces were clear.

"Dinner!" Mom called out. She'd spent a very long time pulling together this special meal for me. She did love to cook, but the majority of her cooking involved mixes and cans, the convenience foods she associated with affluence. It was exceedingly rare for her to prepare a from-scratch meal like this, and she presented it to me with reverence and pomp, as a declaration of her love.

Curried chicken from the *Better Homes & Gardens New Cook Book*.

I'd never tasted it, but this recipe was lore in our family. It called for ingredients far outside the range of our usuals—namely coconut milk and golden raisins. Mom talked about this recipe whenever she reminisced about her own early college days, when she flew off to New York City to study fashion design at Pratt, leaving ignoble Martinsville behind. This creamy, yellow-gold sauce over white rice was sophistication to her, the taste of Brooklyn, 1969.

"Um." I sat for a moment, hating the idea of disappointing her, hurting her. I hated myself for a moment, wishing I could be more of who she wanted. "I'm a vegetarian." Mom had sat across from me at the restaurant Thanksgiving meal yesterday, where I ordered a turkey-free plate. She'd been ribbing me about my weirdo diet for years now. She knew. But she didn't know.

Mom was too deep in denial to be crushed. She told me that it was my favorite dish. (I'd never eaten it before.) She reminded me how difficult it was to find golden raisins, which she'd visited several stores to procure. (Surely true.) She explained that international foods were the same as vegetarian foods. "You love this," she concluded. "You always have."

Dad and I both stood at the stove with her for this Exegesis of Chicken Curry. He and I exchanged a glance and silently resolved together to make it work. We loved Mom. Maybe she was working too hard or was confused, but she very plainly had conflated our two identities and spent all day pouring her soul into this loving gesture for me, all in the name of this midcentury meal that *she* loved.

Sandie was the independent-minded, Beatles-loving, fashionable feminist of Martinsville who'd gone off to the big city to study art and eat chicken curry, confounding her parents.

Amanda was the independent-minded, punk-loving, vintage-clothing-wearing feminist of the Detroit suburbs who'd gone off to the big city to study journalism and eat international foods, confounding her parents.

In our high school senior portraits, taken in 1969 and 1996, we are nearly indistinguishable.

Dad and I were in the kitchen of our messy house, November air blowing in through the broken window, but Mom had found herself in another world. He and I committed to ride along on her spaceship, at least for the evening.

I ate the gravy and the raisins and the rice and slipped the pieces of meat on my plate to the dog. "It's really delicious, Mom."

Later that night, on Mr. Kalamazoo's parents' couch, I tried to explain why I needed to raid their fridge but couldn't quite articulate why I was hungry. I ate some cheese. We watched *The X-Files*. He gave me two vintage LPs with songs he said made him think of me. The magic of this gift was not in the records but in the flash-forward I had, of me in my Chicago dorm some weeks later, spinning these records of songs I'd never heard, trying to discern how he saw me, who I was.

FIFTY-SIX

The records didn't fit in my luggage, and when Mom offered to ship them the next day, I thought that was a great plan. I would be riding back to Chicago in a small Jeep with three other students, and space was scarce.

Mom forgot to send them. Back at school, I realized I'd made a terrible mistake in ceding this task to her. Yes, these were synth-pop records from the '80s that held dubious material or even aesthetic value, but I had my personal, possibly irrational, reasons, and I wanted those records. I wanted the intent and longing behind the gift Mr. Kalamazoo gave me, and I wanted a way to feel close to him. I navigated Privacy Manager to call and remind Mom over and over, but it seemed like the more I reminded her to mail them to me, the more determined she was to not do it.

"I'm working a full-time job, Amanda, and a weekend job, and a contingent job. I don't have time to just rush out to the post office and wait in line. Won't you be home at Christmas soon anyway?" Her job situation might have been a factor but was nonetheless actually bizarre. She had innumerable jobs, and if she interviewed for a job but took or kept a different one, she'd tell the hiring manager to hire her anyway, on a contingent basis, meaning they'd call Mom if they were in a pinch and she could come in for one-off shifts—usually at a time-and-a-half rate. Then she could call in sick to her "regular" job and get paid time off from there and time and a half at the contingent job.

As a nurse, Mom must have been very desirable based on the number of paid positions she was easily able to land. She most often took on visiting-nurse positions in people's homes. These worked well for her given her frequent interpersonal clashes in hospital and clinic settings. Instead, she loaded her car with medical supplies and charts and set off into the suburbs, caring for patients who needed in-home care and setting and keeping her own schedule. Her patients and their families found her empathetic and competent, which astounded us when these reports made their way home to our family. A bonus feature of her employment scenario was that her travels took her to far-flung neighborhoods with different stores. One day she'd discover a new location of House of Fabrics in Allen Park and the next she might find a meat market with good prices in Southgate. She'd add these stores' wares to the gauze and pills and paperwork in her backseat and continue on.

"I need the records, Mom. Is there any way you can ship them this week?" Waiting until I got home for Christmas would mean not hearing them until January. My turntable was in Chicago.

She agreed but first reminded me that her frenetic work schedule was thanks to me. "Did you ever stop and think about how your lifestyle is being bankrolled? We're paying for you to go to college, aren't we?"

I was paying for lots of things but not "college," and I felt bad that I'd been complaining—especially because neither of my parents had finished college. My saved-up Java Joe's money was funding my forays into Chicago, and my student worker job was paying for books, housing, and various other fees. The rest of the financial situation had not occurred to me.

I added an aggressive job search to my to-do list.

Just before Christmas break, the box arrived. When the clerk handed it to me through the mailroom window I could see something was not quite right. A wet splotch spread across the bottom and side of the box, which was far larger than one to ship record albums. I walked across campus to open it in the privacy of my room, and inside I found my records tucked between six cans of Campbell's soup and a bottle of Fantastik. The cleaning solution had leaked and soaked into the record jackets; the soup had bounced around inside the box and cracked the New Order record. Erasure was intact, if wet.

When I unleashed my full and self-righteous teenager fury on Mom, she barely flinched. Even in the moment, I wondered if she'd been hoping for this, trying to find a way to rattle me or catch and kill the part of me that was so joyously independent now.

"Mom, have you heard that I'm a vegetarian?" I asked her. The soups were all Chicken and Wild Rice or Vegetable Beef. Omitting the classic Tomato had to be intentional. I couldn't see her, but I know she shrugged on her end of the landline. "And why why why why why why would you send me cleaning products when I don't need them or I could buy them in Chicago if I needed them?"

"We did talk about this. You can get more use of them than I can."

I was impossible to contain. I couldn't just be angry about the broken records. My grievances were many and deeply felt. I raved about the piles and dirt at home. I accused her of ruining my social life in high school because I couldn't have anyone over. I told her that I would have read many more books in my life if our family had not been banned from the public library thanks to her checking out and never returning two dozen quilting books, and I culminated with a shrill "THERE IS NO QUILT. You never made a quilt. It's been over two years. Libraries don't even have blacklists and I'm on one, and you didn't even begin to make a quilt. NO QUILT."

"Now, wait just a minute," she spoke calmly. "You most certainly could go to the library. You just couldn't check out books or tell them your legal name. Big difference."

I took Amtrak home for Christmas.

Walking into the house, I had the hopeful expectation that the damage I'd undone three and a half weeks earlier at Thanksgiving would have held. If nothing else, maybe out of respect for me and the time I'd poured into cleaning up, they might have kept things on the reasonable side of messy. No one other than me would have been surprised: it was on the unreasonable side of messy. Everything was worse, perhaps purposefully. The bread that was half-green in November was all green now.

I scrubbed the house, spent as much time as possible at Mr. Kalamazoo's or Java Joe's, and angrily got on a train two weeks later.

FIFTY-SEVEN

It would be oversimplifying to say that the rest of my college years progressed as a loop, the same cycle repeating—distance from my parents, wild independence, remorse, tender closeness. We were united by what was most reliable: slovenly and frightening messes in our house, which I cleaned up on periodic visits home. But this was the pattern we'd established and for the most part, we held fast to it.

In the fall of 1997, Mr. Kalamazoo visited, and I took him to a vegetarian restaurant whose basement was an avant-garde theater and comedy club. In the middle of our sesame noodles, a man entered the restaurant, grabbed the purse I'd carelessly slung on the back of my chair, and ran out into the late-October Chicago chill with thirty-five dollars in cash plus my checkbook, keys to my dorm, and a red lipstick I treasured.

Men weren't allowed on my dorm floor, and without my keys, sneaking Mr. Kalamazoo upstairs was complicated, but we managed. In the morning, I called home for advice.

Mom and Dad's worst fears were realized when they heard I was a crime victim. Their sympathy lasted some single-digit number of minutes, until it occurred to Dad—on speakerphone—to press further.

"What were you wearing, anyway?"

I was wearing a vintage black-and-red sweater with bell sleeves and some very cool boots but refused to tell him on grounds it was irrelevant. Dad's worry and kindness turned to something along the lines of *What the hell were you doing out at eight in the evening anyway?* Which was unhelpful.

Campus security would be delivering a new set of keys later in the day, but I didn't know what else I should do. Mom and Dad didn't either. I asked if I should close my checking account or sleep with my dresser pressed against the door in case the robber used my keys to get in.

"Well, the worst is over now. They can't get you." I only had around $150 in the checking account. Dad said I didn't need to do anything at all.

On the Tuesday following, I received a FedEx envelope at my student worker job. The address was filled out in Dad's handwriting and inside were five twenties wrapped in a sheet of white typing paper. There was a check for $100 made out to me and a Post-it note that said "Do not cash until we talk." There was also a blank check.

I called Dad to thank him.

"I've got to go. Counseling session going on here." He hung up. He never wanted to talk about it again. We never did.

That Friday, October 24, 1997, I wrote to him, "Dad, I haven't cashed your $100 check nor have I filled out the blank one. Now that everything's okay, I could just tear those up, so the money is free to you . . . they're safe in my desk drawer. I do not need them, so let me know what you want me to do with them." Eventually, I tore them up.

By this time, I was leasing a 1997 Saturn and working to cover the monthly payment, insurance, and gas. The car allowed me access to parts of the city that weren't well served by the El. I became a regular at the Fireside Bowl, a 1940s bowling alley gone ragged and turned into a punk and emo club that booked all the bands I wanted to see. The entry fee was usually $5 or less. It was all-ages and plenty of patrons were straight-edge, so the fact that I couldn't afford and didn't really want to drink was okay. Everyone else sipped green bottles of Rolling Rock between sets of Braid, Mineral, Boys Life, and the Promise Ring. I was there several nights a week.

I'd taken to heart Mom's concern about the cost of college. They were taking care of my tuition—thank goodness. I had won scholarships to cover some of the academic costs, and I was handling everything else.

I worked a lot in college. I really loved almost all my classes but didn't find them challenging enough to occupy me fully; it was easy to add jobs to fill any vacant stretches of time. I worked, at various times during college: at the campus video producer where I learned to add closed and open captions to everything from the *Veggie Tales* Christian cartoon series to corporate training videos for McDonald's; at the campus art gallery; at the campus library; at a 1920 movie palace–art house theater; at a terribly unhip coffee shop called Lori's Kool Beans; and at a spice factory, which served Chicago's restaurants with daily deliveries of recently imported herbs and spices. My job was to measure the exact amounts ordered by chefs like Charlie Trotter and Rick Bayless and then label them (Ceylon Cinnamon, Saigon Cinnamon, Ground Coriander, Mexican Oregano). I kept a set of spice-scented clothing in the Saturn and changed into and out of it at stoplights along Harlem Avenue four afternoons a week. There wasn't time to change between jobs, and I thought nothing of allowing passing cars to see a brief look at my bra or of putting the car in park and slipping into different pants while waiting for the light to change.

I made a zine.

The school newspaper gave me my own column, which I named after a Minutemen song.

With Mom and her hopes for me in mind, I attended an off-campus party where a tall Lutheran boy named Mitch leaned over me heavily and encouraged me to drink beer from a keg, which I declined.

I picked up something called *Milk Magazine* where I learned that the Promise Ring would be playing in their hometown, Milwaukee, which was only about an hour north. I drove up, alone of course, and forgot my wallet. A stranger in Kenosha loaned me $5 to add some gas to my tank. I didn't eat all day, but I did fall in love with Milwaukee.

I drove the Saturn to Target in the Chicago suburbs so my friends and I could purchase some essentials. At the register, my check was refused. "We can't take a check from you," she said, handing my ID back to me. A month after I'd been robbed in the restaurant, I learned that all the stolen checks in my checkbook had been written for multi-hundred-dollar transactions, which bounced. The $150 that had been in my account was long gone. The bank said I should have sent them the police report the day it happened, which I had not known to do. I called in Dad's counsel again, and he suggested I close the account and pay for all future purchases with cash. That's what I did.

On my Thanksgiving 1997 visit home, I walked up the back stairs and into my bedroom first, to put my suitcase down. I flipped on the light and screamed.

"Mom! Dad!" I summoned them both in. My bed was covered in broken glass and leaves and branches from the tree outside my side window, which was broken.

Had a storm come up just this evening and caused this wreckage on my bed? I was appalled.

"Yep," Mom said. "A storm knocked that branch in a few weeks ago." She was unbothered.

"Yeah," Dad said, "I'd fix it, but it's not our house. We have no equity here."

Too tired to sweep up the glass and change my sheets, I slept on the living room sofa that night and cleaned the bed in the morning, picking glass and twigs off my pillowcase. Mom poked her head around the corner and asked if we could talk.

With great gravity, she told me she had lupus. She suggested I might want to put my education on hold to care for her in her final months or years. This changed everything.

Instead of leaving school, I transferred for two semesters to my college's small Ann Arbor campus. It wasn't all because of Mom. Ann Arbor offered a superior program in visual art—my new major—and a respite from a sticky roommate situation that was beginning to brew in Chicago. Weekends, I worked Friday night and then came home most Saturday mornings to help Mom and sleep over. By my third week back in Michigan, it was clear that something was going on with Mom, but it was unlikely to be lupus. She often booked herself for work shifts all weekend and was, generally, the exact same as she'd been in all the nineteen years I'd known her. It was devastating, but also weird. Nothing about Mom seemed to have changed. I didn't know anyone else with lupus and took her—a medical professional—at her word that her days were numbered.

In the spring of 1998, I was home almost weekly, though I'd stopped cleaning and maintaining their house. Instead, I watched it atrophy as though in a time-lapse video. For weeks I saw that our detached garage was on the skids. We'd never parked a car there; it was a storage area. The wooden building was at least sixty years old with mostly gray slats that had once been painted white. The once-black asphalt of the roof was pure green, caked with pollen and always wet-looking. Saturday after Saturday I pulled into the familiar driveway and observed the unnatural undulation of the roof; parts of it were sinking and drooping. Each week it curled farther downward. It remained intact but wavy, threatening to give way. I did nothing. I said nothing.

I was an observer now.

Mom collapsed on the sofa as soon as she got home from work. "It's my lupus," she reported. Her shoes slipped off her feet, and she grabbed a blanket to spread over herself. "I'm exhausted." The symptoms of lupus were the symptoms of Mom's life—fatigue, aches and pains and headaches, sporadically flaring and waning.

My mother's health aside—that felt like an exception—the choices my parents had made and were making about their housekeeping, their finances, their relationships were their own. Sometimes I would think about their future and thank God I didn't have to deal with it. *How on earth will this end?* I thought when Mom brought home another armload of plastic bags filled with fabric. In 1998, I had not been in the upstairs of my parents' home in two years. *Who will help clean all of this? How will their bills be paid when they are older?* My thoughts went in this direction often, but I found it impossible to put myself into the equation of whatever remedies might be necessary for their future. Chicago had cured me of the nagging sense of responsibility I had for my hapless parents. Instead, I thought, *This will be really fucking terrible for them when they finally have to pay the piper and deal with these messes they've made.*

In my Ann Arbor dorm, I pulled together my things for the weekend—a dirty laundry basket, a textbook I needed to read. The campus was still quiet as I started the thirty-five-minute drive to the Longs'. Dad had proposed a family pancake morning, so I was setting out earlier than usual. Pulling into their driveway, I noticed a larger expanse of sky than I was used to seeing. The garage roof had breathed its last. All of the pieces of the collapsed roof were inside it. From the outside, I could only see its absence.

I lifted the handle and rolled up the door, which still functioned. Spongy pieces of pollen-crusted boards and shingles were everywhere, on top of our boxes: cases of Success Motivation Institute tapes, my never-built Victorian dollhouse, Dad's tools, a binder of Adam's baseball cards. It was too much to deal with this just then. I left the door ajar, knowing we'd all have to work together and deal with this mess while I was in town.

I entered the back door and saw Dad in his threadbare blue robe. Bacon fat sizzled. He held a broken pair of reading glasses up to his face to read a Bisquick box. I hated to be the one to deliver this awful news.

"Dad," I said. "The garage roof is gone. Everything in there is destroyed, or will be soon."

"Yep," he answered, cracking an egg. "Then again, it's not our house."

FIFTY-EIGHT

In the years I was away, I never really kept track of Mom's different jobs except to know that she had begun to work as a hospice nurse. Dad had found his true calling in serving as a Lutheran pastor, and Mom now found hers, as an aide to the dying and their families. She spoke about her new line of work with a cultlike reverence. Instead of trying to keep people alive, a goal in most RN jobs, Mom's role was to keep people comfortable. As she moved from an inpatient hospice facility to visiting hospice patients in hospitals, nursing homes, and their homes, Mom preached the gospel of palliative care. Pamphlets on the joys of dying in pain-free dignity were all over our house. Mom could deftly steer any conversation toward death and dying, and when she did, her face came alive with feeling.

Between Dad's ever-increasing funerals-for-hire and Mom's righteous fascination with hospice, it was beginning to be a death and dying factory over there.

I returned to my Chicago campus in early 1999. I picked up one more job that year: moving lesbians.

An ad in the college cafeteria daily newsletter requested help moving on the following Saturday in exchange for $50. When I called the phone number, I learned that the place was a fourth-floor walk-up. The woman, who was moving into her friend's apartment, told me, "I'm impressed that you're a woman. When I placed the ad I thought only college dudes would answer it." I worked alongside these two women all day and only by our

3:00 p.m. pizza break did it occur to me they were more than roommates. It was a one-bedroom. Apparently, my lack of judgment and willingness to be a girl mover impressed them. Two weeks later, friends of theirs were moving in together, and they passed my number along. In late spring, I was making $50 or sometimes $100 per weekend moving various women between apartments in Oak Park. I enjoyed the money and the exercise.

I completed my final course in August of 1999, and as such I would be scheduled for the December graduation ceremony that year. I'd been packing in an overfull class load whenever possible and finished two semesters early. I was happy to have saved my parents the money, and moreover, I could not wait for my life to begin, fully out from under my parents' financial and other influence. I was ready.

But first, I needed a job. For three weeks I sat disconsolately in the Longs' house using their family room computer to search for jobs. Every time I sent in a resume for a job in Michigan I blanched, imagining my ongoing role in their home's upkeep and in support of Mom's emotional needs. An arts administrator job was advertised at a Milwaukee women's college. I had a very fond feeling about the city based on my previous one-day adventure there, and I had just enough experience at the art house movie theater to land the job.

With great haste, I tried to figure out the finances and logistics. I'd be making $28,000 per year and could start immediately. *Yes*, I said. *Yes, yes, yes*. I was gone in days.

BankOne in Michigan had been keeping my money since the robbery, and I had just under $600 in my account. I tried to transfer it to a Bank-One affiliate in Milwaukee but was advised by the bank to simply close the account and start a new one once I had a Wisconsin driver's license. Dad came along on this errand. Rather than take the cash, we had the bank issue him a check for the $587.

"How about this? I'll top it off. When you get settled, I'll give you a check, or cash, whatever you want, for six hundred dollars," he said. He seemed very proud of me.

Lacking any real knowledge of the city, or any place to stay, the college had agreed to provide me free housing for four weeks. This was mostly a commuter school, and Roman Catholic, with a deep social justice mission. Many of its students were single mothers. Many of its faculty were habit-wearing nuns. I was given a room to myself that shared a kitchen and bathroom with some of the sisters. Seeing them without their headpieces felt sacred and exotic.

My math on payroll taxes and other expenses had me arrive at $500 per month as my maximum rent payment. I found a place for exactly that—a one-bedroom on the ninth floor of a 1950s building right on Lake Michigan. Perfect.

My time with the nuns was running short. I'd gotten my new Wisconsin ID and was ready to sign on the apartment. I called home from the hallway phone in the rectory and explained I was ready for my $600 now.

"I gave it to you. Before you left," Dad said. He was excited about the apartment and said he was sorry I didn't recall that he'd given me the cash already.

"Well, no. We talked about cash or check, and we said you'd give it to me now, like, when I got settled. I need to sign that lease."

"Right. We said cash or check, and you wanted cash."

We went back and forth long enough for me to realize that even if he was right (he wasn't), there was no $600. There was no $587.

I had to ask my new employer for a small advance and then wait a few days for my first paycheck, nearly all of which went toward the apartment. I bought a large (smelly) cushion at a thrift store for $15 and used it for a bed until one of my Chicago friends drove up and gave me her grandmother's old bed. I had phone service at my new office until I could afford to install AT&T, so we arranged this Saturday-morning, bed-drop-off rendezvous on a Friday afternoon, and we hoped she could find my building the next morning. I filled my gas tank and was left with $20, which I somehow stretched into my food money for thirteen days. One of the evenings I popped up to the rectory with a dry bag of lentils and invited myself for dinner with the nuns, leaving the lentils as an offering.

Dad and I never talked about my bank account problem again. For someone who'd had a career in business, then in fundraising, he was remarkably uncomfortable speaking about money, and he tried to never do it.

One of the first pieces of mail I received at my new place was a coupon book from something called Sallie Mae. Apparently, I owed $190 per month on my student loans. Mom and Dad had always said that they were paying for school and indicated that the loans they were taking out would be paid back by them. I don't know why I didn't ask more questions when my college finances were being arranged. I did ask my parents in the fall of 1999 about the loans, and they told me that of course I was supposed to pay them. "Or defer," Dad said. He was a big fan of deferment for loans, he told me.

It didn't take too long for me to get a handle on my finances and my life, which was as glorious and independent and vivid and fun as my early Chicago years, but this time, I was really on my own.

FIFTY-NINE

I don't know—and there are very few records of—what my parents were doing in the years I was in Milwaukee. I visited very occasionally and did not clean their house when I did. We spoke on the phone every few weeks.

"So how did you spend your Sunday?" Mom always wanted to know how I was spending my time. I knew by now she was fishing for details about possible men—marriage material—but I didn't have anything I felt like reporting. I'd drawn a sharp boundary around my dating life and was determined that it was my own and Mom had no business in it.

"Let's see. I slept in. Then I took *The New York Times* in my bag and walked up to Alterra. I sat and drank coffee and read the paper for two hours. Then I went to Harry W. Schwartz Books and browsed for a while, then the thrift store, then there was a dollar theater showing of a terrible Matt Damon movie. Then I walked by the lake and picked up groceries at Koppa's and bought some Vietnamese takeout, and now I'm home and I'm eating and playing records and the sun is setting, and I'm drawing . . ."

"By yourself?"

It was a constant battle between us. I was recharged and energized by doing my own thing, including keeping my own little one-bedroom perfectly tidy. I loved my life more than I could ever explain, but hearing about it definitely left Mom feeling bummed out. I had a one-way ticket to spinsterhood. I was twenty-one.

In the spring of 2000, I was mugged again, this time on my way to a date with a man who worked in the bookstore I loved to visit on Sundays. We were meeting at a bar equidistant from our respective apartments. I was on foot and someone on a bike rode up behind me, grabbed my bag, shoved me down on the pavement, and then stepped on my right hand, breaking a couple of my fingers. I unsuccessfully fought back. I called home to report this and should not have been surprised at the questions.

"Why go out after dark, anyway?"

"If you were meeting a man, I can't really understand what kind of loser wouldn't pick you up to take you out."

"What were you wearing?"

The weeks afterward were terrifying and disorienting even without Dad's suggestions that I'd invited it somehow. One part of my brain asked if it had even happened at all, but the three purply-green fingers on my right hand proved it.

Mom came to visit me in the summer of 2000. I tried to show her the magnificence of my new city—the world-famous art museum, incredible food, the lake! We had fun together in a new way, almost as co-adults and on my very neat and tidy turf. She seemed to be managing okay with "my lupus" as she called it, and I was happy that whatever health news had scared her in 1997 was less prominent now, even if she was a bit lethargic, a bit mopey. It felt like such a change to spend quality time with Mom but not have the anxious dread of her piles of stuff all around us. I gave her my bed and returned to the stinky cushion as my mattress for the weekend. We were tucking in on the first night, and I stood outside the small bathroom, brushing my teeth.

"Go ahead," I gestured toward her in a host-like way. "The bathroom is yours."

Mom declined. She said she no longer brushed her teeth in the evening. Sometimes, she skipped mornings, too.

Foamy from my own brushing, I muttered out a "what?"

She said she was living with lupus, working full-time, and dealing with so much. She liked making her own choices now and then. "There's a point in time when you just do what you wish to do in your life, Amanda," Mom said. "You should try it sometime. It's liberating."

SIXTY

The Wednesday night before Thanksgiving that year, I was back in Michigan for a visit, and Mom was defrosting Stouffer's, and Adam was headed to Ann Arbor to pick up a friend in the dorms. I agreed to drive with the understanding that I'd be ditching the young men at Urban Outfitters and finding my own way to the used record store I liked.

I held a Solomon Burke LP up to inspect it and made eye contact with Frank Uhle, whom I'd met years ago during my time in Ann Arbor. He found a dull pencil on the store's counter and wrote his email address on a slip of purple paper.

We corresponded. I had a computer at my office and therefore access to email forty or so hours per week. Long-distance calls were expensive until I got a phone plan with free calls after 9:00 p.m.

Falling in love with Frank coincided with my wish to move on from my job at the Catholic women's college. I adored Milwaukee and hoped to stay, but we couldn't even consider Frank moving to live near me. He shared custody of a young daughter. The only answer was for me to move there, an unsettling prospect. *Would I be dragged back into whatever drama my parents were up to these days?* I'd love to live anywhere at all except within half an hour of Longs Island. *And was I so foolishly in love that I'd pick up and move two states away from my life I cherished for . . . a man?* Indeed, I was exactly that much in love.

I moved to Ann Arbor with my defenses up. I loved my parents, but I was not about to get into any of their nonsense again, which would now be about a thirty-five-minute drive away. I'd worked very hard to escape it. No money shall be loaned or borrowed, I declared. No meals shall be shared. No emotional baggage shall be unpacked. But for all my firm stances, guileless and sweet Frank worked the other angle. To him, my parents were gregarious and loving people, both in the serving professions of pastor and nurse. They wanted so badly for me to be married with children that they warmly embraced Frank and his daughter, who found in Mom and Dad something more pure and real than I could. Did it matter to my parents that Frank was nineteen years older than me and divorced? Quite the contrary. In private moments, both my parents marveled at my good fortune. They told me they were surprised that I'd actually found someone to love me—at my advanced age (twenty-two) and with my strident viewpoints.

We got married. I was twenty-five, the same age Mom had been when she married Dad and her parents had thought she'd waited far too long, gambling with spinsterhood in her midtwenties. I became a stepmother. I changed my name. Shedding "Long" was both the most feminist and independent thing I could do and a loving gesture to honor the new little girl in my life. It was also the only choice my parents would have tolerated. I'd lived all my life under the bizarre auspices that was my parents' household. Starting my own might have been the only legitimate way out, and I was lucky that escape route happened to be exactly where my own heart was leading me. When I "finally" got married, Mom felt like she'd finished a two-and-a-half-decade marathon of squeezing me into the role of a traditional woman. I let her feel like she'd won, knowing I was the real victor.

Frank and I had our own tribulations in our first years of marriage, but they seemed to bond us to each another, not drive us apart. Frank had lost only a little of the fondness for my parents he'd first felt. Mom and Dad were so truly grateful that someone—any warm body would do—had taken me off the market that they went all in on being grandparents to my stepdaughter and in-laws to Frank.

Largely driven by Frank's sweetness toward them, we spent more time with the Longs than I ever expected we would. Without the experiences I'd had for two decades, Frank saw my parents as loving, if a little goofy. He was not wrong.

SIXTY-ONE

Around the time of my wedding, when Adam was twenty, he and Dad had a terrible argument about something private of Adam's that Dad had seen on the shared PC in our family room.

As with most Long family incidents, this one began at home and then continued over a prolonged car ride. Dad drove and talked. Adam listened. The subject was secrets.

"There's no such thing as a secret," Dad declared. "You can't keep things from people. Every single lie, every secret, will come out eventually."

And then, wholly invalidating this statement, Dad told Adam, for the first time, about the family in Miami, including three half siblings we'd never met.

"Does Mom know?" Adam was hurt, shocked. "Amanda?"

Dad admitted that we'd all known for years and years.

"I wanted to wait until you were ready," he told Adam.

When I still lived out of town, my parents took Frank to dinner. They took my elementary-aged stepdaughter to the county fair. Dad played her silly songs by a local comedian. Mom sewed her Halloween costumes. We visited every other weekend or so, often attending Dad's church and eating lunch together afterward.

They were suppressing their strangeness a bit for Frank, but their performance hardly mattered to me. I was mostly grateful that our financial entanglement appeared to have ended, its only vestige the fact that Mom often referenced "paying for" our wedding. She spent nine or ten months before our 2003 wedding working increasingly peculiar nursing gigs at all hours and days. She sewed my wedding dress. Dad covered the musicians who were already regulars at St. John's, including the convicted child sexual predator who was still the organist. Dad performed the ceremony, and they wrote me a check for $500. Frank and I paid for the rest.

One Sunday in 2004, a new organist was behind the bench, struggling through the hymns, hitting an atonal chord every few minutes. After the service, Frank asked Dad what had happened to the other guy.

"He liked little boys," Dad answered. Nothing more was said.

In spring of 2005, Frank and I were driving around Ann Arbor, still inside the haze of marital bliss we'd built. We were idly looking at real estate listings, hooked on the idea of the foreverness of our life together. My cell phone rang.

"We're in Toledo," Mom reported. Her voice wavered. She started crying. "Something's happened. To Dad."

Frank pulled over, and we sat in a parking lot. I switched to speakerphone. Mom said she was driving, and Dad was in the passenger side. They'd been driving all day.

"We're in Toledo," she said again. Since I'd known them and ridden in cars with them, I had not once seen my mother drive my father anywhere.

In an April 12, 2006, letter to a Martinsville friend, Mom described that day.

It's been hard to know how to start telling you about the events of the past year for us. We are now approaching the one-year anniversary (it was May 1st 2005) that Stephen had a breakdown. Completely unexpected and yet in retrospect, I saw it coming for years. He was preaching, and literally stepped down and said I can't finish today. This was at first service. He called me, drove to the house and picked me up and we spent that day driving and crying. He began counseling the next day, which continued until just this week. With very minimal exceptions, he never spoke to anyone in the congregation again. Someday when we can talk in person, maybe more could be explained. Of course we had to abruptly move out of the parsonage with zero equity and find another house. The only way I know to sum things up from my perspective is that the relationship between him and St. John's leadership was abusive. Abusive from day one and abusive on many levels. Again, in person, more could be said.

PART SIX

Pontiac, Ann Arbor, and suburban Detroit, Michigan

2005 to 2015

SIXTY-TWO

The end was gory. Immersed in those years, it was impossible to know that we were experiencing Longs Island's final decade. They were fifty-five and sixty-two. Perhaps this was a rough patch in a particularly complicated transition to middle age. Alternatively, it could have been the beginning of another few decades of agony. We didn't know the duration, and yet we woke each morning with our minds clear only a moment before the dark realization—again—that we lived in the End Times.

Our decades-long family-wide pact to venerate Dad teetered. Dad—always so determined to conceal any weakness—was all fragility now. Even so, both my parents chose not to tell Adam, who lived in an apartment in Detroit at the time, about the May 2005 incident in which Dad suddenly and finally walked out of the St. John's pulpit during a mental health crisis.

No, Adam hadn't heard anything about it in the eighteen years since, even as our parents frequently referenced "Dad's nervous breakdown" to me. Adam had only known then that Dad was leaving his position at the church. Information regarding this monumental event affecting their health, finances, and very existence was blocked from Adam while the burden of dealing with it was presented to me non-optionally. In fact, it felt to me like a necessary chance to prove myself. I'd been maligned for my feministic rebellion, my weirdness and outspokenness when I didn't comply with their peculiarities. But in 2005, I was young and strong and stable, ready to confront whatever monumental challenges they could put before me, and to atone.

When I say those years were gory, I mean they were savage. Macabre. Some days were so impossibly awful I wondered how we would all physically survive until nightfall. Many more of my days were filled with run-of-the-mill tasks like caring for children and answering emails and filing insurance papers and shoveling snow alongside the knowledge that everything was very and irreparably wrong. Disaster was both imminent and already here.

My mother emailed me from seven different work accounts between 2004 and 2015. (My account with the name "Long" in it was deleted around 2004, following my last name change.) Dad emailed me dozens of jokes on topics like rising gas prices and Andy Rooney's thoughts on Christian prayer in public in America, all forwarded from former church members. One from 2011 begins, "'OLD' IS WHEN—Your sweetie says, 'Let's go upstairs and make love,' and you answer, 'Pick one; I can't do both!'" There are precious few actual emails written by Dad to me. When I read the correspondence with my parents from that decade, many of the events we'd discussed over email felt new to me. Even though I was there, it was like reading the sequel to a novel, familiar characters in an unknown plot. I mostly recognized my parents, though was startled to barely recognize myself in the emails and replies I wrote.

SIXTY-THREE

They needed everything. In 2005, my father walked out on his spiritual calling and twenty-four-hour purpose, not just a full-time job. It would be a matter of months, maybe weeks, until they'd need to find a new place to live and of course they had not earned any equity that might be translated into a down payment.

Mom and I started looking at real estate.

Dad started seeing a Christian counselor, a concept dangerously similar to "therapy," which he'd previously declared the territory of whiny losers.

For years and years, I'd had a lingering worry: What would happen to my parents when all of their terrible choices came due? As apocalyptic as it felt, I saw some hope in the fact that it could have been worse and that finally, finally they could get themselves on track. Their health, their finances, their relationships, their careers, and their home were all in disarray. Resetting was not the worst thing, I reasoned.

They had trained me in supernatural optimism. "Dad, you can start fresh," I told him. "This is exciting."

As much as I had going on with my life, working at an education nonprofit, helping to raise little Liz, I also was aware of how much hand-holding the Longs required. "It's temporary," I told Frank. "It's exciting," I repeated to him, too. "The new start they need."

Given their new level of dependence on me, I suggested that my parents look for affordable places a little nearer Ann Arbor, where we lived.

By midsummer I was driving to their Taylor house several nights per week and at least one weekend day. We schlepped through listing after listing.

"Too small," Mom inevitably declared.

"Too expensive," Dad said.

I continued to see hope, a glimmer of maturity even, watching my parents navigate their new world. Dad was so smitten with the concept of talking through his problems with a trained professional that he decided to become one himself. He enrolled in a graduate-level course at the University of Windsor, in Ontario, with an eye toward counseling as his next career. Decades earlier, when we lived on Long Island, he had a two-hour commute through Manhattan to get to Johnson Wax each day, excellent training for traversing an international border crossing to get to class three times a week.

"It's only half an hour," he reminded me. "Unless there's a holdup with Border Patrol." I talked to him about the drive because I was too scared to bring up the dissonance of the fact that he had been admitted to a graduate psychology department during a full-on mental health spinout.

Mom continued working at least two jobs. Dad drove to Canada and sought other local part-time pastor work, which he eventually found in a northern suburb. They both looked at other houses all over the Metro Detroit area. Whatever house they would land in was only part of the real estate equation. The other part was the house they'd lived in for eleven years now and which was in disrepair and stuffed beyond its limits with things. I was presented with primary responsibility for cleaning up and packing the shambles that was their 1,600-square-foot house. We left the collapsed garage alone.

My dream returned. At night, I imagined taking every last possession my parents owned and destroying them systematically. During the day, I did it for real. They had never lived in a home as long as they lived in this one, and the accumulation of items was intense. Bags and bags of never-worn clothing and never-opened lengths of fabric. Cardboard boxes of random electronics and cords. The back stairs near my old bedroom had narrowed; each side held cardboard twelve-packs of soda, some so old that the cans had split and burst. Syrupy cola eased down the sides of the steps. In the basement, the food I'd meticulously shelved in 1994 sat undisturbed, a museum exhibit of packaged food. Frank helped. I developed a cough.

I had not been in the upstairs of my parents' house since graduating high school, almost a decade ago. I ventured up once while we moved them out, late one afternoon when I was there alone.

Mold enveloped the entire bathroom, a horror movie set.

Across the hall, there was only a small walking path between the door and my parents' bed. It was August, and I was covered in sweat from packing and moving. I stood at their bedroom door and could see Dad's pirate chest on the dresser by the TV, which was on, as ever. My movement up the stairs had jostled free some dust particles, which floated in the streams of sunlight coming through the windows and clung to my wet skin. A commercial ended and a college football game resumed. I'd come up the stairs to assess the damage, see how much more work there'd be up here. The enormity of it was arresting. I wanted to collapse on the floor and take it all in from a seated position. There was nowhere to sit. I walked downstairs.

"We need a second dumpster," I told Mom when she got off work. I'd filled a 22-foot-long, 8-foot-deep, 8-foot-wide dumpster, but I hadn't caught her at home to ask her to order another one. She thought the best she could do for the situation was to keep working. Her back was bad. She now had a type 2 diabetes diagnosis along with lupus.

"My God," she complained. "Are you throwing all my stuff away?"

I was, and I wasn't. A lot of her stuff was pure garbage, as I reminded her. There were remnants of the various basement floods and the garage collapse. In the end, we filled two dumpsters and four PODS moving units, and I threw up my hands at the rest, which we ended up leaving for the church to clean out.

By late August, Dad was emailing me, suggesting that Frank and I cosign on a home loan for them. They'd looked at houses closer to us and found nothing. They'd looked at houses on the low end of their price range and nothing felt right until they came upon their dream home, a newly constructed, 1,800-square-foot home for $210,000, over an hour from my house, and in Pontiac, one of the most crime-affected areas in Michigan. We did not cosign, but by some miraculous combination of Dad's new part-time pastor job and the ARM mortgage crisis, the Longs were homeowners again, for the first time since they bought the Martinsville mansion in 1986. They felt unrestrained hope. My time cleaning out the house had disabused me of hope for their next chapter. I felt a disquieting terror.

SIXTY-FOUR

I had been wrong, of course, to ever imagine that a fresh start would change things. Once we finally settled them in their Pontiac house, their former problems plagued them, and new ones emerged.

The financial commitments they'd made to afford the house and the various tuition loans were truly out of reach for them. Dad had always relied on a special technique for developing household budgets: imagining the best possible scenario that could ever befall them and then assuming it would be at least 15 percent better than that. Spending ensued.

Adam lived in Boston by now, pursuing his own career in business, precisely as they'd envisioned it for him. Neither he nor I could help much, wherever we were. Since we'd both finished college, it had become clear that when Mom and Dad took out college loans—in my name and Adam's—they'd been able to keep some of the money themselves. I'm sure they intended to eventually pay our institutions of higher learning, or us, one day, but that had never happened. Adam and I were still paying loans on funds our parents had spent in the late '90s and early '00s. I didn't receive my college diploma until four years after I'd finished, when Frank paid my overdue balance of $1,740 with the registrar, a Longs Island–style dowry. Until then, my resume included some linguistic gymnastics to indicate I'd finished my bachelor's degree but had not received it.

Dad didn't cut it at the counseling program in Canada, so he transferred to a "correspondence course" in Alabama. He took out an outrageous sum in student loans, which he dismissed as being an investment in his future earnings. He was talking like a twenty-four-year-old future brain surgeon and not the sixty-two-year-old future Christian counselor he was, but none of us could quite break that news to him.

They were lonely—"way up here in Pontiac where we don't know anyone!"—and got a puppy. Neither felt up to walking the puppy, and without exercise he ran roughshod through their newly constructed house. I'd wrongly but fervently designated myself their rescuer, so Frank and I paid for and built a chain-link fence to keep Rocky contained in the yard.

On the sloping lawn where Frank and I sweated and swore, as we dug holes and poured concrete to install their fence over a humid Labor Day weekend, Dad made a flat plank of his hand and leveled it between his eyes and posts. "It's not straight?" He looked at Frank critically. "I mean, I've got a couple of complete amateur fence builders I've put in charge of this." Dad might have seen the edge of righteous rage rising up in one of us, so he tried to make it a joke, but the gift horse had already been looked right in the mouth.

The new house was already feeling "too small" for Mom, so she began renting a two-car-garage-sized storage unit. She soon rented a second one.

The house wasn't getting smaller, but the stuff in it was expanding rapidly. Mom ordered fabrics and home goods constantly. She seemed to want to start over—new dishes, new rugs, new throw pillows. I never understood the byzantine financial arrangement she'd struck with Dad and the mortgage company, but somehow the fall of their move to Pontiac, she had granted herself five thousand dollars to buy furnishings. There was an important catch: the transactions had to be hidden. She often emailed me and asked me to make purchases on her behalf, which were to be ferried to her in secret and reimbursed in cash. I don't know why I agreed to do this. I don't remember whether she paid me back, but for some reason, I told her that October I couldn't do it with my credit card anymore and that she'd have to figure it out herself.

On October 12, 2005, she wrote me, in all caps for some reason, "HI AGAIN -- IF NOT YOUR CREDIT CARD, HOW ABOUT YOUR

DEBIT CARD? I WANT TO ORDER RUG, ABOUT $350, LINENS FROM JCP, ABOUT 250 - 300, MAYBE SOME OTHER THINGS, SMALLER AMOUNTS....."

The things Mom wanted me to do for her multiplied as the things she was willing to do for herself diminished every day. "I don't drink water," she declared boldly over lunch once. We sat at a restaurant, and when the waiter poured her a perfunctory glass, she picked it up and inched it toward me. "You can have mine." She may not have loved water, but this was about Mom seeing herself as a certain kind of unbridled person, one who makes her own choices. By this time, she had chosen to forgo drinking water, brushing her teeth, and exercising in a purposeful way, including climbing any staircase to a floor also served by an elevator. "I don't do stairs," she said happily when depressing the "up" button for a one-floor ride.

Dad seemed to need me, too. A year after they moved, he told me Adam needed money for a car repair. Dad didn't have the cash to help and felt terrible. He didn't want to let either Mom or Adam know he was broke. "I have a great plan," Dad told me. I was instructed to withdraw $500 in cash from my bank account, then take the bills to Adam's bank and deposit them. I offered to just pay the mechanic or write Adam a check. "My God, no. That would emasculate him." Dad himself must have been worried about being emasculated, but these were years in which I just didn't know how to turn down my parents with their desperate and frequent requests. I have no idea why I thought Dad would pay me back. (He did not.) I can't even really conjure a reason why I did it. Guilt that I had the money in my account and they didn't? An inability to say no? On November 6, 2006, Dad emailed with Adam's name in the subject line, "Just put his name on the slip and account # as above and put it in his account at National City. Thanks again, xcuse the cryptic language, but this is the internet ya know. Call me if you need clarification. Love, Dad."

It was into this morass of many lies and very little money that Dad awoke one May 2007 morning to declare, "I am going to die today." He was almost correct.

SIXTY-FIVE

If the nervous breakdown of 2005 didn't scare them straight, why did I think the massive stroke of 2007 would?

The stroke did unloosen other things. Dad, who proudly called himself a motor mouth, who spoke continually, who spun stories, who could not complete an internal thought without talking aloud, stopped. Aphasia is the loss of speech due to brain damage, and it can last a few days, or a few months, or forever following an event like a stroke. For the first time since any of us had known him, Dad was alarmingly and completely silent.

For weeks we talked to him but not with him, never sure he heard or understood a thing. I wondered if he'd die before telling us whatever secrets he was surely hiding. In this disturbing quiet, Dad began healing and learning again to do things like swallow food and support his own weight to walk. He was barely there. Weeks later, he was grunting and moaning, on his way toward vocalizing something. About a month later, he looked at me standing at the end of his hospital bed and spoke three clear words. He hoped to say hello, but his compromised brain wouldn't allow it. My T-shirt had writing on it and seeing it short-circuited Dad's words. "Milwaukee's Polish Grocer," he said reading the words printed across my chest. We learned that if he saw printed words anywhere in a room, his brain would default to speaking them aloud. "Detroit Red Wings," he'd say again and again, trying to say something else but drawn to Adam's sweatshirt. "Employees only." "No glassware in the courtyard." "Oxygen in use."

At the time, I didn't know to appreciate this stage of his recovery. But after Dad's read-aloud period, he ripped forth with every story, every formerly hidden impulse and dark revelation his brain had held for six decades. Another aftereffect of strokes is aphasia's opposite: unfettered loquacity.

"Let me tell you something," he said seriously. He and I sat across a plastic table at the rehab facility where he was working like hell to walk again, and failing. Dad's brown eyes watered a little and he held eye contact for an uncomfortably long time. "This is serious, and I want to be sure you're listening."

I promised I was.

"Around 1980, I'm in LaGuardia. I have to take a leak." Dad rolled his wheelchair back and forth a little, pausing, trying to build some suspense for his story. "I put my briefcase down, and—" Dad cleared his throat. Men always clear their throats when peeing, he always said. "And I'm standing at the urinal and I look to my right, and who's there? Phil Donahue." Dad whispered the name, then waited a beat, wanting me to be surprised. "Now, this guy, it's always like transsexuals and single mothers and you know what else. He's a bleeding heart, and I always think I could teach him a thing or two. But I know that pretty soon I'll be done peeing or he'll be done peeing and then I'll miss my chance." Dad took eons to retell this story. He'd forgotten he'd told it before. It meant something to him to tell it carefully, with detail and anticipation. He finally ended it: "'I've always wanted to have it out with Phil Donahue.'"

Dad curled his fingers forward in a "please applaud" kind of way. "Huh? Huh?" he asked me to laugh, and I did.

In the summer of 2007, in the cafeteria of the rehab center where he lived, every story in Dad's arsenal was dusted off and told and retold. He was the same Dad but different. He couldn't recall which stories were old news and which were simply not appropriate. He'd lost whatever filter used to exist between his id and larynx. A nurse asked him if he wanted a sponge bath, and he answered, "After I shit."

I talked to him about which sandwich he'd like and he told me, "I'm actually a little too horny to eat right now."

He liked telling stories about his wild, younger days, and often ended a story abruptly. Adam pushed him for details, hoping the talking was somehow therapeutic. Dad said, "I may have done that. I don't remember. I was drunk."

"In Philadelphia, we lived in the Thunder Hollow apartment complex," he began. It was familiar. That was the year I was born, a Buickface, with help from the Indian American doctor. It was the year Dad braved the blizzard for peach ice cream.

Impatient, I told him I'd heard this one before. He acted like he didn't hear me and continued.

Dad described it just the way I'd always heard it. Every apartment, every door and stoop looked just exactly the same. He was about to tell the part where the businessmen come home too drunk to discern which door is theirs.

"So I'm walking around, and my briefcase is heavy as hell and I don't know anything about where I am. I knock on a door I think is mine. It's two o'clock in the goddamn morning, and I'm knocking at doors. Your mother is going to kill me." The story has morphed.

"I am so drunk that I have no idea what part of Thunder Circle I live in. And I realize—Sandie is not going to like me knocking, so I'm walking and walking." This might be the hundred and first time Dad's told me this story, but every other time, the drunk businessman was an awful neighborhood nuisance, not Dad himself.

"And I take my best guess at which of these identical apartments is the one where I live, and I stick my key in the door and the damn thing doesn't turn. I'm at the wrong door!" He cracked up. The cafeteria tuna sandwich languished in front of him, entirely forgotten. "I finally gave up. I put my head on my briefcase like a pillow and I slept on the sidewalk until your mother picked my ass up at eight in the morning." He laughed.

Over his soggy-breaded sandwich, I suddenly saw that every story Dad told, every last thing he'd ever said, was up for scrutiny. I thought I'd been wary before, but now things felt newly unclear. The notion of truth was impossible to establish. Then again, it always had been.

SIXTY-SIX

On the evening of July 4 that summer, my mother sat in my yard and told me that earlier that day Dad had shared a new-to-her story about some prostitutes in Hong Kong. By this point, it was impossible to surprise me. I mixed a negroni and told her she should divorce him.

In some weird way I thought that would help us all. If Dad were disabled and divorced, he might have his many debts absolved and become a ward of the state or something. And if Mom stopped using me as her marriage counselor, maybe I'd be able to focus on my own life. Two weeks before my twenty-ninth birthday, I'd started to wonder why every weekend was spent listening to my dad tell sex or booze stories in a rehab facility, and every spare dollar went to shoring up my parents' finances, and every moment of free time was spent hearing my mother's lonely woes or cleaning up her messes.

Mom replied to my divorce suggestion as though this were 1983—the years I was afraid of Colonel Gaddafi and the possibility that my parents might one day separate. "But we aren't legally allowed to divorce. It's not possible." I don't know why she told me this lie when I was five, and I have even less of an understanding of why she'd say it in 2007. Regardless, she'd made up her mind: Mom would be miserably married for the duration. "It's okay, though," she said from her lawn chair in my yard. "You are my best friend, and that's all I need."

The yard grew darker. Mom left. Frank and twelve-year-old Liz went to the park to see the fireworks. I made a second negroni and lay down in the grass alone. Mosquitos bit me. Crabgrass stuck to my damp legs. I drank some gin without the rest of the negroni ingredients. I couldn't see the fireworks, but every few seconds the world boomed and popped. I smelled gunpowder. I felt alone. Tears shot out of the corners of my eyes and slid into my ears. I didn't know what to do. It was gory.

SIXTY-SEVEN

Various bizarre and disquieting things continued to occur. I am scarcely in a position to accurately tell this part of the story of my parents' marriage. I can only report from the few written records that exist.

On December 6, 2007, Mom emailed me with the subject line "New Job!"

I handled all of their tax paperwork in 2008. They had not filed any income tax returns since 1994. I'd known this. When they were buying the house in 2005, Frank asked a tangential question about the possibility of a refund and Dad explained they didn't participate in state or federal taxes. Aghast, Frank pressed. "We *pay* income taxes because they take money out of our checks. We just don't *file* them." Dad rolled his eyes like Frank was an idiot. "Those crooks have enough of my money," Dad concluded, about the IRS.

We learned that their federal handouts for health coverage and disability payments were in some jeopardy because of the back-taxes issue. I laboriously sorted through it, earning experience roughly equivalent to a graduate CPA course, and prepared a 1040 for them. Yes, they owed a lot of money, but getting the paperwork square and getting on a payment plan was the first step and would help them keep their federal benefits. I handed them a sheaf of documents in an envelope with postage on it. "All you have to do is sign it and drop it in the mail," I told Mom. I'd marked the pages with little neon-green SIGN HERE tabs.

I felt powerless about every other bad thing happening, but this math, these forms, seemed like a tangible and finite thing. It was something I could do that would help them and that was out of their range of abilities. I was doing my best to pull away from many other aspects of their financial, emotional, and other needs. Tax preparation would be my contribution. I was willing to do it all, save forging their signatures.

Around my birthday in the summer of 2008, my cell phone rang, and I could see it was the Longs' landline. Mom called me often from her cell phone, but this must be Dad, likely calling to declare that Mom had died upstairs and I should rush over.

"Thanks for fucking up our taxes," he said in greeting. He was flaming mad. The IRS received my package, the result of countless hours of careful work, and they'd returned it to the Pontiac house because it was incomplete.

"Oh my god, Dad, I am so sorry. What's incomplete? What happened?"

"It's not signed! No signature on this. How could you mess this up, Amanda? You can't just fuck around with the IRS."

I was breathless defending myself. I felt crushed by guilt. In the course of that call, Dad had turned the real situation into a subverted reality. The real situation was that my parents had not paid or filed taxes for more than a decade, and they owed about $75,000, and all they had to do to get on track was sign the 1040 I'd organized. The version Dad and Mom asked me to believe was that I'd ruined them financially.

I stopped knowing what was true or real. And in those psychedelically gory years, important things became less important. Stupid things became priorities. Life was upside down.

Mom's health deteriorated, and she developed kidney disease. She stopped talking about having lupus and apparently, according to records I discovered in 2022, she never had it at all.

Dad developed heart disease and had heart surgery. Then he was diagnosed with cancer.

Mom continued hoarding, though we still only called it "clutter" or Mom's "mess." People who hoard, or who shop compulsively the way

Mom did as a coping mechanism, usually are trying to deal with their own anxiety or fear or insecurity, things Mom obviously always faced. The garage in their Pontiac house was filled with food, much of it perishable. Animals got into it. Summer arrived. The toxic smell of rotted food was inescapable, but that was the least of our problems.

I developed a pernicious stress-related skin rash to go along with my stress-related migraines.

In February 2008, I emailed a friend of mine, "I left town in a rush yesterday because my dad was rushed to the hospital, with what they thought was another stroke. Unfortunately, he's having seizures. AND, my mom's hospitalized w. pneumonia. Frank and I are up in Pontiac. Ugh. It's been pretty wild. Let's try again soon."

That time, my parents were each in the ER of two separate suburban Detroit hospitals, dueling patients. They both had severe health issues, but in Mom's case, there was another layer—of competition. After years of little exercise, no water, and a fistful of ibuprofen every day, her kidney problems were very real. However, she refused to take any restorative action. Several times in those difficult final years, I believe she caused herself to be hospitalized by overdoing it with liters and liters of Diet Coke, which overloaded her urinary system and seemed to send her into a state similar to a coma.

If things ever felt slow or steady, one of them went to the ER. If they'd been at the ER in Pontiac too recently, they went to one in Rochester Hills or in other suburbs. It was hard to accuse them of purely faking—these were decidedly unhealthy people, both physically and mentally—but the symptoms were often vague, and the timing was often suspect. When the stove at our house gave out and Frank and I bought a new one, Mom couldn't stop needling me about my luxury lifestyle. "It must be so nice to be financially comfortable enough to just buy yourselves a new stove at the drop of a hat. What's it like having six hundred dollars to toss around?" This was Mom's recurring "it must be nice" theme, which I found exhausting but could never figure out how to stop. She admitted herself to the ER the week of the stove delivery.

The summer of 2009—the summer I was pregnant—Dad went to the ER for chest pains. They had not been able to reach me to come up and help him out of the house, so they called the Pontiac Fire Department. Firefighters went through the garage, piled with boxes of fabric and odiferous, spoiled food, and attached Dad to a stretcher to transport him to the hospital. They found the garage impassable and had to navigate the front steps. A couple of hours after I missed Mom's call to come help, the phone at my nonprofit's office rang. It was the Pontiac fire chief reporting that my parents' house was a hazard and they'd be ticketed if the fire department ever returned and found similar conditions.

"First, how did you get this number?" I recall asking, even though I knew Mom had given it to them. She felt I devoted too much time to my work—and not to her—and often sought ways to gently embarrass me there. The chief was not in the mood for my bullshit or my mother's, and he told me that if my parents themselves were not able to clean it up, then it was my own responsibility. There would be no more warnings.

I hung up and sat very still at my desk for several minutes. Now I'd have to leave directly from work and go up to Pontiac and see Dad in the ER. I couldn't imagine what I could do to ameliorate the garage nightmare. If my predictions were correct, Dad would be discharged around dinnertime, so I'd be schlepping them home and feeding them and getting home myself at 10:00 or 11:00 p.m. We'd done this before.

Earlier that summer, Frank and I had been at an ultrasound appointment where we learned we'd be having a girl in September. He and I sat in our Toyota afterward, and I whispered to him, "I do not know how to be a mother to a daughter."

My colleagues at work were swirling around, working, talking, but I had yet to snap out of the daze induced by the fire department phone call. Even if my marriage and career and being a stepmom could somehow be on autopilot, how could I ever care for my parents and also care for a new baby? I wheeled my office chair closer to my desk and dialed the switchboard of the Pontiac Fire Department. "I'd like to report a fire hazard," I said.

SIXTY-EIGHT

In early 2010, they were simultaneously hospitalized in the same building, in separate Medicaid-funded beds. I shuttled between the third floor and the seventh floor checking on them both. It was the first time I'd spent a night away from my daughter, and therefore the first time I tried to use a breast pump, which I'd borrowed from a friend. After several unsuccessful attempts in the hospital parking garage with my shirt half off, I threw the breast pump across the pavement like an angry toddler. It was well-constructed and in a padded bag. Nothing happened. I walked over to it and kicked it, hoping a car would run over it and crush it. I returned to the car and saw myself in the rearview mirror: the scabby stress rash on my chin, dirty hair. The older I got, the more my face resembled my mother's. What if I just let my parents be? What if they had to find a way to solve all their own problems from here on out? I envisioned getting in the car (backing over and crushing the breast pump first) and driving directly to Ann Arbor and leaving them both in the hospital with no ride home. As satisfying as this scenario was, I was not up to the task. I thought, and still believe, that without my intervention my parents would be homeless or dead or starving. The thing was, they were already at the precipice of all these things, and I didn't have any more time, or money, or anything to give.

I had no idea how things could ever change.

I'd begged the fire department to intervene and was rebuffed. ("Can you arrest them?" I'd pleaded.) They lived in that house until they could no longer afford it, and then some. They stopped paying on the mortgage. "We're not going to be able to keep the house anyway, so we might as well use the money for rent at a new place," was Mom's reasoning.

They continued living in Pontiac for months after they quit paying. We speculated on whether the bank would change the locks. They never did, but they did eventually shut off the utilities.

Frank and I packed what we could and moved them from the Pontiac house to a low-income, assisted-living facility about half an hour away. They continually broke the rules and were called to account for their actions and threatened with eviction, but they did not change. The manager called me sometimes to report on their misdeeds. "They left a full trash bag outside their door in the hall. Can you drive here and pick it up?"

SIXTY-NINE

Most Saturdays I drove up to see them in their new place. Anytime I spent a Saturday the way I wanted to—reading, going to the farmers' market, walking in the park with my daughters—I felt such unimaginable guilt that it wasn't worth it. It was easier to just go deal with my parents and check it off the list for the week.

The front desk attendant caught me as I walked in. "Oh, guess what I'm listening to?" I had no idea what was on her Discman. "*Naked*," she said. She was holding back a guffaw. "It's hilarious," she said.

Mom had told this woman, and many other people she encountered, that I knew David Sedaris. I didn't. I did have a significant professional connection to another well-known author with the first name David, but it wasn't Sedaris. This was a mistake I didn't have the energy to correct.

I smiled and headed toward the Longs' apartment to take out the trash. The chute was about 14 feet from their door and Mom walked past it six times a day, but she seemed to like leaving the trash for me to do.

Trash deposited, I collapsed on their couch and handed them their Tim Hortons coffees with the number of sugars and creams they each liked. The TV was on. Dad was in his wheelchair, looking rough. He wasn't mobile enough for a traditional shower and his sponge-bath-only lifestyle had left him dandruffy, ruddy. The melanoma on his face was raw. I felt sad for them. They were sixty-one and sixty-eight years old. I wanted their lives to be better.

The apartment was outfitted in their comfort zone of maximal clutter, and they'd struck a precise interior design gestalt. There was new stuff Mom had bought for the Pontiac house, like a puffy, blood red, overstuffed sofa. There was also Dad's medical equipment: a hospital bed, bed pans, and wheelchair attachments on the dining table. And notably, there were prominent vestiges of their Hong Kong furniture purchases from the '80s. When I first entered, I'd confront the onyx folding Chinese screen inlaid with mother-of-pearl and delicately painted with thin, gold lines. It featured agrarian scenes and women with folding fans. Food that didn't fit in the kitchen was in brown paper bags throughout the living room. I noticed the unsigned packet of IRS forms I'd prepared and was sent back to them in 2008 still sat on their end table. It was 2011. They never signed them or returned them.

"Two bad animal stories," Dad announced, savoring his coffee.

Once I sunk into the big red couch, I was immobile myself. The clutter and the sadness had a slowing effect on me, as it must have had on my parents. I tucked in for a Dad story, sipping my own cup of Tim Hortons.

"Wait, turn the TV down," I requested. We looked together at the screen; it was a story from last weekend about a horrific opioid-motivated shooting at a pharmacy on Long Island, right by where we used to live. I'd read about it in the paper, but seeing the building on cable news made me realize this was the very same place Mom and I used to go until the day she left me in the car and I started the engine and pulled down the gearshift when I was four. We'd never told Dad what happened, and I didn't bother bringing it up that day in 2011. It had been thirty years, but I couldn't help imagining *what if we'd been shopping when this shooting occurred? Or what if I'd actually driven the Mercury Cougar into the pharmacy in 1982 and it was destroyed and the pharmacy had closed and none of this ever could have happened?* I often imagined parallel realities, who we would have been if only some certain thing hadn't happened, if only we had evaded consequences somewhere else. Life on Longs Island was a life of perpetual near-misses.

"Let's hear these animal stories," I told Dad, clicking the TV to mute.

First was a snake story. Mom had seen one in one of the storage units where she kept fabric, food, and other various things. *Well, alright*, I thought. Maybe she'd finally give up paying for the units. Nothing was more motivating than a snake. Mysteriously, though she was terrified, she kept the units and visited them often, if warily. She also visited the Pontiac house. Both of these errands were daily reasons for her to escape spending the day in the depressing apartment with Dad. The bank never did change the locks, so Mom came and went freely from the Pontiac house, which had no electricity or water service. "Toilet is only for pee now," she explained. And she told me she didn't mind being there in the dark, with no heating or cooling.

To this moment in my life there is nothing sadder than imagining my mother sneaking into that house alone to paw through her fabric in the shadows. I repeatedly asked her not to. She couldn't stop herself.

"What's the other animal story?"

"I'm so mad I can't even speak about it," Dad said. His jaw set hard. "It's the goddamn raccoons." Dad was incredulous that wild animals—raccoons, he'd seen them—were eating the food they stored on the apartment balcony. Dad explained they'd gotten into some sliced cheese, a Jell-O salad, and some hamburger meat. There was loose meat scattered all over their little wooden balcony facing the courtyard. We'd lived this scenario before, when people would scavenge food off our backyard air-conditioning unit in Taylor. Dad was equally angry at the raccoons. "They ought to know better," he maintained.

I considered pointing out the intellectual differences between humans and racoons or reminding him that they were keeping food *outdoors*, where racoons *lived*. I knew these were not arguments worth starting. "It's awful, Dad," I agreed. "They are really selfish raccoons."

SEVENTY

Whatever accident was waiting to happen, it was miserable to be the one waiting.

The summer of 2011, I joined a support group called Children of Hoarders and was invited to speak to the local monthly magazine about my situation. I chose to do so anonymously. "Another Ann Arbor woman told me tearfully about her repeated, unsuccessful attempts to get her elderly mother to acknowledge her hoarding problem. Both her parents are physically frail, and she believes that their home is an accident waiting to happen," the *Ann Arbor Observer* said in its October issue.

I had a low-level headache almost all of the time, and Saturday mornings it spiked. My parents felt I was supposed to spend my free time helping them. If I did, I was miserable. If I didn't, I was more miserable. Christmas 2011 was the first one I didn't spend with my parents. I told Frank I felt incapable. I might implode. I bought them gifts and meals, and I saw them in the days before and after. I didn't really miss their overblown holiday ritual, but I did keenly miss my childhood years—Mom tending to me by fussing with my clothes, Dad shining his charismatic attention my way. It was hard to imagine that these people had ever been the ones caring for me.

I continued seeing them approximately once a week. I did their chores, paid for groceries, ran errands, but something in me had turned off. I saw through their untruths and knew they were taking advantage of me. And yet, I didn't know how to stop it. And I didn't know how to walk away.

On August 22, 2012, while I was at work, Mom called.

"I'll need to be taken in to the hospital," she told me. She spoke in a normal voice.

I pressed for details. This was a boy who had cried wolf before. "What did your doctor advise?" I asked. "Why do you have to go to the hospital now more than you did yesterday?" I can imagine how those questions would have sounded to an outsider. Her answers were flimsy. I told her that if it was very bad, she should call an ambulance. She said she didn't need an ambulance; she'd driven to Kroger earlier. "Then drive yourself to the hospital," I told her.

Mom said she'd wait for the weekend—"risking death"—and would go to the hospital when I could drive her. "If I die in my bed, Dad will call you."

When I turned down driving her to the hospital, they'd tried Adam. Dad asked Adam to fly home from Boston to drive Mom to the ER. Or, he suggested, Adam could PayPal them the money for a taxi. Adam, like me, suggested they call an ambulance.

I emailed my parents, with Adam on cc, on August 23, 2012.

Hi Mom,

Once again, I'm so sorry to hear that your health news is not good. I spoke to Adam last night, and we agree that this sounds serious enough that I don't think it's a good idea to wait to go to the hospital. If your doctor suggested you go directly from his office yesterday, that sounds like an urgent need. I want to encourage you to go as soon as possible. Also, I've looked at my schedule, and I just can't get away to take you on Friday. I also called St. Joseph on Woodward and learned that their parking is totally free, even overnight; I even spoke with the security department to confirm this. There should be no reason for you to wait on this, and I really believe you should go to the hospital in your own car (which also gives you the flexibility to be discharged without depending on my schedule). I will visit you there on Saturday, of course.

Hope you are feeling well today and taking good care of yourself.

love,
Amanda

The answer came the next day, from Dad.

Dear Amanda & Frank, Cindy, our friend from Church picked up Mom to take her to the Hospital earlier today. Thank you for your prayers for your Mom. She truly needs prayer in her last days. She needs her rest so she has asked me to tell everyone no visitors please. Love, Dad

Adam, Frank, and I strategized over email that afternoon.

Frank: "No Visitors Please—!!??!!??!! These people are getting more twisted by the minute."

I replied, "Please visit me. I'm struggling." Frank came to my office with a coffee.

Adam: "It keeps getting better. Should I come back or not? I really can't decide . . . spending $1k on travel isn't what i had in mind for the immediate future, but if something really is wrong, I'd feel horrible."

I replied, "Something is very wrong, but I can't tell what the fuck it is. I think I'll call that hospital in a bit and ask how she's doing. I'll also go tomorrow (and be banned from entering?). Maybe you should decide after I try to go tomorrow. Did you try calling them today? They won't take my calls."

I called the hospital where she was and heard she was being processed in the ER and would be discharged in the morning. There was not a medical reason for her to stay. Mom and Dad wouldn't speak to Adam, Frank, or me. Our calls rang once and were declined. She was at the hospital briefly enough to not even be assigned a room and a phone. I considered visiting them at their home in Pontiac that weekend but decided against it.

On August 29, the day before I was supposed to leave on my annual Labor Day weekend vacation, Adam and I were both blind copied on an email.

> Dear Christian Friends, Please pray for my wonderful Christian wife, mother of Amanda (Uhle), Adam, and Grandmother of Beatrix Eleanor Uhle—as her Doctor has given her "weeks" to live. As you already are aware she is suffering from diabetes, end-stage renal disease—she recently entered the hospital (to get "re hydrated", and get her blood sugar under control, as it was over 500); much to my alarm, while in hospital she suffer a "silent heart attack". Thank you for all your prayers, cards. good thoughts! In His Service, Pr. Stephen Long.

Dad was in the habit of calling me to report Mom's sudden death, but this was his first go at writing a near-obituary, which he sent to dozens of their former church members, many of whom wrote to me or called me in alarm. I don't know why Dad erased Frank and Liz from the announcement of Mom's impending death. But it was less impending than he thought. I knew that some or all of the week prior had been a play to get me to stay home from my vacation. Anguished, I went anyway.

I felt as though I'd poured all of my attention toward my parents the last many years, and even all I could give wasn't cutting it. They begged for more. Death was their last resort. They went all in.

Dad, not Mom, was enrolled in a hospice program in 2012. It was not his first. Mom had been enchanted with the notion of hospice since she started working in the field in the '90s. As soon as Dad's poor health inched toward possibly needing hospice care, she signed him up. "Terminal?" she asked his doctors knowingly in multiple conversations.

He was very sick, indeed. But hospice programs usually have a six-month term, and Dad had "graduated" several times over. One program let him re-enroll, but when he wasn't dead a year in, they wouldn't take him back for a third go-round. Henceforth, every six months Mom enrolled Dad in a new hospice program. She said it was for "the services," like volunteers who would play Scrabble with him. Dad was mentally in no shape for word games, but another feature of these programs was narcotics. Hospice is about increasing comfort for the dying, so little vials of morphine came rolling into the house with every changing of the guard. Dad rarely, if ever, took a dose of morphine. He simply wasn't that kind of sick. He couldn't walk. He was telling inappropriate stories all the time. He'd had heart trouble, brain trouble, and a very serious skin cancer was developing. However, like Mom, he was mentally and physically miserable as well as broken, but medically he was relatively stable. He was not in any narcotics-level pain.

Mom wrote to Adam October 13.

> I suspect Dad's cancer has metastasized (not sure of spelling - spread) to his brain. His behavior has become unpredictable, erratic, weird, etc. The tumor on his face is bigger every day and more and more difficult to take care of. Amanda is planning to get Dad's name on the waiting list at Arbor Hospice. Financially, I don't know how to make it work. Amanda suggested I send the income figures and monthly obligations to you to take a look at, so that information is below. If we place Dad in Arbor Hospice, we would have to apply for Medicaid to pay for the care, but they will take his Social Security money to offset the cost. I would not be able to stay in this apartment, nor am I able to move, either financially or physically. The social worker at his current hospice agency is looking into this for me too.

Adam, who had an MBA and a successful business career, wrote back with a series of financial suggestions, closing with, "The long and short of it is, with some creativity and willingness to both own your finances and make some changes, you can make this work. Having $2800/mo in gross income (that's assuming you lose dad's benefits) is something a lot of people don't have. I hope this helps. Don't take offense to any of my comments or questions; I'm trying to help you examine your own finances and empower you to find a way to make things work."

She did take offense and never replied.

Anyway, Dad was messed up, but he wasn't dying. Until he was.

The cancer on his face flourished in the fall of 2013. It was dark black with patches of pus, red around the edges, exposed. His skin disappeared under its awful appetite. It was impossible for anyone to care for him at home. We moved him to a nursing home. He died overnight the Monday after Thanksgiving.

How to imagine a Long family without Dad? His jokes and stories—his love—were at the center of whatever it meant to be the Longs. He and Mom created an equilibrium together, looking the other way at each other's mistakes and championing the other regardless of logic. A united front of unreasonable love. I couldn't imagine Dad without Mom, but now I'd have to confront Mom without Dad.

Mom came over at 8:00 a.m. the day he died and fell asleep on my couch. Frank took our daughter to school. Early-winter sun shone in my window, and I sat in my vintage kitchen chair watching Mom sleep. I knew she was all my responsibility now. She wouldn't listen to Adam's advice, even when she sought it. She often called me her only friend in the world. Without Dad to tether her to the apartment or whatever psychological counterbalance they'd been enacting for one another since 1975, it was all on me.

SEVENTY-ONE

I put my arm around Mom and walked her through the casket showroom. We chose the least expensive one. She pulled out a printout of the hymns we knew he wanted, and we planned the funeral with a kind mortician named Ken. We made headstone decisions. The total would be $6,700, an impossible sum. Their debts towered over us, always.

"There will be life insurance," Mom told Ken. They had already tapped most of the life insurance they had to pay for various emergencies, but there was a $25,000 policy due to Mom thirty days from the death, which would be early in 2014. Ken reviewed the papers and agreed she could pay the bill in a month.

The year 2014 swallowed me whole. I finally understood the word *endless*. It had been seven years since I lay crying in my backyard on July Fourth with the gin. It had been nine years since Dad's nervous breakdown. We kept churning ahead in these gory years, but it had stopped feeling like a journey some time ago. Whatever we were doing was interminable. Gory was a perpetual state of being.

Weekends, I did things like clean out Mom's freezer or drive her to the storage units where she'd root through boxes and bags to find a certain piece of fabric she wanted. We often did a northern Detroit suburbs loop between her credit union and bank branches' ATMs. A certain check would go in a certain account, then we'd put another check in one seven miles away. Cash would be withdrawn from another spot while we rolled around wasting my time and gas. Mom timed it all exquisitely so funds would float just long enough to cover various automatic payments. She knew the number of days in the grace period for being overdrawn at each place. Mom was conducting an orchestra of hundreds and writing the music as she went. These calculations must have been exhausting. What if they'd put a fraction of this meticulous energy into an alternate lifestyle? That was too far-fetched to be worth the speculation.

On one of these weekend excursions, we also stopped to see her doctor. Before exiting the car, Mom squinted at a prescription vial in her backseat, memorized the dosage, and then tossed it behind her in a pile of a few dozen of the same drug. She asked me to come into the exam room with her.

"TMI, Mom," I told her. But she reassured me she'd just be consulting with her doctor about a prescription. It would be quick.

"I'm completely out," she told him. Mom generated a single tear. She said the name and the number of milligrams she'd just read out a few minutes ago in the car. "It helps me so much and my prescription coverage is maxed, and . . ." The doctor put a gentle hand on the knee of Mom's cotton pants and told her he was going to look in the closet for some samples. Maybe that would help. He left.

"Mom, is that the same stuff?" By my count she had thirty or more little bottles of the same medicine in her car. Who knows how many she had at home? She wouldn't answer. She was in another realm. She didn't speak again until she was thanking the doctor. He handed her twenty-some little boxes and sent us on our way.

Mom put herself in the hospital on my daughter's fifth birthday in September of 2014. The medical chart said "dehydration." Mom was saying: "Choose me. Choose me."

She called me from the hospital and said she hated to miss the birthday party. She explained she'd like to take a cab 63 miles each way to attend the party and then return to the hospital. The only catch? "Can you pay the cab driver when I get there and then give me cash for the ride back to the hospital?" She also wondered if I would have a wheelchair waiting in the parking lot so I could roll her up to the picnic table area where we'd be serving cupcakes and popcorn.

I didn't own a wheelchair. I asked her why she was in the hospital at all if she could come and go for a party. I asked her if hospitals let you just come and go like that. She deflected by speculating that I must have overspent on other things, like the party at the city park. "It's okay if you can't afford it," Mom said.

I did bring a rolled wad of cash to my daughter's birthday party, stuffed into my bra strap because my sundress didn't have pockets. And I did frequently check over my shoulder to see if Mom would materialize in the parking lot, an oxygen tank on wheels trailing behind her. She didn't. I drove up to see her after the five-year-olds and their parents went home.

Back in her apartment, things had naturally deteriorated since Dad was no longer there. The hospital bed was gone, but piles of clothing had replaced it. Mom slept in their old king-sized bed, but 70 percent of the surface was covered in foot-high piles of clothing on hangers, little, white retail tags still attached to everything. She never changed the sheets, just slept in her nest within it. Every time I walked in, I wondered who would clean this up one day. Wondering was a way of protecting myself from the reality I knew: it would be me.

"Can you sign this before you go?" Mom presented me with a paper form, half filled out. She was adding me to her checking accounts, in anticipation of her imminent death. I'd already endured a dozen conversations about her choice of funeral hymns and what I should do with her fabric. (Save it.) I'd also been admonished that I shouldn't wholesale toss the contents of her apartment. Indicating that she'd been planning a sadistic treasure hunt for me, Mom had said that around two thousand dollars in cash was hidden somewhere—maybe several somewheres—and I'd only find it by meticulously going through her possessions. I thought she was lying at the time, but I still asked her to tell me where she'd hidden it. "I'm not dead yet," she'd answered. End-of-life planning had kind of been her thing for a while.

This was different. "I never agreed to be on your bank accounts, Mom."

"You have to be. Who else will inherit all my money when I'm gone? And deal with my finances?"

I reminded her there wasn't a windfall coming my way. "Don't be so sure," she menaced. Also, I said, I'd deal with her finances when she was gone, but I'd do it the way children deal with their parents' finances, as heirs, not joint account holders. Their IRS debt was at least $100,000 by now and I knew that was the beginning of a vast chasm.

It was hard for me to say it. I knew it was hurtful. "Mom, I can't tie my financial life to yours. It's just a hard no." I told her that I had done, was doing, and would be doing many, many things to love and support her in life and death, but this one wasn't going to happen. I felt good setting this boundary. "Unfortunately, I can't let you provide your banks any of my personal information."

"Too late. I already did." I looked closer at the form. She'd officially added me and my Social Security number, but without a signature it wasn't final. Afraid that she would forge my signature, the next Monday I called all of the banks we usually visited Saturdays and asked to put a letter on file that said I was not an account holder and would not be opening an account or sharing one with Sandra Long.

SEVENTY-TWO

I would have taken almost any opportunity to leave the state of Michigan at that point, and I rejoiced that I had a necessary business trip to Boston that June. I looked forward to catching up with Adam. I looked forward even more to being away from my mother for three days.

The plane and the hotel room both had cable TV, which I didn't at home. There were two prominent stories the week of my trip: Donald Trump's ride down an escalator to announce his candidacy for president and the escape of convicts Richard Matt and David Sweat from the Clinton Correctional Facility in Dannemora, New York.

Trump, I ignored. He was a joke.

The convicts captivated me.

Richard Matt and David Sweat had spent months plotting an elaborate prison escape. When they broke out, via a five-hundred-foot tunnel they'd been digging, upstate New York and all of New England were terrorized. For twenty days in June 2015 the two men were at large. The idea of desperate murderers running around sent people into a panic. Schools closed. Bounties were issued. Every law enforcement division was hunting Sweat and Matt through the woods, at the Canadian border crossings, and anywhere else. They had vanished. It was riveting television.

Like a lot of other people, I couldn't stop watching and reading about the escape and the manhunt. I wasn't afraid; I was exhilarated. Every day they evaded capture, I silently thought, *Go! Go! Go! Keep running.* I was too embarrassed to say that I was gripped by this story of two convicted murderers because I felt empathetic toward them. Whether or not they deserved it, I saw that the two of them had been in an untenable situation with a lifetime sentence—which is just how I felt. Sweat and Matt escaped. It took them months of planning and deception, but they wanted out of that state prison and they dug themselves out. I wanted out so badly. Mom's needs enveloped me constantly. There was barely room for my household's needs, my work, myself. And I was out of ideas. By summer 2015, I truly believed I had tried everything, short of simply walking out and abandoning my mother, a decision I'd weighed and decided wasn't for me. I didn't have the courage.

And yet here were Sweat and Matt. If they had figured out how to steal tools and dig a tunnel through concrete in the middle of the night, then they deserved to be free.

Mom worsened. She could no longer drive. She didn't have the energy to make herself coffee or pull laundry out of the dryer.

On the weekend of July Fourth, I checked Mom into an inpatient hospice facility. Her health no longer allowed her to live on her own. We didn't think we could afford a home health aide for the level of support she needed. She'd tried to get me to live in her apartment with her and I declined. Devastating and miraculous all at once, we found a private home that accepted up to five hospice patients at a time. Colloquially, you'd call it a McMansion—a big, open, quiet, and very tidy house with many bedrooms in a rural neighborhood. A huge-hearted social worker ran the place with two nurse assistants. Treacly signs with words of inspiration were everywhere. The place exuded love and care, and it was unquestionably a place to go to die.

Packing Mom to go was awful. She was well enough to walk and to pick out clothes she wanted and to tell the social worker which variety of Little Debbie cinnamon rolls to have on hand. She was also well enough to understand that when we packed her things, she wouldn't return to the apartment. I could go to retrieve anything she needed, but she was extremely unlikely to return herself. We didn't discuss the fact that her stuffed-to-bursting apartment and car would be my responsibility. We were both too sad.

I was sad she was dying. I was angry at myself for wanting so desperately to be free of the responsibility of her. I was horrified to realize that it was indeed time for her to go, at sixty-four years old. And above all, I was in anguish that Mom's last days or weeks or months were so undignified. Every possible thing was a literal and figurative mess. For years she'd thought of hospice care and dying as a pampered chariot ride into the clouds of heaven. I surveyed our scene and found raccoon-ravaged food on her balcony, piles of clothes and papers and canned goods everywhere, and our two broken hearts. This had not lived up to expectations.

To live at the hospice, Mom had to surrender everything. I still don't know how she did it, mentally. I don't know that I could do it now. No purse. No money or keys of her own. No car or means to leave. Her agency was entirely stripped. She carried with her only a suitcase of clothes and a backpack of makeup and other personal care items. She was allowed to open the alarmed front door in the foyer only if I signed her out. I moved her in on Monday, July 6, 2015, and brought my family to visit that weekend. The next weekend, Adam came to town and we picked her up together on my birthday, July 18, and we ate a memorably miserable dinner together at a restaurant nearby.

Adam, taking on a Dad-style role, floated a few corny jokes as we ate our french fries. Neither Mom nor I could laugh.

Knowing we had to pay for the care facility somehow, I spent any free time in those two weeks pawing through the apartment looking for important paperwork, family photos, anything I might need if we had to stop paying and the place was repossessed. I assumed that would happen sooner or later, and I wanted to make my best effort at cleaning it out first.

I received her mail, and the bills that arrived were astounding. Along with a dozen catalogs every day, there were notices of massive debts to the IRS and others. There were numerous loans and credit cards she'd taken out with various mail-order catalogs to buy clothes and fabric. She owed small amounts to several dozen such operations. On a total bill for which she owed just under $200, Mom was having an autopay minimum of $12.99 taken out, as well as a service fee of $7.99, and then she was charged interest on the balance so her bill the next month would be larger even if she didn't buy anything else. It went on and on and on. I took her laptop to my house and stayed up until four in the morning, paying off and closing account after account by impersonating her. "Please close my account. It's paid in full," I wrote over and over from her email account. Her passwords were either saved or easy to reset with access to her Gmail account.

The apartment itself was a trove. I found plenty of photos and documents. I was astonished to find $4,100 in twenties in her underwear drawer. I found several copies of most all of David Sedaris's oeuvre. The bindings were pristine. She'd never read them.

Tuesday, July 21, I received a phone call from the hospice. The backpack she'd carried was not full of makeup and shampoo as she'd reported to me. It was stuffed with little vials of morphine, a drug that was not prescribed to Mom. Even if it had been, only the licensed medical staff were allowed to dispense medication. Mom knew this; she had to ask the staff when she wanted ibuprofen. She knew she wasn't supposed to have narcotics under her bed, which had been discovered when the cleaning service vacuumed and the bag tipped open. Mom was now being kicked out of the hospice, and it was my job to pick her up within twenty-four hours.

SEVENTY-THREE

"Well, I can't," I explained to Frank. I thought about going there and packing her things, like rewinding a VHS tape from two and a half weeks ago, doing the hellish move-in in reverse. I thought about getting her backpack of drugs and the boxes of Little Debbie cinnamon rolls and case of Diet Coke and driving her and her stuff back to the apartment. I wondered what I could possibly say to her. I determined that this task was one I just couldn't physically complete.

"I will," Frank answered. For as much as I did for my mother in the dystopian era near her life's end, it's important to know that Frank, and Adam, and my coworkers, and even my daughters stepped up, too. They couldn't do much; almost all of the dark things that transpired in those years were exclusively between Mom and me, because of our long history, because of how she viewed what a daughter was supposed to do. But when I stumbled, they were there. Frank agreed to take the day off work and do the move-out. He figured he could do it dispassionately.

He handled the car ride by remaining largely silent. It was better than I could have done.

Mom and I decided I'd be in charge of trying again to find a home health aide for her that we could afford. I placed an ad on Care.com the day Frank retrieved her and deposited her back in the apartment.

The last texts I ever received from Mom were from the same day, July 24, 2015. "Did Frank accidentally unplug my recliner when he plugged in my computer?" Followed by, "Never mind-Got it to work" four minutes later.

We hired two nursing assistants in late July and early August. The first one quit. The second one was fired by Mom. Her health continued to decline.

She normally paid the storage units' rental fees via check, but neither she nor I had paid for them in August. I wondered what family treasures or valuables might be there. I'd been avoiding even thinking about those mountains of stuff, but it was clear that my final chance to salvage anything was imminent. I had the keys to the locks on each unit, but Mom's keypad entry code to the gate had been reset due to nonpayment. I lurked by the entrance one Saturday morning, hoping I could slip in behind someone. I loitered for twenty minutes before seeing a pickup truck approach the gate. Its slow arm rose and I darted inside. If the truck driver noticed, she didn't care. Like a scene from a poorly written movie, my plan worked. I was in.

I found boxes of photos. I found some of my old toys and clothes from Long Island days. Adam's homework assignments from Martinsville days. Dad's framed credentials from the seminary. The history of our family was tucked in crumbling cardboard boxes amid and among all the detritus of Mom's hoarding. I dug and dug. It was sweltering in the storage units and I gulped water I'd brought and then broke into a semi-ancient case of some sort of aspartame-sweetened beverage Mom had stored there. I was terrified at the idea of a snake popping out of a corner and approached every torn box and pile of fabric with caution. That afternoon my daughter was playing a soccer game in Ann Arbor, which made me feel more lonely than guilty.

By the time the fluids caught up with me, I realized that there were no bathrooms, and I couldn't leave and return without an entry code. I scouted around for some way, but the place was surrounded by a high fence and a busy road. Appealing as it would have been to squat in the weeds, all the people driving out of the Kroger parking lot across the street would have seen me. There were decades of our lives in these boxes and somehow these artifacts were going to be tossed away while I'd be left inheriting thousands of never-worn tagged garments on hangers and cans of corned beef hash. Desperate, hot, angry, and lonely, I gave up and hovered over one of Mom's '80s CorningWare pots, which I emptied alongside the fence along with a gross and unintelligible stream of profanity. Rage shook me. I invented new swear words. *Why is this happening? Why am I here? Who am I? I am thirty-seven years old and peeing in a cooking vessel while my mother is dying and my daughter is playing soccer.*

I finished the job. I was sweating and crying. Whatever I could rescue from the two units went into my car. I surely missed many important things. Locking the rolling garage doors of the units seemed futile. We'd never return to clean up or collect this stuff. I locked them anyway. The sun had set.

I approached the gate, which opened automatically upon exit. It lifted, but I suddenly put the car in reverse instead. I didn't know what would happen to all Mom's stuff. I hated all of it. I never wanted to see any of it again. And yet the thought that nagged me was that some poor soul in the distant future would come upon the CorningWare dish I'd used as a toilet and take it into their household and use it to make casseroles. I was in no position to feel responsible for anyone else's future misery.

I unlocked one of the units and quickly found the dish, wide and white with a blue cornflower motif on the front. I held it over my head and hurled it to the concrete floor. The CorningWare released into several jagged shards and some ceramic powder. I swore again, shut the door, fastened the padlock, and left forever.

SEVENTY-FOUR

She was very sick. We had no one to help. I called the hospice that had evicted her in July, and I begged. The social worker agreed she could return, but she had to have all of her possessions searched beforehand, which I told Mom we had to allow.

Mom and I reenacted six weeks ago, when we'd sat together in agony in her apartment, deciding what she should take with her to the place where she would die. The first time we did it, it was nightmarish and devastating. I wouldn't wish those three hours in July on anyone. When we did it the second time, in late August, it was—indescribably—worse.

Late August 2015 was exactly two years after Dad had emailed her near-obituary to everyone he knew. I visited her almost daily then. She was sleeping constantly, only conscious part of the day. We talked a little. We tried to talk about big topics but reverted to mundane ones. I sat with her, and when she was not awake, I worked inside my heart to reconcile whatever we'd been through. I wasn't sure I could. She moaned loudly when she was unconscious. The hospice staff explained that when people are dying with unresolved business, there is often an uncomfortable vocalization of their repentance, their misery. "Terminal Anguish," they called it. I found it almost impossible to listen.

The hardest part of those days was leaving the hospice and returning to Ann Arbor where I'd find a stressful work email and learn my daughter really wanted me to take her to the pool that evening, one of the last of our summer days. I felt pulled apart into shreds. I took my daughter to the pool. *Is this what a person does when their mother is dying?* I replied to difficult emails. *Is this what a person does when their mother is dying?* My mother continued to die in a McMansion.

On Thursday, September 3, I sent a group text from my mother's phone to church members and some of her friends. "She has declined severely these last few days. If you are interested in visiting, please do so soon."

I spent Labor Day weekend giving her apartment the treatment I'd given the storage units. I swept the whole place for papers, money, sentimental things, clues. I did a rough sort of what might be garbage, what could maybe be donated. The mess was unreal. To prove that it existed, I took several blurry photos of Mom's bathroom vanity, the food stacked in the living room, the chaotic kitchen counter. In the bathroom, amid the mess, I'm visible in the mirror holding my iPhone and wearing a hoodie. I am a beast.

The Tuesday after Labor Day I worked at my job.

Wednesday was for my errands. I'd scheduled Don to clean out the place all day, during which I'd visit the church, florist, and mortuary for funeral planning. The church was fine. Don and his crew were wonderful, even if I had to make a trip back to retrieve the garbage bag of morphine. The florist enraged me. She was one of many people I encountered in those years who were probably trying their best but who had no understanding of my history on Longs Island. "You only have one mother," they'd say. Or "You can't let her down now." Hospice staffers, friends of mine, church members, even strangers who learned what we were going through all had their own diagnoses, and it was usually some version of indicating I could do a little more for my mother, could be a little more empathetic, a little more selfless. It was hard to explain how little I had left to give and how close I was to ruin myself.

After the florist was the funeral home. I'd made an appointment with kind Ken, who helped Mom and me in 2013 when we were planning Dad's services. The funeral home was the family business of a nationally renowned poet, and I felt oddly at home there. It was tidy and crisp and quiet inside. The people were warmhearted and free of judgment. I sat in a tufted leather chair across from Ken's desk, the thick carpet swallowing every sound but our low voices.

"I'm very sorry for your loss, Amanda," he spoke with authenticity even though I know he said this phrase all the time. He'd said it to Mom and me eighteen months earlier when we sat together selecting Dad's casket. Ken gently walked me through every detail. He knew that Mom was still alive and that we were planning for the inevitable. I answered his questions. I made selections. I asked for the total cost.

We were lucky that fall. In 2007, when Dad's stroke changed everything, he had recently been prescribed the medication Avandia. Shortly thereafter, a class-action lawsuit began against GlaxoSmithKline, its manufacturer. Mom was invited to join and she did. The paperwork and the lawsuit itself took years. It was successful in 2011, and in the fall of 2015 we learned we'd finally be receiving a payment of $7,100. I had already signed my name and forged Mom's on the documents. A check would be arriving any day now. I wondered if the check would arrive before Mom died. It felt like both would happen around the same time: soon.

"How much will the interment and other services be?" I asked. I hoped inflation hadn't increased costs drastically since Dad's, which was $6,700.

Ken told me it would be just under $7,000. I smiled and stood with relief. I scooted my fancy chair toward his desk. "Thank you," I said, extending my hand. He didn't reach for it. Ken clasped his own hands together and looked down. It pained him to get the words out, but he slowly explained that Mom had never made good on her promise to pay for Dad's funeral with the life insurance funds she received. We still owed for that one, and in fact, that's the reason there was still no headstone placed at the cemetery above Dad. We owed money. Mom had said something about the ground being too stiff.

We were now paying for double funerals. It was a circus act keeping

Mom's bills paid for the apartment, the hospice, regular stuff like her cell phone and car payment. The cash I'd found in her underwear drawer had paid one month of rent at the hospice. My own bank account had been tapped for so many nickels and so many dimes from my parents' needs over the years. Another seven thousand was impossible. Equally impossible—leaving Ken and his family business with an unpaid bill. That was a total Longs move, and I had sworn off of those years ago.

"Adam?" I called him in the middle of his workday in Boston. I stood in the silent hall outside Ken's office, hearing the echo of my own voice asking Adam for seven grand. He would find a way. He planned to fly back to Michigan in two days, and he told me he'd bring a check for Dad's funeral invoice.

SEVENTY-FIVE

After my meeting with Ken, I returned to the apartment. Don's crew had done magnificent work. The place was unrecognizable. Garbage was gone. Clothes and food were stacked and boxed and ready for the charity truck pickup. Don had spent one very long day enacting the recurring dream from my childhood. He did so expertly.

Don handed me a small, white leather Bible. "Sandra Long, April 12, 1975" was engraved in silver on the lower right corner.

"Looked important," he said.

For all the times I'd heard that my parents lost all of their wedding gifts, I'd forgotten about this: a Bible given to Mom from Dad the day they married in Martinsville. I guess it had not been tied to the roof of their car on the drive to West Virginia.

Don and I settled up, and I brought the garbage bag full of morphine back into the apartment. I couldn't quite imagine where to put it at home.

I pulled into my driveway in Ann Arbor after eight that night. It was Wednesday, September 9, 2015. My daughter's birthday was tomorrow. She would be six. I had neither bought her a gift nor planned anything at all. I wondered what kind of mother I was. Or what kind of daughter. I was so tired.

Inside, my daughter hugged me. Frank said that a friend of mine made us a meal, knowing what we were going through. At the table, Beatrix sat on my lap, still five, still a baby. Frank warmed the food on the stove and delivered it to me. I was voracious. My friend had made basmati rice and mung beans with garlic. I ate and ate. I felt mothered. My daughter braided my hair while I piled rice into my mouth.

On Thursday, I made my daughter a birthday card. I went to the hospice. Mom was not conscious. She moaned. I stayed as long as I could. In the evening, family friends came to our house. They brought my daughter toys and brought us Chinese takeout. Our teenage neighbor came over with her new-model Polaroid camera and took photos of us in the backyard. We are surrounded by square white cardboard boxes and pink plastic toys. My daughter is smiling. I am barefoot in a white dress. I am a ghost.

Mom died overnight—officially an hour or so after Beatrix's birthday. Adam arrived in the morning.

He dove in alongside me. We went to the apartment together, and I explained about the charity truck coming, about the morphine garbage bag. I delegated things to him. "You're going to have to call that fucking florist," I told him. We spent the weekend dealing with all of it. Our manner of settling the estate was to leave it, Longs-style, unsettled. All the things the Longs had not dealt with in the forty years since 1975 we did between his arrival Friday morning and the funeral on Monday morning. I say "we did them," but truthfully, I can't properly remember most of those three days.

Monday night we drove around Taylor together. It was a warm evening. We got donuts and drove through the scrubby neighborhood where we lived in the '90s. I pulled into a bowling alley, where we ordered a pitcher of beer. "Orphans," he said, raising a mug.

We both felt nauseous but kept going with the donuts and beer regardless. He told me a story. The story was so sharply detailed that I can see it perfectly in my mind, even though I wasn't there. Adam's story remains the one vivid thing I've retained from the hellscape that was Mom's funeral weekend. We may have lost it all, but we were still the Longs. We were still telling stories.

"So, you told me to deal with the drugs," he began. Adam said he'd looked up responsible disposal of narcotics and found that a local fire department would take stuff Saturdays and Sundays, no questions asked.

The bag was in his car and he approached the fire station but couldn't seem to park nearby. The surrounding streets were closed. He called the station. I wondered if this was the same fire station I'd called to report my parents six years ago. The fireman told Adam they'd be happy to take the drugs but that day was a county fair and it would be hard to park. He asked Adam to come by next weekend instead.

"Nah," he told them. "I have to get rid of this stuff today." Adam didn't want me to have to deal with it myself after he was back in Boston. "How do I get these drugs to you right now?"

Adam parked a quarter of a mile away. He gathered the loose plastic at the top of the black bag and hefted it over his shoulder like Santa Claus. He walked into the fair. Kids shrieked. Families ate elephant ears. Clowns' makeup bled in the warm sun. Unreliable carnival rides clanked and hummed. Everyone wore a neon wristband. The Survivor song "Eye of the Tiger" blared. Adam trudged through the joyful crowd carrying our family's narcotics contraband. The illicit burden was slung on his back in a black Hefty bag. No one but us knew what was inside.

EPILOGUE

I set out to document whatever was real about the forty years of my parents' marriage. I still don't know. Surety was not a Longs thing.

Dozens of times my work on this account of my parents' marriage has provided moments of intense, surprising validation. My process was to write sections first from only my memory, then return to them with a reporter's eye, seeking news articles and other data to buttress or refute my first draft. Again and again, I found that contemporary research corroborated and enhanced the view I'd held of the '80s and '90s. Yet the gory years of 2005 to 2015 were much more elusive to me. They are more recent. They are years in which I'd already begun writing—about this very subject—and yet I find those memories very hard to access and untrustworthy because they lack order. Gaps exist. Inconsistencies are common. Timelines and the relationships between events are indecipherable. I have deeply felt memories, cinematic in their specificity, of driving my father to an outpatient surgery to remove a cancerous growth on his face and of cleaning up my mother's vomit from the cupholders and console of her Hyundai Elantra. I also cleaned her smelly freezer of spoiled food and watched Dad spread a thick layer of soft butter on top of a Panera Bread cheese Danish two days after his discharge from heart surgery. But to connect those events in any kind of sequence and to report on the forty years that compose my parents' marriage, I had to consult my diary at the time, my Hotmail account, endless newspaper clippings, interviews, photographs, audio recordings, maps, and numerous other incomplete and partly accurate records. I was exacting in my research, yet I can stand by this story as accurate only insofar as my ragged, imperfect first-person vantage point allows.

Adam was a primary source, tolerating my questions, reading various drafts. Only once, in tens of thousands of words, did his recollection of something clash with mine. The pinkish, feather-shaped scar on Dad's cheek was a birthmark, Adam said. I'd always heard it was a football-related injury. We talked and tried to remember together. I examined photos from Dad's boyhood in the '40s and '50s, hoping to see the scar or its absence. Nothing was conclusive. I wondered whether I couldn't properly recall because my most recent memories of Dad's face were its final months, when cancer destroyed it. How the scar appeared is one of a hundred unanswerable questions. The football story is true. The birthmark story is true. They are both false. Or they are both true enough, for us.

My reporting uncovered more mysteries than it solved.

I don't know what Dad knew about the organist at our church or when he knew it. It's possible that he turned a blind eye to abuse, but knowing my father, researching him the way I have done, I very much doubt that's what happened. Another possibility is that as soon as Dad learned the truth about the past, he was the one to take decisive action and fire the organist. I can't know the secrets Dad never told me. I choose to believe he did the right thing on this one.

I don't know why my father quit college and got married after one year at the University of Florida. I had assumed, and Mom had indicated, that a surprise pregnancy prompted it. But their first child, my half sister, was not born until five years after the marriage. I'll never know.

Some of the people who I imagine could have provided essential perspectives on this story eluded me. I tried to locate Uncle Brian and thank him for years and years of *National Geographics*. I tried to find some of Dad's '80s business partners and failed to find them, too. I learned that in addition to Tim, another of my half siblings is dead. I considered contacting the third one and ultimately decided that leaving her in peace is the only gift I can offer her.

I don't know whether Mom ever took a single dose of morphine. As naïve as that may sound, as far as I could tell, Mom's interest in the morphine was as nonsensical as her interest in accumulating anything else. She was deeply compelled to hoard food, clothes, fabric, shampoo. She felt more secure and happy by avoiding a feeling of scarcity. She may have used morphine occasionally, compulsively, or not at all. I never wanted to ask her.

To survive having a relationship with my parents for thirty-some years, I preemptively forgave them or forgot things or lied to myself about things they did. Facing them was painful. It still is.

In my research, I found a letter Mom wrote to her biological father, who apparently was still a down-and-out alcoholic in the '80s when he asked Dad to hire him. Mom's reply was a long letter in a spiral notebook. I wonder if the letter was transcribed to stationery as is, or edited, or if it was never sent at all. In it, Mom firmly told her father that his poor choices in life and his parental relationship to her did not constitute a responsibility on her part. They would not be employing him or sending money. It wasn't fair to ask her to rescue her father, she told him. They would not jeopardize their own financial stability to clean up the many mistakes he'd made. "Love, Sandie" she signed it. I felt deeply betrayed when I read this letter in 2021. I had understood the rules to be that we took care of our parents no matter what. What had I spent all those years doing? The Longs were always changing the rules anyway. I tried to lose the letter. I hope I never see it again.

I developed a mantra: *People are not their parents*. They don't have to be. The Longs were incoherent with anything related to finances. They engaged in personal relationships like soldiers of fortune. Their housekeeping standards were abhorrent. Was I destined to be and do all of these things, too?

My entire childhood, my parents' poor reputation dogged us all. I felt shame. I never knew who they'd defrauded or how. I always knew I would be lumped in with the Longs no matter what I did. I'd listen to them argue every Tax Day and declare that I'd never ever be in that position myself. The ever-present messes and piles made it impossible for me to feel relaxed at home, and I dreamt of the neat apartments and sparely furnished homes I hoped to inhabit. I promised that I'd be a different kind of adult. I wanted to fully disassociate from them and still love them and be loved in return. I didn't know if that was possible, but that's what I hoped maturity would mean. I ached to grow up and establish myself as someone new.

I think I was wrong. People indeed are their parents. I am my parents. I have a striking resemblance to my mother. In odd moments, I may catch myself in the bathroom mirror or in a storefront's glass and see my mother: middle-aged, a little dissatisfied. Our faces are shaped the same. My hair was straight until the year I got married and in the twenty years since then it's been curling and spiking outward in an imitation of Mom's. Six months after she died, I paid almost $400 to straighten it, to disguise myself. This was futile.

As uncomfortable as it is, I am my mother as much as I'm not her. Thirty years later, I'm doing some of the same things Mom did: negotiating with my teenage daughter, figuring out how to put dinner on the table after a long workday. I have her hazel eyes and crippling fear of snakes. I don't accumulate the way Mom did, but I collect books. I have far more vintage plates and thrift-store jewelry than one could say I need. Whether I'm doing these things in emulation of her or in defiance, she's still there. A vestige, or an obstacle. A ghost.

Learning about my half brother was a gift. Discovering how short his life was, and why, will always plague me. My half brother was our father, too. Braggadocios about money, charming, gullible. These two men only spent about a year together, but Tim seems a precise echo of Dad. We may be better housekeepers or more frugal with our money, but Adam and I are echoes, too. Remnants of both my parents show up in my daughter. There is no escaping this.

There is a primary mystery I hoped my research would solve: Why did they treat me the way they did? Even as a child I found their behavior toward me and others—toward themselves—inexplicable. Their self-defeating choices made everything more challenging. I could never understand it. I could absolutely never convey it coherently to anyone else. The dreadful summer Mom was dying, a well-meaning friend of mine heard me make an offhand complaint about Mom's messy apartment, and she beseeched me to sit down and talk. My friend said, "I know you are struggling, but this is your only mother. You have to be better for her." My friend worried that Mom would die and I'd have regrets that I didn't do enough or wasn't sympathetic enough. Like most people, she saw only the surface of the tsunami. She couldn't see or imagine its depth.

"There's so much more to tell you," I told her, defensive.

"So tell me." My friend thought she was seeing a dark side of me—selfish, cowardly, lazy. She thought she was helping.

"I don't know how," I answered. "All I can say is that what you're seeing is my best. It's all I have." My friend, who had normal, respectable, even vibrant parents, didn't get it. I absorbed her disappointment in me as I would soon absorb the florist's disappointment and so many countless other well-intentioned disappointments. "I swear. It's the absolute most I'm able to do."

Trying our best is the one indisputable thing I have in common with my parents. Their best fell frustratingly short of what I needed and wanted. Their best was bizarre. Craven. Outlandish. Deranged. Hilarious when it wasn't dangerous. Confounding. If there is another key to unlock the mystery of Longs Island, I don't have it. To thoroughly report on the madness of their forty-year reign, I've had to piece together not just their documented actions but also their inferred and imagined motivations. Why did they act so strangely? Why defeat their own best interests constantly? I won't know, but boldly, as is my birthright, I will guess. This is what their best looked like.

We sometimes joked about having an adjective as a last name. "The long one!" cried the Vietnamese donut shopkeeper when Dad rolled up to his drive-through after church, looking for Long John pastries. Or Dad would goof with Adam and me about our height, about being "long." They both joked about the "Long-Cox Wedding" headline because we were never above a good male anatomy joke in our house. *Long* was our descriptor. We never recalled its verb form. It was always there. We'd never noticed.

The dictionary definition does the near-impossible in capturing a familial ethos to reflect my generation and my parents', maybe even those before us and those to come. All my life I've been knocking on doors, digging through boxes, grasping for answers. *Who were these people? What drove them? How did all of this happen in our strange lives? Why am I me?*

And why, in our malaise and our love and our stories and savagery and tenderness of all those years together did we never remember that *long* is a verb?

"To feel a strong desire or craving especially for something not likely to be attained. To pine. To yearn."

ACKNOWLEDGMENTS

Primary thanks are due to my parents, whom I have loved deeply all these strange and long years. During our time together, they presented me with challenge upon challenge. They also showed my brother and me, and each other, a fierce and immeasurable sort of love. My mom and dad met life's vagaries with confidence and humor, and they created a household unlike any other. We made improbable choices. We figured out sticky situations. We laughed all the time. I know they loved me. To the extent that I am brave, it is only because of them. What else should parents do but equip their children with courage and love them?

My parents were extraordinary.

And in the years since they've been gone, creating this book and documenting their lives has been a private and personal pursuit, aided exponentially by a wide community of people I hold dear.

My brother Adam is owed my eternal thanks for his steady support as both reader and interview subject, for bravely retreading some of our Indiana path together in 2022, for his ever-present wit and insight, and most of all for sticking by me. We shared an odd childhood. Adam made it, and all the years since, much more joyful.

Once in 2007 when my father was hospitalized, Amy Sumerton looked up from her desk at 826michigan and said to me, "I'll help you when you decide to write this book," planting an idea in my mind. It was a constant comfort to know that someone held the opinion that this was a viable story and that I was competent to tell it. In the summer of 2022, when I admitted to her that I'd been wrestling my way through since the year before, she marched us forward, line editing with affection and exactitude, posing the specific questions I needed with both humor and the whip-smart rigor I've always admired in Amy. Her work improved every page. I am so fortunate she lent her talents to *Destroy This House*.

Jenny Traig and I started discussing this project in February of 2021, a time when most socializing occurred outdoors by pandemic necessity. It turns out you can drink old fashioneds outdoors in winter in the Midwest and we did, eventually moving indoors for countless evenings of conversations during which Jenny allowed me to ramble and ponder. To accept her wise book recommendations. To ask her counsel. Jenny's own memoirs and other nonfiction deeply inspired me and encouraged me, just as she did. I can't imagine a more trusted first reader, or a more cherished friend.

Generous friends read early drafts. Their notes and their kindness meant the world to me and enhanced the manuscript in untold ways. Nana Asfour, Sara Billups, Hadil Ghoneim, Joe Malcoun, and Phil Stead provided the magnificent gift of their attention and time in the summer of 2023. Special accolades to Sara, who handed me a letter I'd written her in 1994 during a recent Lansing, Michigan, rendezvous. And to Phil, whose precise and thoughtful word-by-word edits came along with his game-changing idea to change the title to *Destroy This House*.

So many others provided the support necessary for me to write this book, from working space to thoughtful conversations to historical resources. I'm grateful for Geeta Makhija, Erin Stead, Alvan Uhle, Isaac Fitzgerald, D'Real Graham and Gail Taylor, Carol Davis, Scott Goldsmith, Jeff and Jeanna Cox, Art and Betty Ann Brill, the Indianapolis Public Library and Indiana Historical Society, Christina Ferguson, Kathy Mulder, Anthony Reale, and Scott Silsbe. Thank you to the wonderful editors who have encouraged my writing, especially Jacob Brogan and Elizabeth Ralph. Thank you to the incredible humans I get to call colleagues at McSweeney's: Brian Dice, Sunra Thompson, Dan Weiss, Annie

Dills, Daniel Gumbiner, Rita Bullwinkel, Vendela Vida, Raj Tawney, Chris Monks, Lucy Huber, Ginger Greene, Claire Astrow, Beth Haidle, Lily Ulriksen, Jade Howe, and Nikky Southerland.

Thank you, Dave Eggers, for innumerable gifts, and for the unending adventure of our work together.

Enormous thanks to the unstoppable Julie Stevenson, whose strength and intelligence are a ceaseless comfort and whose acumen landed the book into the expert hands of Judy Clain at Summit Books. Judy's vigor and warmth are matched only by her prowess. To be guided and championed by Judy is a profound honor, especially because of the masterful literary professionals surrounding her. Immeasurable thanks to Josie Kals, Kevwe Okumakube, Luiza De Campos Mello Grijns, Anna Skrabacz, Laura Perciasepe, Jackie Seow, Patty Romanowski Bashe, and everyone at Summit Books and Simon & Schuster whose work has helped this book come into existence.

Conditions must be favorable for any project to come to life, and I benefited tremendously from so many large and small things falling into alignment, whether by chance or by arrangement. There is no better place to write than the swing on my front porch. There may be no better time to write than the depths of a once-in-a-lifetime pandemic. Encouragement came from unexpected corners, from the songwriting of Matthew Milia to the flight delay that kept me awake all night in a Manhattan hotel room in a thunderstorm, writing about my father selling motivational cassette tapes. Working for so many years in the family of 826 organizations, I internalized the message that writing is egalitarian, a message I implore everyone to repeat and understand.

But the condition most meaningful to me and to the gestation of this memoir is the family that's formed around me now that I have grown out of my parents' home. For a time I wasn't sure how to be a mother. Thank God for Liz Uhle Teixeira, who showed me how, and for Beatrix Uhle, who taught me everything else I know. These treasured daughters, and my very dear son-in-law Lucas Uhle Teixeira Martins, fill my life with love. And one paramount condition—the unfettered support of my spouse—makes possible all that I do. Frank Uhle encouraged me in every way, insisting I write every Saturday morning and shoehorning other writing time for me into our active lives. He delivered hot coffees, stayed up late listening to my weird stories, felt my triumphs and anguish as acutely as I did, and joined me in building an enduring new kind of home together.